SCHOOL DEVELOPMENT SERIES

General Editors: David Hopkins and David Reynolds

DEVELOPMENT PLANNING FOR SCHOOL
IMPROVEMENT

DEVELOPMENT PLANNING FOR SCHOOL IMPROVEMENT

Edited by
David H. Hargreaves
and David Hopkins

CASSELL

Cassell
Villiers House
41/47 Strand
London WC2N 5JE

387 Park Avenue South
New York
NY 10016-8810

First published 1994

British Library Cataloguing-in-Publication Data
A catalogue record for this book is available from the British Library

ISBN 0-304-33101-5 (hardback)
        0-304-33103-1 (paperback)

Typeset by Litho Link Ltd, Welshpool, Powys, Wales
Printed and bound in Great Britain by Redwood Books, Trowbridge, Wilts.

Contents

Contributors

Madeleine Atkins, University of Newcastle upon Tyne, England
Charles Beresford, Institute of Education, University of London, England
Colin Biott, University of Northumbria at Newcastle, England
John Braithwaite, School of Education, Macquarie University, Australia
Pat Broadhead, School of Education, University of Leeds, England
Hilary Constable, School of Education, University of Sunderland, England
Peter Cuttance, Quality Assurance Directorate, Department of School Education, New South Wales, Australia (formerly Education Review Unit, Education Department of South Australia)
Neil Dempster, Griffith University, Australia
Grace Distant, Griffith University, Australia
John Dunford, School of Education, University of Leeds, England
Patrick Easen, University of Newcastle upon Tyne, England
David H. Hargreaves, Department of Education, University of Cambridge, England
Janet Hodgson, School of Education, University of Leeds, England
David Hopkins, Institute of Education, University of Cambridge, England
Chreston Kruchov, Royal Danish School of Education, Denmark
Daniel U. Levine, University of Nebraska, USA
Barbara MacGilchrist, Institute of Education, University of London, England
Peter Mortimore, Institute of Education, University of London, England
Elizabeth Newman, Faculty of Education, University of the West of England, Bristol, England
Andrew Pollard, Faculty of Education, University of the West of England, Bristol, England
Viviane Robinson, University of Auckland, New Zealand
Jane Savage, Institute of Education, University of London, England
Louise Stoll, Institute of Education, University of London, England (formerly Halton Board of Education, Ontario, Canada)
Mike Wallace, School of Education, University of Nottingham, England (formerly National Development Centre, School of Education, University of Bristol, England)

Foreword

Development planning has recently become a commonly adopted strategy for school improvement. Building on the experience of schemes for school self-evaluation or school-based review in the 1980s, development planning has in the UK, as well as in many other countries, become in the 1990s a more inclusive and sophisticated school-based strategy for managing change.

Although development planning is now widespread, its success or effectiveness in terms of improving most schools has yet to be fully established. The research to support claims for success has not been undertaken on sufficient scale or in sufficient depth. Several chapters in this book contribute actively to the creation of a better research base.

At present, the effectiveness of development planning has been best monitored and evaluated in England and Wales by Her Majesty's Inspectorate (HMI). In April 1994 the Office for Standards in Education (OFSTED) reported in *Improving Schools* that, on the basis of the evidence from school inspections, planning for improvement has not been a strength in the majority of primary and secondary schools. HMI do show, however, how a number of schools had, against the general trend, succeeded in improving themselves.

In *Improving Schools* three case studies of schools – one primary, one middle and one secondary – are presented. Each of these schools broadly followed the advice given by the DES-funded School Development Plan Project, which was subsequently written up by us as a book, *The Empowered School* (1991). The three schools, each in very different circumstances, planned for and achieved demonstrable improvements. It is evident that development planning can be an extremely effective tool for improvement and that the contributing elements can be replicated in other schools. But as the report points out (*Improving Schools*, p. 7):

> There is no magic formula for bringing about school improvement; nor is it easily achieved, particularly by schools in socially deprived areas. Nevertheless, as several of the examples in this document testify, even schools suffering from high levels of deprivation can achieve genuine improvements through careful rational planning and the commitment of teachers, heads, pupils and governors.

That development planning can be effective is thus no longer in question. But it is not fully clear in what circumstances and by what mechanisms the process of improvement is achieved. Even more important, it needs to be shown in what circumstances and in what ways development planning, when adopted and put into some kind of practice, fails to lead to school improvement. Unless we can clarify what can go wrong as well as what goes well, development planning will fall well below its potential in many schools. Indeed, it may even be rejected as an improvement strategy when in fact the tool is simply not being applied to best advantage.

This book reports on the 'state of the art' of development planning. Through the selection of research and commentary from a range of national contexts and our editorial overview, we seek to identify the main and recurrent themes in an emergent field of study. The chapters contribute to our knowledge and understanding both of best practice in development planning and of how and why it does not in some circumstances lead to the promised improvement. This is a progress report on an approach to school improvement which, when it is better understood, can be more effective still.

David H. Hargreaves and David Hopkins
Cambridge
May 1994

Acknowledgements

We are most grateful to the contributors to the book for allowing us to use their material and for responding so promptly and graciously to our inevitably tight deadlines. We also wish to acknowledge: Gill Kimber, at the Institute of Education, Cambridge; Naomi Roth, our editor at Cassell; and David Reynolds, the co-editor of the School Development series, for the support they have given us.

Introduction

David H. Hargreaves and David Hopkins

In the United Kingdom, as in many countries, development planning, though a relatively new concept, is becoming a standard word in a changing educational vocabulary. Different terms are being used both within and between different countries and the same term does not always have a shared meaning. There is, however, something of a common core in both the genesis and definition of the concept, whatever particular name is used. Development planning is a response to the management of multiple innovations and change and the perceived need for a systematic and whole-school approach to planning, especially where schools are expected to be more self-managing.

In societies where the education system is in a relatively stable state, where there is general consensus about the purpose and function of schools and where the public, especially parents and politicians, are broadly satisfied with the quality of education provided by schools, the energies of teachers and heads (or principals) can be predominantly devoted to maintaining the school: that is, ensuring the continuation of the status quo as effectively and efficiently as possible. In such a world, innovation makes a relatively rare appearance. When innovation does occur, it usually:

- is introduced by the individual teacher rather than the headteacher;
- is a product of that individual's enthusiasm and ambition;
- may have to compete with other innovations since the prudent headteacher encourages only limited innovation;
- will be successfully implemented if the innovating teacher wins the support of the headteacher;
- dies when the innovator leaves the school for promotion.

This age of simple innovation has passed into history. Often today innovations:

- are introduced as required by the headteacher who is conscious that the extent and pace of change is too high, but who nevertheless has a duty to implement them;
- are a product of shifting external political pressure or legal imposition;
- do not have to compete with other innovations since the headteacher expects everyone to be innovating ceaselessly and a wide range of innovations to be implemented simultaneously;
- will only in exceptional circumstances be implemented fully and successfully in the short time-scale allowed.

In both cases, but for rather different reasons, there is a high risk that the history of an innovation will more often be one of failure than of success – an increasingly recognized outcome which has led to the popularity of books such as Michael Fullan's *The New Meaning of Educational Change* (1991), the most recent of successive editions. The advocates of development planning in various forms are seeking to learn lessons from the past so that, in spite of the new landscape, the success rate for innovations can be improved (Hargreaves and Hopkins, 1991).

But why did this landscape of educational innovation change so fundamentally? For it is changing in many parts of the world, not just in the United Kingdom. In many places educational standards have almost certainly been rising, not least because more young people now stay in formal education for longer periods. These standards may not, however, have been rising fast enough to meet the world's expectations of schools and teachers which have risen even faster. In a climate of severe international competitiveness, politicians across the spectrum have become more critical of schools and their performance. There has been a tendency to enhance the autonomy of schools, to devolve budgets to them, to increase the power of parents, the local community and business interests in school governance, and to provide greater choice of school to parents. At the same time, teachers are expected to be more accountable for the character of educational provision and the quality of educational outcomes. In particular, there is now considerable pressure on schools to improve on the levels of achievement of the students, as unskilled and semi-skilled jobs progressively disappear from advanced economies.

Expectations of the education service, then, are rising at a rate that is difficult, even impossible, to meet – to everybody's frustration. Politicians are using various methods, some more directive than others, to pressure schools to improve themselves. In consequence schools find themselves subject to substantial innovation overload – multiple innovations have to be implemented simultaneously within an unreasonably short time-frame. Pleas for greater consultation and for periods of consolidation fall on deaf political ears. Schools are heavily constrained, sometimes by legal requirement, to change. The traditional focus on maintenance is weakened as the demands of development bear upon headteachers and teachers. The past, whether glorious or inglorious, is forgotten; the present is often experienced as confused, unstable and hectic; the future is all. To move from where the school now is to where the school is expected to be requires sophisticated planning and management. *Development planning* is simply a description and more formal explication of the process and actions required to plan and manage change with the intention of improving the school.

Development planning was not, in its original form, an innovation that could be imposed on the school from the outside. It was simply the more systematic and self-conscious approach to the management of development and change adopted by those heads who recognized that a more explicit and somewhat different approach to school management was essential in new and often unwelcome circumstances. The idea then became more systematized by educationists of various kinds, leading to the production of guidelines or advice to schools, and books such as *The Self-Managing School* by Caldwell and Spinks (1988). These publications are compilations of, or derivations from, existing best practice, sometimes combined with as much common sense, untested as it might be, as the authors could muster. Headteachers and teachers wanted active help in coping with multiple innovation: these guidelines rapidly gained high levels of circulation, for they were meeting a felt need. But some schools were much slower than others to respond to the demands for change. Politicians and administrators were then tempted to *impose* development planning on reluctant heads, rather than simply commending it. Or heads would accept the notion of development planning, but then impose it on an unpersuaded or sceptical group of teachers. As we shall see, in such circumstances development planning could become part of the problem, namely an addition to the already long waiting list of troublesome innovations, rather than part of the solution.

Recently it seems that this 'imposed' approach to development plans is being furthered by the new inspection system in England and Wales. Inspectors are using the school's development plan and associated documentation as the basis of the school's planning and management, and expecting clear evidence that what is in the plan is actually being implemented and evaluated. In many respects, it seems reasonable for inspectors to take account of any development plan in making their judgement on the quality of education provided by a school. However, we fear that, perhaps unintentionally, this approach serves to require schools to construct a development plan – which the headteacher knows will then explicitly be used as a basis for accountability – and to do so in a managerial, bureaucratic and unduly rigid way. This may subvert the more collegial, participative and pragmatic approach which we are convinced is necessary if development planning is to be empowering. At its best, development planning draws the school staff and the school's partners together in the creation and implementation of whole-school policies and planning. In this way planning helps a school to shape its values, mission and culture, and to do so in a more self-conscious and explicit way that improves morale, communication and commitment to the fundamental purposes of better teaching and learning.

It will be very easy for inspection, or any other accountability system, to stunt such institutional growth by undermining the processes of planning, which involve delicate human relationships, by focusing heavily on the written plan, which looks robust and open to interrogation. Worst of all, it may reinforce the gap between senior staff with management responsibilities and the majority of classroom teachers who feel distanced from development planning, as either process or product. In such circumstances, when accountability is seen as the major instrument for promoting school effectiveness, development planning, originally designed to assist schools in their growth towards greater effectiveness, could lose all its potential as a means of school improvement.

This, then, is the background against which development planning is emerging in various countries. In the series of chapters from several countries that follows, various themes are explored. It is immediately apparent that, although development planning is now a widespread innovation, it is no panacea. Indeed, it seems likely that some schools may be abandoning the notion of development planning, because either they saw it as an easy way to manage change, or they found that it did not seem to work in the first year – in both cases predictably running into problems. Whatever the advantages and disadvantages of development planning as an element of school improvement, it seems that it is not a 'quick fix' solution to innovation overload nor is it a technique of school management that can be kept insulated from the life and work of the school. Advice here, as in many areas of educational policy, will at this stage have to go beyond the evidence. More evidence is essential if better advice is to be provided. Such evidence depends on more and better research, and on a more sophisticated picture of how schools actually 'tick', manage change and improve themselves, which is not by any means always as the theoreticians and advisers suggest and expect. The HMI report *Improving Schools* (1994) advances our knowledge of how development planning works within the complexities of school dynamics.

THE CHAPTERS

In the opening chapter Neil Dempster, Chresten Kruchov and Grace Distant provide a most useful cross-national comparison of the documention on, and approach to, development planning. It is essential to set the United Kingdom experience within a wider context if the strengths and weaknesses of present practice are to be better understood. Differences as well as similarities between Denmark, Australia and the United Kingdom indicate the difficulties in generalizing about development planning: the differences between countries are themselves in need of explanation and it may be that the differences will be consequential in ways that are at present hard to discern. More detailed descriptions of the variety of approaches to development planning, both within and between countries, are essential. Dempster and his colleagues go beyond taxonomic work, suggesting a general trend from a 'public sector management style' in schools towards a 'corporate managerialist style': the different dimensions to these styles permit a more subtle and systematic comparison between countries. In a concluding section, they raise interesting questions about whether, in countries where development planning is associated with new financial responsibilities for schools, the market-oriented approach to devolution, with an underlying economic rationalism, may not be at all emancipating for the school's stakeholders. This may require a more explicit concern with political forms of devolution and an intention to enhance democratic processes.

In England and Wales the devolution of financial responsibilities to schools' governing bodies may reflect government dislike of local education authorities (LEAS), which were regarded as even less trustworthy than headteachers and governing bodies. In other spheres, such as curriculum, assessment and (more recently) pedagogy, the teachers were so strongly distrusted that they had to be *made* to change their practices in ways approved by government through newly centralized powers. Whether a function should be centralized or decentralized is always likely to be contentious, since there are benefits and costs involved in either. Devolution is likely to be empowering only when the benefits greatly outweigh the costs involved. Empowerment implies not just greater control but enhanced abilities to deploy new powers. One neglected aspect of empowerment is that whenever a school implements some innovations it should *at the same time* strengthen its general *capacity* to improve itself, that is, beyond the specific innovations at hand. The United Kingdom government has not at any stage understood this notion, being more convinced that its specific reforms, rather than a wider capacity for self-improvement, would lead to greater school effectiveness. Exactly what empowerment means and what forms of empowerment affect what kinds of school improvement in what ways remain major topics on the research agenda.

Much of the literature on development planning is concerned with the promise that the processes involved will enhance school effectiveness. An alternative is to turn this approach back to front by identifying the most effective schools and then working out what causes them to be effective. This is another way of providing guidance on how best to plan and develop a school towards greater effectiveness. In Chapter 2, Daniel Levine draws on his work in the United States on unusually effective schools, emphasizing the factor of site-level planning and professional development as a known correlate of effectiveness. As with many of the handbooks on development planning, it is essential for Levine that teaching and learning ('the instructional program') is a central focus of the professional development. This school-based staff development is, however, best described as a 'professional development culture' at work rather than the more traditional approach to in-service training which just happens to take place in the school. Far more than a change of site is involved. Like the concept of 'participation', that of 'staff development' is a common and favoured item of the contemporary educational vocabulary. Research is now making it essential to clarify precisely what we mean by these terms and then to treat them, not as self-evident and simple entities, but as complex areas that must be refined both conceptually and empirically if anything of value to policy and practice is to be said.

Levine, in company with some other contributors to this book, touches upon the dilemmas of autonomy and accountability. Simply empowering teachers, in the sense of giving them more decision-making authority, does not automatically improve schools. (There is, of course, nothing whatever which *automatically* improves schools and the sooner the notion of foolproof formulae or simple panaceas is abandoned the better for us all – Secretaries of State for Education please note.) Indeed, school improvement often requires painful change in teacher practices, which is why their active participation in some form is a prerequisite for commitment to innovation. This is a well-established principle, but one which continues to be regularly broken or ignored with predictable consequences. Headteachers and teachers often need professional development and support to handle these matters: it cannot be assumed that all the appropriate skills are already held. Indeed, in the schools which potentially have most to gain from development planning and are in greatest need of improvement, they may be singularly lacking.

Like many in the field, Levine confesses that, despite everything we know about schools, teachers and students, 'little is known about how to shape and carry out the planning process'. He draws as far as he can on ideas and evidence from a range of sources to support his advice and suggestions, which are given an unusually rich level of illustration. We share his view about the difficulties of changing an organization's culture – yet another of the key ideas where there is an urgent need for conceptual refinement and more research evidence. Levine is also surely right to emphasize that school improvement and so development planning are almost always sources of conflict. Sir John Harvey-Jones, the former chairman of ICI, has pointed out that 'It is much more difficult to change things when everything is apparently going well.' In such circumstances efforts are made, not unreasonably, to preserve the status quo and this sometimes combines with a leader's anxiety to avoid conflict at almost any cost. The result can be a headteacher's claim that development planning is going very well when behind this happy front little is in fact changing, sometimes in spite of much activity. Levine, like other contributors, puts a premium on the quality of the heads and their interpersonal skills as a key ingredient of successful school improvement.

Pete Cuttance's chapter, which reports part of the work of the Education Review Unit in South Australia, develops further some of the themes in the previous two chapters. At the heart of his concern and the mission of the unit is the tension between accountability and improvement. In many parts of the world politicians appear to adopt the view that an increase in accountability from schools will itself, almost automatically, be a spur to school improvement. It is widely felt by heads and teachers, in contrast, that the two are not easily compatible and that the pressures of accountability threaten to undermine the drive towards improvement. A crucial issue facing those (like Cuttance) with responsibility for school systems is whether the concept of *quality assurance* can be used as an umbrella for both accountability and improvement, providing a synthesis that allows each to be not merely consistent with, but actively supportive of, the other. If this could be achieved, it would constitute a significant reconciliation between what are seen as contradictory trends within education systems – and potentially be a boost to teacher professionalism rather than a threat to it.

Cuttance opens his chapter with a short review of work on school-based review and school self-evaluation. There follows a discussion of the range of factors which are held to explain the disappointing results of an approach that promised school improvement driven from within the profession rather than by external demands for accountability. If self-evaluation is a failure, or (just as consequential) the politicians perceive it to be a failure, then some external form of assessment will be considered as an alternative. For Cuttance, Her Majesty's Inspectors (HMI) in the United Kingdom represent a paradigm case of the strengths and weaknesses of external review. As it happens, HMI have recently been reformed (for rather obscure and doubtful motives) and made part of OFSTED (Office for Standards in Education), which oversees the inspection of schools by independent, registered ('privatized') teams, who will visit every school once in four years. At the same time, external inspection has been now expanded at school level as well as into the field of higher education, including the old universities where hitherto HMI had no rights of entry. The universities' own attempt at quality assurance, a rather reluctant one initiated under external pressure, has not satisfied the government, which has now insisted upon external quality assessment. In short, the trend in the United Kingdom is towards a combination of internal and external approaches to evaluation and quality assurance, rather than a replacement of the internal by the external – though there is little doubt that the external is seen as the more important.

Ironically, as Cuttance explains, this combined or dual approach was first adopted by the Inner London Education Authority (ILEA), which was abolished by the Conservative government. Indeed, one of us (Hargreaves) was Chief Inspector in the ILEA at this period, and introduced the reconsideration of school self-evaluation, which was more popular among inspectors than headteachers, with the intention of replacing it by a school improvement strategy. This approach would be spearheaded by development planning, but backed by external inspections that would feed into the school's own self-evaluation (or internal audit). In the case of schools causing greatest concern, they would also be supported in addition by the Inspectors Based in Schools (IBIS) team: these inspectors worked jointly with teachers on the diagnosis of weaknesses and then the subsequent remedial action. At the same time, and in the interests of accountability, inspection reports on individual schools were published, and each year the Chief Inspector made a public report on the quality of all aspects of education. Before these developments – a dual system of evaluation and improvement (Hargreaves, 1990) – could be adequately monitored and researched, the ILEA was abolished in April 1990.

The work of Cuttance and his colleagues stands as one of the most sustained and sophisticated of the combined approaches to school development planning, and one that is being monitored. (Recently Cuttance has moved to New South Wales, where he is developing a new form of quality assurance.) The findings about the effectiveness of development planning are described in terms of *stages* reached by the schools, though whether indeed all schools have to pass through all four stages in sequence remains open to question. The failure to involve the participants in the process of development planning and the failure to turn the plan into detailed action plans that guide and support implementation are likely to be characteristic of the difficulties experienced by schools in other countries; the finding certainly applies to England and Wales. Cuttance also reports – an issue that becomes relevant in this book – that heads tend to overestimate their success with, and progress in, development planning, a finding which needs explanation but seems to corroborate the value of a dual approach.

In his concluding section, Cuttance doffs his research hat and with the enthusiasm of an official who has a formal responsibility for and to schools turns what he has learnt as Director of the Education Review Unit into practical advice for more effective development planning.

In countries where rapidly rising expectations of the performance of schools are combined with the devolution of powers and responsibilities to more self-managing schools, there arises an acute tension between the accountability of schools to a range of partners and the professional autonomy of the school staff. First, there is the question of who has the right to make what kinds of decision about the work of schools. Until recently, in decentralized systems such as the United Kingdom, the curriculum had been left in the hands of the headteacher and teachers of each school. The introduction of the National Curriculum came as a severe erosion of the profession's autonomy in this regard. (Though it needs to be borne in mind that, by standards applying elsewhere in the world, the curriculum autonomy enjoyed in the schools of England and Wales was exceptionally high.) The 1988 Education Reform Act, however, forbids ministers to prescribe how schools choose to organize the curriculum and select teaching methods. Five years later, ministers have recognized that pedagogy may be as important as curriculum content (perhaps even more important, indeed) in the raising of educational standards and probably regret their earlier decision to leave choice of pedagogy to the professional judgement of teachers. They are today far less neutral on organization and pedagogy than they appeared to be in 1988, the time of the Education Reform Act. The battle over the boundaries between the rights of politicians and those of the profession is likely to continue and will affect the culture of schools and approaches to school development. We would expect similar debates to assume greater importance in other countries, especially Australia and New Zealand, over the next few years.

Secondly, the tension between accountability and autonomy is expressed in the relationship between internal self-evaluation and external assessment or inspection and the difficulty in making them complementary and mutually supportive. This is a recurrent theme in this book.

A third form of the tension inheres in schemes of staff appraisal or performance review: is it meant to be a supportive form of professional development or is it a device for assessing teacher competence, rewarding the effective and disciplining the ineffective? Much of the tension is played out at the national (or state) political level, in running battles between teachers' unions or professional associations and ministers or their officials. But behind the public facade, the tension is also played out within the micro-politics of life in school. Heads want to foster the professional growth of their colleagues, but they are also caught between the outside pressures, from politicians and parents, to 'discipline' or dismiss weak or incompetent teachers. Can this conflict be resolved? And can it be done in a way that avoids arousing a justified suspicion among teachers that they are being *manipulated* in the guise of being *managed*? To busy heads it may be easier to turn a blind eye to the problem: most teachers in most countries are familiar with the way schools avoid confronting the issue by assigning the weaker teachers to smaller groups, easier classes or even non-teaching duties without fuss.

By exploring one of its forms at the level of the individual school, Viviane Robinson through her research extends and elaborates on this tension in a way that makes it a foreground rather than a background issue in development planning and school improvement. For development planning, as both practised and preached, requires the head to foster a collegial or collaborative climate in which teachers feel both active participants in the shaping of the agenda and recipients of support in the task of implementation. Most heads accept that this involves a significant investment in staff development programmes for a school's teaching staff by which existing strengths are built upon and weaknesses remedied through the acquisition of new knowledge and skills. At the same time, however, there may be pressure on a head to insist upon particular procedures and practices that are held to be prerequisites of innovation and/or to attend to the problem so often avoided, that of identifying and taking action against teachers who for whatever reason fail to display the appropriate levels of competence. This may not be easy where among teachers there prevails a second version of professional autonomy, the right to be left alone and uncriticized, not by outsiders, but by one's professional colleagues and superiors. Moreover, as we have found in England and Wales, heads sometimes learn that one of the major barriers against successful development planning is a 'rump' of teachers, usually a distinctive minority, who resist all the changes, decline to participate and persist in attempting – sometimes vociferously, sometimes surreptitiously – to undermine the morale and commitment of other teachers who are at worst responding neutrally and at best positively to development planning.

Robinson's research draws a persuasive account of not only how this tension can be expressed, but also how it may be so analysed to discover a way through the dilemma. The interpersonal skills of the head once again emerge as a central feature of successful school development.

Although the growth of development planning has undoubtedly been stimulated by external pressures for change, all schools have to face the question: whose plan is it? In the report of their research in Chapter 5, based on fifty-seven schools in nine

LEAs, Colin Biott, Patrick Easen and Madeleine Atkins confirm that in many schools, secondary schools in particular, the participation of the whole staff in development planning is uncommon. However, participation is not necessarily a good thing in itself: it has to be experienced as worthwhile by those who participate. It would be impossible as well as undesirable for everybody to participate in everything. Participation needs essentially to be *selective* about who is involved in what issues for what purposes in what ways and on what occasions. One suspects most headteachers could not produce a justification specified in these terms for many instances where they invite or decide against teacher participation. Participation *of some kind* may be a necessary condition for a collegial school culture, but it is certainly not a sufficient one. How to decide on what kind in each instance is the problem.

Important questions are thus raised about whether the involvement of teachers in all or merely some whole-school planning is legitimately to be regarded as empowering. This may reinforce the view that the *process* of development planning is far more important than the *product* (a written plan) and provides one more justification for classroom issues – the curriculum, teaching and learning – being a central feature in any development plan. If these elements are ignored, then there are few rational grounds for teachers to be interested in, or committed to, development planning. It also suggests that, however a head chooses to promote staff participation, it should build upon the ways in which teachers *already* work together and collaborate. Participation in development planning should not be an *additional* feature to social relations among staff but an *extension* of their existing relations and a further expression of their existing values. It is only by research of the kind done by the Newcastle team that the subtleties of many aspects of development planning become exposed and that what to some seems obvious good practice ('teachers should be participating') is shown to be more complicated and to require more careful consideration if wise decisions are to be made.

The Newcastle team take up one of the themes from the opening sentences of this book: how development planning means different things to different people. To portray its complexity in practice, a typology of development planning is proposed, with six dimensions: construction, management, content, change, participation and control, and quality assurance. Each dimension is treated as bi-polar with several intermediate positions. By this means a profile for an individual school can be drawn across different positions on the various dimensions.

There is scope here for considerable empirical and conceptual progress in research into development planning – and perhaps for self-diagnostic purposes within a school or at LEA level. It is an open question whether the finding that, in terms of content, schools tend to choose as priorities curriculum and staff development will be sustained over time. The experience in other countries, with other traditions and current national reform priorities, is likely to be different.

In her chapter, Hilary Constable elaborates on the dilemmas faced by headteachers. Like Robinson, she sees the headteacher as 'caught between the pulls of collegiality on the one hand and a managerial style on the other'. The breathtaking failure of some of the headteachers in her study to allow even the most basic forms of teacher participation seems hard to credit, since they defy common sense as well as contravening all published advice on development planning. The causes are obscure, but they need to be uncovered since relatively simple mistakes in handling the basic processes in development planning are probably far more widespread than is usually imagined. Are the reasons given, such as the pressure of time, genuine explanations or are they excuses and rationalizations for the fear of allowing a participation many headteachers feel unable to control? When, in our own research, we asked one head-teacher why he had not allowed his staff to participate in the selection of priorities for the development plan, he replied, 'Oh, I couldn't possibly have let them decide the priorities: they would have chosen all the wrong things.' Again from our own research, we suspect that where headteachers are *required* to produce a school development plan, for example by the LEA, especially if the time allowed is short, then severely adverse effects tend to follow – the necessary preparation is neglected and a bureaucratic and manipulative rather than a collegial approach to the construction of the plan is encouraged. Time pressure can lead headteachers to find convenient 'short cuts' to the production of a document at the expense of the underlying process of school improvement.

Constable's analysis explores three areas of tension. She offers no easy answers to the problems she uncovers, but suggests that if school leaders are at least aware of them they may be able to review their practice and so adopt a better approach. We have become more and more convinced that preliminary and concurrent in-service training or consultancy is essential if headteachers and teachers are to be adequately prepared for, and supported in, the tasks of development planning or any related approach to the management of change and school improvement. The skills involved are greater than has been acknowledged and Constable's analysis, like that of Robinson, documents the point.

Development planning is held to be related to collaboration among teachers in two ways. First, it *requires* collaboration among teachers in the selection, planning, implementation and evaluation of selected priorities if it is to be successful. Secondly, it *stimulates* collaboration by bringing together teachers to pursue these various activities. The first point is asserted as self-evident: if people plan and work together they are more likely to achieve agreed goals than if they do not. This remains open to verification from research, since there are alternative ways of running a school which might be equally successful. The second point is more obviously an empirical question demanding research, since it is possible that development planning will stimulate more conflict than collaboration and this could then reduce the morale, confidence and effectiveness of individual teachers as well as the effectiveness of the school as a whole.

In Chapter 7 Newman and Pollard question whether the research led by Nias and Southworth, which has been influential in inspiring primary school teachers to work in more collaborative ways and thus indirectly supportive of development planning, has presented an idealized picture of collaboration. In their own research, from which only the most tentative conclusions can be drawn since it is based on a single case study, they reveal, as do other contributors to this book, the key tension for headteachers in a time of externally imposed change and increased pressures to greater school effectiveness: on the one hand, staff need to be encouraged to adopt a more collegial approach to decision-making and to work in more collaborative ways on agreed policies, but on the other hand, the head wishes to take, and often feels driven to take, a strong leadership role in shaping the direction of the school and managing the means for moving forward. Newman and Pollard describe how in-service training of a collaborative kind within a development planning framework did to some degree stimulate a more collaborative culture, but this was not achieved without some real conflict, which led to disillusionment and departure for a minority of the staff.

Conflict may be an interim stage in many schools along the path towards more collaborative relationships among teachers. Research is needed to show just how typical this might be. At the same time, we suspect there are schools, probably a minority, where such conflict is minimal. In these cases research is needed to show why the conflict abates. Is it a product of the social skills of the headteacher? Is it a consequence of the departure of the disaffected and the progressive recruitment of replacement staff who from the beginning are committed to collaboration? Pollard, Newman, Nias and Southworth are all working in primary schools. In secondary schools, where the sheer size of staff militates against agreement and collaboration, the conditions for conflict are much higher. We believe from our own experience, there are some schools, particularly the larger secondary schools, where there remains a persistent minority of teachers – the 'rump' referred to earlier – who resist the development of more collaboration and who assume the position of an oppositional minority. Again, research is needed to expose the dynamics of such social processes and their consequences in terms of both school effectiveness generally as well as the capacity to manage change in an era of reform.

Those who have worked with schools on various forms of curriculum development, action research, self-evaluation and school development or school improvement know that the processes involved are so complicated and variable between schools that it is difficult, indeed, dangerous, to provide guidance for schools that might be read as simple recipes for the management of change and improvement. The pressures on schools to look for such recipes have increased rapidly at the very time when it has become more difficult for many schools to seek the support of outsiders during the hazardous process of school development, as traditional supporters of in-service training, LEA advisory services and institutions of teacher education in higher education, are themselves going through a change of role, if not actually disappearing.

In their chapter, Hodgson, Broadhead and Dunford describe a project between three higher education tutors and six primary schools, the purposes of which were:

- to develop an understanding of evaluation processes in all school staff;
- to use evaluation processes in the review and development of a school development plan;
- to strengthen teamwork and collaboration within the school;
- to improve the quality of teaching and learning.

The chapter reports some of the experience and outcomes of the project – detailed research did not begin until 1994. However, it is clear that one of the forms of successful partnership between schools and higher education is beginning to emerge. There have been three major models for the relationships between schools and higher education staff. The first is the provision by higher education of in-service courses, varying in length between a half day and the (now rare) year of full-time study, which are attended by one teacher (occasionally two or more) from each of a wide range of schools. In the second model, more recently developed, the higher education staff visit the school to provide some form of school-based and school-focused professional development, probably on one or more professional training days. Both these models will continue, but we suspect will to some degree be displaced by the third model, whereby a group of university staff work with the whole staff of a small group of schools on an agreed project over a sustained period. This model has several advantages, among the most important of which are:

- the schools have an outside input from persons who are familiar with the emerging evidence on school development and school improvement and can feed such knowledge and advice as and when appropriate to the particular circumstances of the project schools;
- the staff of all the project schools can meet together to share experience, both problems and achievements;
- each school is able to call on support both from a lecturer who acts as a continuing link with the school as well as other lecturers with particular interests and skills as and when appropriate.

The University of Leeds/LEA project described by Hodgson, Broadhead and Dunford is clearly in the third model, as is the Cambridge Improving the Quality of Education for All (IQEA) project. IQEA is a school improvement project that involves schools in working collaboratively with a group from the Institute of Education at Cambridge, and representatives from their Local Education Authority or another local support agency. The overall aim of the project is to produce and evaluate a model of school development, and a programme of support, that strengthens a school's ability to provide quality education for all its pupils by building upon existing good practice. The goal is enhanced learning outcomes for both students and teachers. Over the past four years the team from Cambridge have provided training and support for a network of over thirty schools in East Anglia, north London and Yorkshire (Ainscow and Hopkins, 1992; Hopkins *et al.*, 1994).

IQEA works from an assumption that schools are most likely to strengthen their ability to provide enhanced outcomes for all pupils when they adopt ways of working that are consistent with their own aspirations as well as the current reform agenda. This involves building confidence and 'capacity' within the school, rather than reliance on externally produced 'packages' – although good ideas from the outside are never rejected out of hand. At a time of great change in the educational system, these schools are using the impetus of external reform for internal purposes.

The project in each school is based upon a contract between the staff of the school, the LEA or support agency and the Cambridge team. This contract is intended to clarify expectations and ensure the conditions necessary for success. In particular, it emphasizes that all staff be consulted, that co-ordinators are appointed, that a 'critical mass' of teachers are actively involved in development work, and that sufficient time is made available for classroom observation and staff development. The Cambridge team co-ordinate the project, provide training for the school co-ordinators and representatives, make regular school visits and contribute to staff training, provide staff development materials, and monitor the implementation of the project.

The style adopted in the IQEA project is to develop a strategy for improvement that allows each school considerable autonomy to determine its own priorities for development and, indeed, its own methods for achieving these priorities. This is a similar approach to that adopted in a number of other school improvement projects in the United Kingdom and elsewhere, whereby individual schools devise their own projects within an overall framework for development. In IQEA and other projects such as the Halton project (described in Chapter 9), the planning process provides a common structure for development work in all the schools.

The intellectual source of Louise Stoll's chapter, based on her Canadian work, lies in the field of school effectiveness and school improvement, which has played such an important role in North American research. Headteachers, teachers and other practitioners could with advantage raid these two literatures for ideas and practical guidance, but are in danger of being caught between them since they have differing theoretical and conceptual frameworks as well as differing research traditions and findings. Happily the two fields are increasingly being considered together and even reconciled, under the influence of writers such as Stoll who has the invaluable experience of working in both school effectiveness and school improvement projects. This poses considerable intellectual challenges because of the very different conceptual and methodological preferences in the two fields, but a convergence of the two is potentially a rich resource for practitioners seeking inspiration and advice about school improvement.

Stoll draws some very useful contrasts between the different approaches of school effectiveness and school improvement, pointing out that their relationship is in many respects complementary. The effect is to highlight, in a period of self-managing schools, the conception of the school as both the focus and centre of change. Her account of the Halton Effective Schools Project, essentially school development planning but called school *growth* planning, mirrors experience in this and other countries. Like most projects on school improvement, the study is stronger on accounts of the processes involved than on the product or outcomes, but Stoll rightly raises questions about, as well as difficulties associated with, evaluating the effectiveness of school improvement projects.

Yet in the absence of agreement on how this might be done – and researchers might well not agree with politicians on criteria for judging such projects – is there not a danger that teachers will become cynical about school improvement schemes simply because the research community cannot produce research quickly enough to provide useful feedback to schools that are often hungry for guidance? But then educational research is always in danger of being used selectively by politicians and practitioners alike to justify what they want to do or are doing anyway.

One future task is to link the research done by school improvement project leaders, such as Stoll or Cuttance, with the more personal evaluations and reflections of practitioners and also with the independent researchers such as Braithwaite or Wallace (in their chapters), in ways that advance policy-relevant knowledge and understanding. This means partnerships between academic researchers, project leaders and the senior staff of schools that are not easily organized and then, more difficult still, appropriately funded. Until there is substantial investment in more sophisticated action research projects we have to rely on the more limited range of conventional research that does gain funding. One of the greatest failures of the United Kingdom government's education policy in recent years has been the reluctance to devise pilot action research projects in which new ideas can be tested and revised before dissemination to all schools. Is there any hope that, following the Dearing review of curriculum and assessment, which exposes the disastrous folly of the government's approach to the implementation of reform since 1988, there might be a change of strategy?

In his contribution from Australia, John Braithwaite works on a wider, national canvas than Cuttance (who reported mainly on work within the state of South Australia in comparison with the United Kingdom), and so provides more detail on the distinctive features of the Australian background to the emergence of development planning. His research approach is necessarily limited in depth but it covers a sample of schools in seven states and territories. All except one of the schools he contacted on a random basis had been involved in development planning in some form – an interesting index of the speed with which the notion has spread across Australia. There were a number of perceived benefits, but heads made the complaints that commonly arise in the United Kingdom and other countries – too little time to do development planning properly and too few resources to implement selected priorities. Most worrying of all perhaps is the perception that too often there was little impact on the central concerns of schools and teachers, namely the character and quality of teaching and learning. These are, as Levine insisted in his chapter, at the heart of school improvement. If development planning becomes dislocated from school and classroom improvement then in our view it is an innovation which will quickly die out – and deservedly so – as no more than a short-lived fashionable idea that was supposed to help schools with the management of change in a period of innovation overload but in the end made little difference at the point where it matters most, student achievement. One advantage of the dual approach is that external monitoring or inspection almost always focuses on student learning and achievement: it potentially helps internal review and planning to maintain the same emphasis.

Like that of Braithwaite, Mike Wallace's research report is derived from relatively small-scale projects. His chapter (Chapter 11) shows a number of strong parallels in work on development planning between England and Wales and Australia. Wallace's headteachers, like Braithwaite's, found it necessary to alter their development plans as they went along. In Wallace's cases, heads were, for instance, often overtaken by events beyond their control or their capacity to anticipate: matters to which a response was essential arose after the development plan was compiled. In environments that are as turbulent as that in England and Wales, suggests Wallace, schools may not be helped by approaches to development planning that are overly rationalist and require a rather rigid adherence to a regular cycle of stages which presume little disturbance during cycles. Since in most countries the educational environment qualifies as 'turbulent' rather than 'stable' in Wallace's detailed specification, the point is probably applicable far outside England and Wales. When heads appeal for a period of 'consolidation' – and is not this the ubiquitous cry? – they are taken by politicians to be resisting change when they may reasonably be seeking a more stable environment in which great activity is more likely to lead to effective implementation and less likely to run into the troubles described by Wallace, which easily result in failure and demoralization. Wallace's 'contingency model' will make sense to many practitioners and needs to be taken into account in prescriptive advice on school improvement and development planning.

More importantly, it needs to be understood by middle-level administrators in local government, since it may be they who, in pressuring schools to document development plans for bureaucratic and accountability purposes, reinforce the over-rationalistic approach and so unintentionally undermine the effectiveness of the very school improvement they seek to promote.

Our experience coincides with Wallace's that innovation overload is not reduced if the development plan is handled in a rigid mechanistic manner. Yet a headteacher can use the plan as a device for controlling the overload by using the school's mission or vision as a filter. This process of filtering externally induced reform may be an act of resistance and self-defence or a means of avoiding or emasculating an imposed innovation. It may, on the other hand, be a more positive process of selective transformation, whereby undesired features are eliminated, selected elements are allowed in and the whole innovation is infused with and made subservient to the school's own vision and goals. Unless the whole staff of a school are, by one means or another, involved in the selection of and committed to the emergent priorities, and such priorities are consonant with, or contribute to, or are filtered through, the school's vision of itself, then the chances of successful implementation are greatly reduced. If a school lacks a vision, one that is collectively shared, there is nothing through which to filter the external reforms. But even when a school has used its vision in this transformative way, there must then be recognition that implementation has to be actively *managed* and thus appropriate structures for implementing change may need to be devised. The school must be willing to examine whether the existing structures are adequate to sustain the development processes, even though they are known to work well enough for maintenance purposes. Because not everything is in process of change, some maintenance structures continue to run alongside change activities. This is why any new structures emerging to handle the change process are easily marginalized and take the form of an extra bureaucratic layer which then fails to make a significant impact on the classroom work of teachers. As we expressed this in our own work, in some schools the challenge of change requires a transformation to the management arrangements and the culture of the school to create the structures and the commitment that support innovation (Hargreaves and Hopkins, 1991). The energizing of the teachers is a necessary but not sufficient condition; innovative activities have to be steered and given direction. Or so, in the light of our current knowledge and experience, we would hypothesize.

The final chapter is an early offering from a funded project which is likely to become the most important research into development planning in England and Wales. One of the difficulties of previous United Kingdom research into this field is that the projects were too modest and/or that most schools were still in their first 'cycle' of development planning and their experience was very unlikely to be typical of the school after two or three years. The two principal researchers bring a range of relevant experience to their tasks. Peter Mortimore has impeccable credentials in mainstream research into school effectiveness, but also has experience as an inspector and an LEA administrator. Barbara MacGilchrist was a headteacher and then Chief Inspector of ILEA. As appropriate to this book, they set their research within a wide, not just national, context. It is hoped their research will throw light on school management and the management of change as well as the impact of development planning on teachers and pupils, but the intention is to do so in collaboration with researchers in other countries, such as Australia and Denmark. They describe their research methodology in detail, which may be directly useful to others who are planning research into allied areas. The research is to be guided by six expectations culled from the literature. Early findings are reported provisionally. It is evident from the 100 per cent response of all 135 LEAs that, since all but two LEAs have policies on development planning, in under ten years the vast majority of schools in England and Wales, and probably Scotland too, have become involved in development planning of some kind – despite the fact that this has not been a requirement of central government, most of the encouragement coming from LEAs.

The intensive phase of the research includes nine schools in three LEAs. Mortimore and his colleagues are very aware of the difficulties in generalizing from such a small sample. Cross-national comparisons in such circumstances become even more hazardous. There is the added problem of a Hawthorne effect common to any intensive study of a school: there is bound to be some impact of the researcher. They are also alert to the difficulty of making a causal analysis – one that has dogged researchers in the United Kingdom at least since the publication in 1979 of *Fifteen Thousand Hours* by Rutter *et al.* (which included Mortimore, of course), which led many an incautious head or education officer to turn correlation into cause and then cause into a simple recipe for school improvement. If only it were so simple!

A continuing risk for those working in the field of development planning and school improvement is that whatever is written will soon be raided by practitioners eagerly searching for guidance or even for 'answers' as national and local pressures for school improvement continue to mount. The more central to the concerns of headteachers and teachers that researchers make their investigations, the greater the dangers in moving from research to applied policy and practice. It is excellent news that this research 'will seek to assess how much impact the processes of planning have on the four target areas: school management; classroom management; the individual teacher; and – ultimately – whether it makes a difference to the opportunity for learning offered to students within the school.' This will be widely welcomed but will also cause policy makers of various kinds to drool in anticipation. If, during the course of the research, the degree of international collaboration between workers in the fields of development planning and school improvement also increases, then confidence that policy appetites may be reasonably be satisfied in the not too distant future will also be strengthened.

EDITORIAL CONCLUSIONS

In these concluding remarks we do not attempt to raise all the important issues concerning the design and implementation of development planning as an approach to school improvement. Many of the most pertinent issues have been touched upon, albeit fleetingly, in this introduction or will be discussed in the chapters that follow. In this final section we wish to focus on three related themes which appear, on the basis of the chapters and our experience, to have national and international relevance, and to raise some implications for practitioners, researchers, and policy makers.

The Developmental Nature of Development Planning

There are two aspects to this: the way in which development planning has evolved from school self-evaluation and other school improvement strategies; and then the way development planning is implemented in schools and continues to evolve in the light of experience. Both require comment, because both have implications for the linking of development planning to classroom practice which is, as we have insisted, the crucial link in securing better student achievement.

One of the most commonly advocated means of achieving school improvement, by enhancing the teaching–learning process and improving the school's capacity for providing quality education, has been through a continuous process of school self-evaluation. The relative failure of self-evaluation to promote substantial improvement led to an emphasis on school-based development, and the management at the school level of complex change and multiple innovations. More recent efforts at school improvement have been characterized by attempts to enhance student achievement through the use of specific classroom-based strategies that also have an impact on the organization and culture of the school. In many countries there is clear evidence of a move to a more holistic approach to school improvement that uses the development plan as a means of linking together a series of strategies that focus on student achievement (Hopkins, 1994).

A further aspect concerns the operation of development planning. From our own work with schools we have begun to recognize a fairly predictable sequence of stages through which a school passes as it engages with and understands the process. When a school embarks on development planning for the first time, attention is focused on the plan in the form of a document. People ask questions such as: What does a plan look like? What makes a development plan a *good* plan? These are reasonable questions. Although they are the ones that first spring to mind, they are not in our experience the best place to begin the activity of development planning.

The second stage is when a school realizes that the process of development planning, rather than the plan as a product, is the heart of the matter. The plan is more than a statement of intentions: it is the quality of the process that determines success. The identification of appropriate priorities, the production of a good strategy with action plans specifying tasks for implementation and evaluation, well-established staff development opportunities, a system for ensuring that everyone is consulted and involved – all these depend upon a sound grasp of the processes involved.

The third stage is reached when there is a realization that the quality of the management of planning is the key to success. This requires skill, sensitivity and flexibility on the part of school leaders, and may entail a review of the school's organizational structures and culture, resulting in substantial, even radical, changes, many of which were neither planned nor anticipated but lead to a reshaping of the character of the school. Fundamental changes to how the school understands, manages and organizes professional development form one of the most likely indirect effects of development planning. At this point 'development planning' as a distinctive feature may even disappear as it is absorbed into transformed ways of working and the new partnerships sought and sustained by the school. In the absence of such sophisticated views of the management of development planning, any immediate impact on student achievement cannot be expected.

Development plans can and do create conditions favourable to student achievement but by themselves have little *direct* impact on pupil progress. For example, development planning creates the 'space' for teachers to collaborate on acquiring a new range of teaching strategies. Such changes in timetabling and resource

17

allocation are necessary but not sufficient for enhancing student achievement. What are required of course are the more specific and sustained modifications to a teacher's classroom practice that the collaboration allows.

In many countries, schools are now faced with a number of innovations – self-evaluation, development planning, staff development policy and practice, and teacher appraisal – that are 'content-free'. Although all these have a carefully specified process or structure, the *substance* of each is for the teacher and school to decide. In combination, these strategies can form an 'infrastructure' at the school level that facilitates the implementation of specific curriculum or pedagogical changes that can have a direct impact on student learning. The virtue of development planning is that it helps create the conditions in which other innovations can flourish in the interests of school improvement.

The Importance of the Internal Conditions of the School for Sustaining Innovation

It is now well established, in this book as well as in the broader literature, that unless the school works on its internal organization at the same time as its chosen developmental priorities, then work on curriculum and teaching method can quickly become marginalized. As Fullan asserts:

> Without a direct and primary focus on changes in organisational factors it is unlikely that [single innovations or specific projects] will have much of a reform impact, and whatever impact there is will be short-lived ... school improvement efforts which ignore these deeper organisational conditions are 'doomed to tinkering'. . . . Strategies are needed that more directly address the culture of the organisation.
>
> (Fullan, 1990, pp. 248–9)

This much is now known, though the degree to which it is accepted by practitioners is unknown.

Important questions, however, remain unanswered. Everybody talks about the importance of *school culture* in sustaining innovation and change, yet there are real difficulties in defining school culture and even more in knowing how to change it. Certainly culture is not changed simply by talking about it: some action is needed. We suspect that it is changes in certain underlying *structures* that produce the necessary cultural change: indeed, the cultural change may be an index of the more subtle structural modifications that are causally significant. In our own work (Hargreaves and Hopkins, 1991, Chapter 3) we used the term *management arrangements* to signify this combination of structures and culture. Management arrangements we see as consisting of three elements: *frameworks* (largely structural); *roles* (both structural and cultural); and *working together* (largely cultural). There are many varieties of management arrangements, because of the possible combinations of different structures and cultures. They can be changed and adapted according to the preferences and circumstances of the teachers. We doubt whether there is one ideal set of management arrangements, a recipe of culture and structures for improvement that could or should be adopted by all schools. It is for this reason we believe caution needs to be exercised in talking about the *culture of the school* and its importance. The concept is convenient, but when used in a simplistic way it may hide more than it reveals.

Our division of the management arrangements into three analytically distinct dimensions is a limited first attempt at simplifying the structure-and-culture complex that underpins school organization and so also development and improvement. *Frameworks* consist of structures that any school has to establish, such as means of devising organizational aims and policies, a system for decision-making and communication, mechanisms to allow members to meet and co-ordinate their activities. *Roles* refers to the relationships between members and partners – the expectations held by and towards the people involved, the allocation of responsibilities, the groupings of people. *Working together* refers to the quality or character of relationships: the nature and extent of co-operation or conflict, the forms of leadership and style of management.

Each dimension overlaps with and influences the other two in a complex interaction of structural and cultural factors. Schein may be right to observe (1985, p. 2) 'that the only thing of real importance that leaders do is to create and manage culture', but we need to disentangle the dynamics involved. Most of the school effectiveness literature reports research in the form of correlations between *process* data (what happens in schools and classrooms, the attitudes and practices of teachers and students) and *outcome* data (students' achievements, attendance, etc.). For many heads and teachers these are technically difficult to read and only by distortion and inference are they turned into accounts of what causes lead to what effects – though eager policy makers and practitioners are desperate for such. Current wisdom does indeed focus on culture – now a rather more fashionable concept than ethos – and especially on the power of *collaborative* cultures. But this is, in our view, to focus unduly on one element of our scheme, working together, at the expense of the other two and to privilege culture over structure.

Researchers and practitioners alike are still substantially ignorant of how structures generate or influence cultures and how cultures generate or influence structures. How do leaders create certain forms of social organization that generate and sustain certain values and belief systems (from structure to culture) and vice-versa (from culture into structure)? Do successful leaders begin by asking what cultural changes will generate the new structures that are needed to make the school more effective or do they ask what structural changes will stimulate new cultures? If they do both, under what circumstances and in relation to what issues do they adopt the one tactic rather than the other? Unless we rescue the notion of school culture from having to do too much work at the analytical level, questions such as these will go unanswered, and possibly unasked as well.

As already noted, we doubt whether a school culture is readily changed by teachers talking about it or as a result of exhortations by the school leaders. But significant structural changes, especially ones that bring teachers into working more closely together, will affect how teachers talk to one another and define their professional relationships – and perhaps also with various kinds of 'outside' partner. It is through the new relationships and the content and style of talk arising from structural changes that the culture begins to shift; in turn, the emerging culture then stabilizes, legitimizes and even routinizes the structural conditions which form the essential foundations for the new culture.

In terms of development planning, we now think it useful to pose further questions to cast light on these issues. Development planning requires the selection of a set of priorities and plans to implement them. There are various grounds on which, as well as ways in which, priorities can be selected and then sequenced. In *The Empowered School* we were mainly concerned with how priorities might be selected and sequenced to create some coherence and mutual supportiveness within the school's development plan. We might now be equally concerned with the impact (intended or unintended) of the selection and sequencing of a particular set of priorities on the deeper level of school structures and culture. The degree to which implementation is effective may reflect the dialectical relationship between changing structures and cultures that are not easily detected or measured by researchers.

Our subsequent experience has enabled us to understand more fully another dimension we introduced in *The Empowered School*: the distinction between a school's development activities and its maintenance activities. Perhaps the most crucial challenge facing schools today is how to balance change and stability effectively; how on the one hand to preserve what is already admirable and fine in a school, and, on the other, how to respond positively to innovation and the challenge of change. We suggested that it was the school's management arrangements that were crucial in achieving the correct balance. We still feel this is sound advice, but we are also realizing from our current work that the most successful schools are deliberately creating contrasting but mutually supportive structural arrangements to cope with the twin pressures of development and maintenance.

Schools are finding out quite rapidly, or eventually more painfully, that maintenance structures established to organize teaching, learning and assessment cannot also cope with developmental activities which inevitably cut across established hierarchies, curriculum areas, meeting patterns, and timetables. The innovative responses required for sustained development, for example delegation, task groups, high levels of specific staff development, quality time for planning and collaborative classroom activity, are inimical to successful maintenance. Maintenance structures, however well developed, often do not cope well with development. In our experience, structures that attempt to do both, usually do neither satisfactorily.

What is required are complementary structures each with their own purpose, budget and ways of working. Obviously the majority of a school's time and resources will go on maintenance; but unless there is also an element dedicated to development then the school is unlikely to progress in times of change. Decisions are made as to what aspect of maintenance requires development and it is that priority which gets the 'treatment' for that period of time. In practice, however, the development structure acts as a support system for the maintenance activities. A priority on teaching and learning, for example, will inevitably spread across a school's curriculum activities to the darkest realms of its maintenance activities if carefully managed. After any particular development phase another aspect of maintenance is selected and so on. Over time most aspects of the school are subject to some form of development activity.

It is in this way that successful schools respond to the challenge of centralized imposed reform within a decentralized system. The school will embrace some changes immediately and place them directly into the maintenance structure. This will be because the school either has no other legal option, or because it has a particular expertise or penchant for that change. Other changes, where experience is perhaps lacking, are selected as development priorities and sequenced over time.

Some centralized initiatives, however, are resisted, either because they are incompatible with the school's central purpose, or perhaps because they may just be wrong headed.

How Schools are Improved through Reform

In most countries there is a political demand for school improvement: any differences are those of pace, style and method. The politicians, with their own ideas for reform, tend to be impatient with what is often seen as resistance from teachers and scepticism, caution or even open hostility from academics. There are unlikely to be solutions which are quick, easy and cheap – or even just one of these! It is now abundantly clear that simple decentralization or centralization provide no panacea. A more integrative and action-based approach holds greater promise, but it is easier to say what will not work than what will work. It is the insistence by politicians on using strategies that have repeatedly been shown not to work that heralds the breakdown of communication and relationships between governments and both practitioners and researchers.

The pathology of policy implementation has been described by Milbrey McLaughlin in her re-analysis of the large-scale Rand Change Agent study undertaken in the USA in the 1970s. Many of the conclusions from the study still hold true today:

> A general finding of the Change Agent study that has become almost a truism is that it is exceedingly difficult for policy to change practice, especially across levels of government. Contrary to the one-to-one relationship assumed to exist between policy and practice, the Change Agent study demonstrated that the nature, amount and pace of change at the local level was a product of local factors that were largely beyond the control of higher-level policy-makers.
>
> (McLaughlin, 1990, p. 12)

She concluded that the relationship between 'macro-level' (for example, government) policies and 'micro-level' (for example, school) behaviour is paramount. This general observation has two specific implications: that 'policy cannot mandate what matters'; and 'implementation dominates outcomes'. We do not want to argue at this point for a specific set of policies. But we, like other contributors to this book, are certain that with regard to school improvement it is very difficult for schools to go it alone. So we doubt much beneficial effect from the rapid erosion in many countries of the 'middle tier' – the LEA, the district office, the State education department – not because we give uncritical allegiance to such bodies, but more because no school is an island and it is dangerous to weaken LEAs until frameworks for collaboration between consortia of schools with some alternative form of outside support or consultancy have been established. There is much in favour of decentralization, but it should not be at the expense of loss of support for schools in the management of change. The arguments adduced in this book make development planning a means of combining accountability with help and intervention with collaboration. This is what 'pressure and support' is about.

It is also becoming clear that change and development is a relatively long-term process, which conflicts with political timetables (one period of office). In these time-scales it is virtually impossible both to establish the partnerships between schools and a middle tier or other form of consultancy or agency to produce confident 'self-managing' schools and at the same time to implement major reforms in curriculum, pedagogy, governance and finance. The haste in implementing a hugely ambitious programme of reform, arising from a political timetable, has without question been responsible for some of the profound mistakes made by government in England and Wales since 1988. In addition there has been too little understanding of how schools work, and, even worse, too little interest in finding out how they work. In consequence far less is being achieved in terms of realizing the ultimate purpose of the reforms – raising the quality of student learning – than was possible. At the same time, we are optimistic in that schools seem to be making faster and greater progress than many would have expected, though our faith is tempered by a realization that there remains at the political level a persistent arrogance that understanding the complexities of school improvement processes is not an essential ingredient for the effective implementation of reforms aimed at raising student achievement.

These, then, are some of the themes that seem to us to be important if development planning is to fulfil its potential contribution to school improvement. We conclude by highlighting some issues for research, policy and practice.

With regard to *research* we would encourage colleagues to continue to:

- examine more closely the chain of events that connect planning to student achievement;
- identify the ways in which structure and culture affect each other in school development;
- ascertain the optimal balance between pressure and support in successful innovation.

With regard to *policy* we would encourage makers and advisers to:

- treat the (longer-term and more subtle) process of change as important as the (more immediate and obvious) content of change;
- provide more and better organized professional development for school leaders and teachers as a key element of resource provision;
- provide better and probably new forms of support for schools as both decentralization and centralization are insufficient in themselves.

With regard to *practice* we would encourage teachers and school leaders to:

- build a support system within the school that over time fuses development planning into school development and the improvement of classroom practice;
- examine carefully the school's 'management arrangements' as part of the process of development planning;
- invest in teams and partnerships within and outside the school and to be willing to take significant risks in so doing.

Above all, we hope that all three parties – policy makers, practitioners and researchers – will talk seriously together and learn from one another about school development and school improvement. As these chapters show, the knowledge base of what we do is fragmented and far from complete. Dialogue between the three parties is a necessary condition for rapid progress. We hope that this book will make a small contribution to this crucial endeavour.

REFERENCES

Ainscow, M. and Hopkins, D. (1992) 'Aboard the moving school', *Educational Leadership*, **50** (3), 79–81.

Caldwell, B. and Spinks, J. (1988) *The Self-Managing School*. Lewes: Falmer Press.

Fullan, M. (1990) 'Change processes in secondary schools: towards a more fundamental agenda', in McLaughlin, M., Talbert, J. and Bascia, N. (eds) *The Contexts of Teaching in Secondary Schools*. New York: Teachers College Press.

Fullan, M. (1991) *The New Meaning of Educational Change*. London: Cassell.

Hargreaves, D.H. (1990) 'Accountability and school improvement in the work of LEA inspectorates: the rhetoric and beyond', *Journal of Education Policy*, **5** (3), 230–9.

Hargreaves, D.H. and Hopkins, D. (1991) *The Empowered School: The Management and Practice of Development Planning*. London: Cassell.

Hopkins, D., (1994) 'Institutional self evaluation and renewal,' in Husen, T. and Postlethwaite, N. (eds) *The International Encyclopedia of Education*. New York: Pergamon Press.

Hopkins, D. Ainscow, M. and West, M. (1994) *School Improvement in an Era of Change*. London: Cassell.

McLaughlin, M. (1990) 'The Rand Change Agent study revisited', *Educational Researcher*, **19** (9), 11–16.

Office for Standards in Education (1994) *Improving Schools*. London: HMSO.

Rutter, M., Maughan, B., Mortimore, P. and Ouston, J. (1979) *Fifteen Thousand Hours: Secondary Schools and Their Effects on Children*. Wells: Open Books.

Schein, E. (1985) *Organizational Culture and Leadership*. San Francisco: Jossey-Bass.

Chapter 1

School Development Planning: An International Perspective

Neil Dempster, Chresten Kruchov and Grace Distant

Over the past decade governments in many Western democracies have been faced with concerns over increasing drains on the public purse caused by burgeoning educational expenditure (Hughes, 1992, p. 2). At the same time they have been unconvinced that increased funding has been translated into improvement in student outcomes from the schooling system. As a result, a number of Western governments under the influence of economic rationalists have sought ways to ensure that schools are made more accountable for what they do. To do so, they have taken lessons from private enterprise and adopted corporate managerialist approaches to public sector management (Dempster, 1991; Knight, 1990). These business, commercial and industrial approaches to organizational management demand that authority and responsibility be devolved closer to the work site so that employees are made more responsive to client needs within the framework of corporate strategic plans.

In recent years an increasing number of governments in the Western world have sought to prescribe an operational framework for schools by defining the curriculum, assessment and accreditation procedures centrally. At the same time, they have decentralized the focus of control over school management, in many cases placing school governance in the hands of locally constructed school boards (Hughes, 1992, p. 89; Harman *et al.*, 1991, p. 20). It is clear from these moves that the concept of self-managed schools is vital to political and bureaucratic strategies for the devolution of authority and responsibility to the point of educational service delivery.

The cornerstone of effective self-managed schools, it is argued by education system managers, is the school development plan, the school's equivalent of the corporate strategic plan referred to above. As a result, a great deal of effort has been placed on getting schools to commit themselves to a strategic planning process. At the present time these efforts are evident in Denmark, Australia, the United Kingdom and many other Western democracies.

It is to an analysis and comparison of school development planning in these three countries that we turn our attention in this chapter. In doing so, we construct our analysis in three parts. First, we provide a concise summary of three school development policy documents. Second, we describe the similarities and differences between the school development planning approaches adopted in the three countries under scrutiny. We then tie up this discussion with a summary which presents a comparative profile of the rationales, purposes and legitimating sources for school development planning in each country. In the third part of the chapter, we argue that as a result of pressures that are also affecting the world of business, industry and commerce, there are a series of management changes which schools are being 'driven' to make. These we categorize as movements from a 'public sector management style' to a 'corporate managerialist style'. We then set up a series of categories within these two poles as tools to extend our analysis of school development planning approaches in the United Kingdom, Australia and Denmark. We speculate on whose interests are being served by the school development planning process, questioning whether the process is liberating or controlling for the school's stakeholders. In concluding, we provide a summary of our arguments together with a projection of important areas for future research.

SCHOOL DEVELOPMENT PLANNING APPROACHES

In this section of the chapter, we describe approaches to school development planning contained in documents influential in the United Kingdom, Australia and Denmark. In so doing, we provide a general summary of each document before concentrating our attention on comparing and contrasting their rationales, purposes and legitimating sources.

The United Kingdom

The first document we examine comes from the United Kingdom. Entitled *Planning for School Development*, the document was produced by a team of researchers (Hargreaves *et al.*, 1989) and the research project was funded by the Department of Education and Science (DES). The document puts forward an approach to planning that is consistent with much of the strategic planning literature drawn from the worlds of business, industry and commerce (Strong, 1989). The approach includes (Hargreaves *et al.*, 1989, pp. 6–17):

- carrying out an audit of a range of school functions;
- determining priorities for development;
- constructing and agreeing on a plan;
- drawing up action plans, targets, tasks and success criteria;
- implementing the plan;
- checking the progress of implementation; and
- checking the success of implementation.

The United Kingdom approach places the planning in the hands of school governors, heads and teachers with encouragement to delineate the roles of each contained in a second document, *Development Planning: A Practical Guide*, published by the Department of Education and Science (1991). The expectation is that by emulating the process of school development planning outlined in this document, schools will be better placed to organize what they are already doing and what they need to do in more purposeful and rational ways (Hargreaves *et al.*, 1989, p. 4). While the DES has made it mandatory for schools in the United Kingdom to produce a curriculum development plan, school development planning is not yet a formal requirement. The DES considers the document *Planning for School Development* (Hargreaves *et al.*, 1989) as advisory, leaving schools free to employ the school development planning approach or not. However, as a result of local education authority (LEA) policy, many United Kingdom schools are formally required to produce a school development plan. Consequently, a range of different approaches to school management may still be found (Beresford *et al.*, 1992).

Australia

There is a great deal of similarity between the development of strategic plans in Australian schools as essential tools in the movement towards self-managed schooling and that which is occurring in the United Kingdom. However, even though most public schools across Australia are now involved in the development of strategic plans as part of the process of self-management, planning documents differ slightly in nomenclature from state to state. For example, whereas Departments of Education in Queensland, South Australia and Western Australia prefer the classification 'School Development Plans', the Victorian and the Northern Territory Departments of Education place their strategic plans under the rubric of 'School Renewal Plans', while 'School Improvement Plans' is the name given to plans developed by schools in New South Wales. While we acknowledge that these differences in nomenclature exist, we argue that the difference is of a superficial nature only. The underlying rationale for the development of strategic mangement plans in Australian schools and the general structure of these plans remain consistent with the corporate managerialist style we outlined earlier. For this reason and for reasons of scope, we restrict our analysis to one of the eight Australian state and territory documents, the Queensland document entitled *Collaborative School Development Planning and Review*.

The Queensland process signals two important underpinning principles:

1   participation of school stakeholders; and
2   review and evaluation as explicit parts of the planning process.

With these principles in mind, the Queensland document (Department of Education, 1992, pp. 7–9) lays down the following elements in developing planning:

- details of the participative planning process (who is involved and how);
- a school profile (school description and analysis of school environment);
- a mission statement (a statement of guiding principles and purposes);
- values and beliefs (a statement of values and beliefs that will influence the way the school addresses the school profile and mission statement);
- goals and strategies (an outline of school goals for the next three years); and
- internal review and evaluation (a brief description of processes to be used in the internal review and evaluation of the plan's components for the next three years).

The Queensland approach is directed at all major elements of a school's operations, namely, management, curriculum or studies, human resource management, resources and administration. Schools must write their plans under the headings outlined above and submit them for approval to Regional Offices of the Department of Education.

Denmark

The Danish document we examine, entitled *Development, Quality and School Management*, was not produced by government agencies as was the case in Australia. Researchers from the Royal Danish School of Educational Studies were commissioned by the Danish Ministry of Education to report on school development. The researchers, Kruchov and Hoyrup (1991a), carried out their study in a cluster of schools called the Gladsaxe Commune.

Their document bases its approach to development planning on evaluation themes. This has been done because the researchers have concluded from their work (Kruchov and Hoyrup, 1991b, p. 9) that school development rests on a systematic prospective analysis of educational leadership. They say that views about educational leadership can be clustered around nine themes:

- close pedagogic leadership;
- administration;
- personnel welfare and development;
- organization;
- dealing with conflict;
- school development;
- visibility in management;
- responsibility of management; and
- delegation.

The document suggests that people with a stake in the school should use the evaluation themes to focus their thoughts on the kind of school they would like to have, thus avoiding the defensiveness that often accompanies analyses of present circumstances. It is suggested that a series of discussions accompany each theme and that consideration is given to lists of concrete examples for possible initiatives. The result of these theme discussions is a comprehensive sense of direction about where the school should be heading. The document concludes with a set of questions to guide the development planning which is seen as a logical outgrowth of the evaluation process.

Throughout the Danish document, it is clear that what is provided is advisory only. The report carries no system authority or expectation obliging schools to undertake thematic evaluation and development planning.

A COMPARATIVE PROFILE

This section of the chapter compares the three documents, their legitimating sources, rationales and purposes. Table 1.1 contains a summary of that comparison. Even though the overarching rationale for development planning in each of the three countries examined is part of a quality and accountability trend, our analysis exposes variation in the approaches to and legitimating sources for development planning. As Table 1.1 shows, school development planning in the United Kingdom is legitimated through reference to the Education Reform Act (1988) and in a *de facto* way through the documentation produced by the Department of Education and Science (now the Department for Education). In Queensland, Australia, it is legitimated through ministerial policy and system-wide documentation produced by the Department of Education, while in Denmark legitimacy is claimed through recourse to research evidence. In both Queensland and the United Kingdom, there is an official expectation of compliance placed on schools. In Denmark, school development planning is not considered a policy requirement until it is pursued as policy by school communities themselves.

Table 1.1. *A comparison of legitimating sources, rationales and purposes for school development planning.*

Countries	Legitimating sources	Rationale	Purposes
United Kingdom (England)	Education Reform Act 1988 Department of Education and Science (*de facto*)	School development planning aids the development and management of change. Benefits include: focus on aims; totality of planning; sets manageable short-term priorities; relieves stress caused by change; promotes recognition; enhances staff development; and strengthens school–community relationships.	To assist governors and teachers to answer four fundamental questions: Where is the school now?; What changes do we need to make?; How shall we manage change over time?; How shall we know whether our management of change has been successful?
Australia (Queensland)	Queensland Department of Education policy, documents	Devolution of greater responsibility to schools improves decision-making and accountability through collaborative school development and review. Benefits include: reduces teacher stress; enhances school effectiveness; improves school–community relations; and has positive effects on student outcomes.	To assist the school to reflect on its total practice to assure quality education experiences for students. To encourage participation of all stakeholders. To foster decision-making about resources and services with regard to priorities. To support on-going review and evaluation.
Denmark	Research reports	The results of research into educational leadership and management indicate that there are benefits in democratic school planning. Schools will benefit by examining nine themes as significant fields for development. Separate controlled evaluation procedures are part of development. Effective development involves school boards.	To provide advice and support to school boards on evaluation and development. To focus actively on priority areas. To facilitate active planning for development by the school community.

A comparison of rationales in Table 1.1 exposes the 'benefits-selling' approach adopted by Queensland and England. The researchers responsible for the United Kingdom document (Hargreaves *et al.*, 1989) report that headteachers and teachers to whom they had spoken found that school development planning broadened parent and community participation which produced better quality decisions, increased student achievement and credible public accountability. However, Hargreaves *et al.* (1989, p. 5) qualify these advantages by suggesting that such benefits are 'far from automatic'. The Danish document makes no such claims. It offers the results of inquiry as starting points for participative evaluation and development by schools. The conclusion is drawn from this analysis that the United Kingdom and Queensland documents are much more assertive about the effects of school development planning than is the Danish document.

The last column in Table 1.1 lists school development planning purposes in each of the three countries. There is some similarity amongst the ideas presented but it is clear that the Queensland approach places a heavy emphasis on planning and review for quality assurance. The English and Danish approaches seem to concentrate more on successful development than on public accountability.

In summing up this part of the chapter, we make the point that there are both explicit and subtle differences in the approaches to school development planning contained in the three documents we have examined. The explicit differences have already been identified and discussed. The subtle differences we note lie in the 'softness' of the Danish approach and the 'hardness' of the English and Queensland approaches, the bureaucratization of development planning in England and Queensland, the Danish respect for community democracy and finally, the centre–periphery press for conformity in Queensland and England and the respect for and protection of local school community controls in Denmark.

We turn now to explain a series of trends in educational management which we argue are influential in our present discussion of school development planning.

MANAGEMENT CHANGES INFLUENCING SCHOOLS

Some of the keynotes of public sector change we referred to in our introduction have been increased market and consumer control, decentralization, reorientation of management from a regulation-based to a goal- and structure-based strategy, and increased competition between public institutions and between public and private institutions. Public institutions have had to justify their existence by documenting quality and accepting some degree of external participation in administration and management. Taken together, these demands comprise the general structural characteristics of change. In the internal workings of public institutions (including schools), these tendencies are reflected in the adjustment of salaries in relation to performance and transferral or dismissal based on qualifications.

It is not our intention to discuss and evaluate these general characteristics of change in any detail. However, two aspects impinge on our present work. First, we argue that there is a relationship between, on the one hand, documentation of an institution's *raison d'être*, competition with others and response to market mechanisms and consumer demands and, on the other hand, decentralization and self-management, which provide greater freedom of action and organization for the individual institution and claimed improved management structures. Second, when a school enters into competition, opens itself to its community and provides consumer-oriented service, it can no longer be managed by outside bureaucratic directives with little local authority. The school must have organizational latitude to decide how it will meet the demands of its future.

As a result of these pressures, we suggest that there are a series of positions towards which schools are being or have been driven; gently in countries such as Denmark and more forcefully in others, such as the United Kingdom, Australia and New Zealand (Harman *et al.*, 1991). As a base for our argument, we sketch two poles of contemporary change which define the directions of development in school systems as a manifestation of change in the public sector (see Table 1.2). We set up these categories as tools to extend our analysis of school development planning in the three countries referred to earlier.

Table 1.2. *Directions of contemporary corporate managerialist change in schools.*

Public sector management style		Corporate managerialist style
From public control	towards	market and consumer control
From judgements of quality based on educational criteria	towards	judgements of quality based on financial criteria
From management by civil servants	towards	governance by directors
From institutional monopoly	towards	open competition between institutions
From centralization	towards	increased decentralization and individual decision-making based in the school
From fixed salaries	towards	salaries based on qualifications, extent of responsibility and merit
From predominantly top-down leadership and administrative management	towards	shared leadership and collaborative management
From implicit quality control	towards	explicit quality specification and public accountability of the school
From management by regulation	towards	goal and structure oriented management

We have already stated in this chapter that school development planning is intrinsic to increased decentralization and individual decision-making based in schools. We apply seven of the trends illustrated in Table 1.2 to our understanding of approaches to school development planning (we make no comment on salary trends because these fall outside our present purpose). We now take each of the seven in turn and comment on its influence and effect on school development planning in the United Kingdom, Denmark and Australia.

Market and Consumer Control

Each of the three countries under examination is experiencing a shift towards market and consumer control to some degree. It is our opinion that a 'quasi market economy' is most evident in education in the United Kingdom (Harman *et al.*, 1991; Dempster *et al.*, 1992) and that it is least evident at present in Denmark. However, both Australia and Denmark are moving towards the United Kingdom position through policy changes associated with the self-management of schools (Caldwell and Spinks, 1988). These policy changes, as we indicated at the outset, are led by the devolution of authority and responsibility to school communities and they rely on participative strategic planning by the consumers of school education.

Judgements of quality based on financial criteria

Our examination of Danish policy documents has not revealed the same strength of commitment to management by financial criteria as exists in Queensland or the United Kingdom. In Queensland there is a clear direction to school managers to place the budgeting process at the heart of school development planning to ensure that what is projected can be accommodated within the block grants provided by government. At present, in Queensland the only available research into schools that have been through a complete cycle of planning, review and evaluation shows that there is concern that financial criteria have not been as influential in management decisions as policy makers would like (Highett, 1992). Knowing that block granting is commonplace in the United Kingdom, we suspect that management by financial criteria will become much more important there, as it will in the future with Australia, throughout the 1990s. If this is the case, then school development plans will continue to be refined as a management instrument even more than they have been to date. As yet, Danish schools have not been drawn into linking school development planning tightly to budgets.

Governance by boards of directors

The United Kingdom has moved rapidly down a 'corporatist' path by creating boards to take responsibility for the governance of schools. Denmark has had community councils acting in a governing capacity for many years but these councils do not have the same level of financial responsibility as do their United Kingdom counterparts. In Australia, the management of state schools has been progressively moved away from civil servants towards parents and community members since 1984. In that year, the Victoria government introduced a new Education Act, part of which created school councils as the principal decision-making body for every school. Since that time, other Australian states have followed suit. Queensland has acted rather more slowly than some, only trialling school advisory councils in 1992 (Department of Education, 1992). The shift towards this form of school governance has important implications for school development planning. In the United Kingdom, the policy documents call for direct involvement in development planning and approval of plans by governors as they do in a number of Australian states. The Queensland policy requires a collaborative approach amongst parents and members of the school community, but where there is an advisory council the active participation of councillors is encouraged. We believe that the trend towards participative planning for school development involving the governors of schools will increase during this decade in all three countries.

Open competition between institutions

There is little about competition on which we can comment from the school development planning documents on which we are focusing. The potential for comparisons amongst schools in all countries based on the scope and quality of their plans is already a reality in Queensland. The research to which we referred earlier

(Highett, 1992) identifies shortcomings in development planning amongst nominated schools. Such research is in keeping with emerging reporting practices in the United Kingdom and Australia which concentrate on a league table approach to the publication of school activity. The Danes have not yet moved in this direction.

Shared leadership and collaborative management

Collaborative management and shared leadership have become dominant themes in educational administration and management literature in recent years (Harman *et al.*, 1991; Caldwell and Spinks, 1988; Smyth, 1991; Kruchov and Hoyrup, 1991a,b). These authors, among others, argue that this style of leadership and management is essential if school plans are to be realized in practice. In addition, the implementation research of the 1970s and 1980s (Fullan, 1991) has shown that for plans to be implemented successfully, there must be a sense of corporate ownership of both what is intended and the strategies to achieve those intentions. With this as background, school development planning has been conceptualized as a process requiring collaboration by major stakeholders in each of our three subject countries. We contend that the trend towards this participative leadership and management style seems set to continue for the remainder of this century. However, we argue that its effects on the school development planning process are not well researched in any of the three countries yet.

Goal and structure oriented management

There is little for us to comment on with respect to this trend. Schools in the United Kingdom, Denmark and Australia are encouraged to use their development plans as management tools. The plans outline school missions, goals and strategies to achieve goals. Moreover, when budgets are tied to plans, a base for recasting school structures to support implementation is established. It is our view that school development plans are a direct manifestation of the move away from management by bureaucratic general regulation, particularly in the United Kingdom and Australia.

Explicit quality specification and public accountability

We assert that school development plans in the United Kingdom and Australia are expected to respond to the call for more explicit quality specification and public accountability. In both countries, plans are public documents, approved by school governors or by regional authorities. The plans are meant to focus review and evaluation procedures, irrespective of whether these procedures are carried out by inspection agencies or by a combination of school stakeholders. In contrast, judgements of quality in school performance in Denmark are not so tightly linked to development plans. Our analysis of Danish practice shows that judgements of quality are more broadly based in research into the school system in general and in the views of school communities. Nevertheless, we recognize that the Danes are moving towards individual school accountability and that this movement will increase reliance on the outcomes of the school development planning process. The 1990s may see the school development plan assuming an importance for accountability that may detract from its collaborative use as a cohesive management tool.

CONCLUSION

On the basis of the shift in school management style illustrated in Table 1.2, and our analysis of school development planning documents in the United Kingdom, Australia and Denmark, we draw a number of conclusions.

Our main conclusion is that collaborative school development planning of the 'harder' kind adopted in Australia and the United Kingdom does not necessarily result in the emancipation of those involved. In keeping with the work of Marginson (1992) we assert that the catalysts for devolution may be of a political or economic nature. In so doing, we argue that this distinction explains some of the differences between the approach to school development planning occurring in Denmark and that which is unfolding in the United Kingdom and Australia. Figure 1.1 illustrates two forms of the concept of devolution: a political form incorporating democratic processes and an economic form incorporating market processes. It is the economic/market-driven form of devolution that is most consistent with the merging corporate managerialist style referred to in Table 1.2.

| Political forms | Economic forms |
| (Democratic processes) | (Market processes) |

Figure 1.1 *Forms of devolution.*

We suggest that a politically motivated democratic form of devolution is found in Denmark and that this results in a 'grass roots' approach to management, decision-making and developmental planning, and the possible local liberation of stake-holders. On the other hand, we say that a more strongly market-oriented approach to devolution, school management and planning exists in the United Kingdom and Australia. This market orientation is firmly rooted in economic rationalism. At worst, economic rationalist approaches to school system restructuring result in the incarceration of stakeholders at the local level through a strengthening of the policy control of central agencies. Paradoxically, while schools are encouraged to become self-managing, the policy controls in Australia and the United Kingdom mean that school development planning must be accomplished within a restricted planning framework and with a set budget.

Finally, research into the effects of school development planning in countries such as Australia, Denmark and the United Kingdom is far from robust. For example, in a recent review of research since 1985 in Australia, Dempster *et al.* (1993) found forty-two reports of studies into development planning. All of these studies investigated the processes associated with planning rather than the results. We suspect there is a taken-for-granted assumption that a corporate managerialist style of school system operation produces tangible benefits for all concerned. Such an assumption needs to be tested through rigorous research into questions such as the following:

- What is the relationship between effective schooling and the process of school development planning?

- What is the relationship between effective schooling and political and economic forms of devolution?
- What are the actual effects of school development planning on school management, classroom management, teachers' work and children's achievements?

Answers to these questions require systematic studies into the impact and effects of school development planning. Research of this type is now under way in the three countries that have provided the focus for this discussion, some of which is reported in subsequent chapters of this book.

REFERENCES

Beresford, C., Mortimore, P., MacGilchrist, B. and Savage, J. (1992) 'School development planning matters in the UK', *Unicorn*, **18** (2), 12–16.

Caldwell, B. and Spinks, J. (1988) *The Self-Managing School*. Lewes: Falmer Press.

Dale, E.L. (1989) *Professionalism in Education*. Oslo: Norsk Gyldenal.

Dempster, N. (1991) *Partnerships in Australian Education*. Canberra: Australian College of Education.

Dempster, N., Logan, I., Sachs, J. and Distant, G. (1993) 'Planning in primary schools: a national study in Australian schools', Paper presented at the International Congress for School Effectiveness and Improvement', 3–6 January, Norrkoping, Sweden.

Department of Education (1992) *Collaborative School Department Planning and Review*. Queensland: Department of Education.

Department of Education and Science (1991) *Development Planning: A Practical Guide*. London: Department of Education and Science/HMSO.

Fullan, M. with Stiegelbaues, S. (1991) *The New Meaning of Educational Change*. London: Cassell.

Hargreaves, D., Hopkins, D., Leask, M., Connolly, J. and Robinson, P. (1989) *Planning for School Development: Advice to Governors, Headteachers and Teachers*. London: Department of Education and Science/HMSO.

Harman, G., Beare, H. and Berkeley, G. (eds) (1991) *Restructuring School Management*. Canberra: Australian College of Education.

Highett, N. (1992) 'School development: an overview of the Queensland process', *Unicorn*, **18** (2), 17–24.

Hoyrup, S. and Kruchov, C. (1991) 'School leadership for an improved school', in L. Monsen and T. Tiller (1991) *Effective Schools*. Oslo: Ad Notam.

Hughes, P. (1992) *Managing Curriculum Development in Queensland*. Brisbane: Department of Education.

Knight, J. (1990) 'Current reforms in education implications for teachers', *Unicorn*, **16** (3).

Kruchov, C. (1988) 'School development and strategies for change', *Danish Educational Journal*, **3**.

Kruchov, C. and Hoyrup, S. (1991a) *Development, Quality and School Management*. Copenhagen: Royal Danish School of Educational Studies.

Kruchov, C. and Hoyrup, S. (1991b) *School Development and Quality in School Leadership*. Copenhagen: Danish Ministry of Education.

Marginson, S. (1992) 'The market in schooling: issues of theory and policy'. *Choice Theory and Education*, Occasional paper No. 19, Australian College of Education.

Norgaard, E. (1989) 'On content and management', in Arnum, J. (ed.) *Who Makes Decisions?* Copenhagen: Gyldendal.

Smyth, J. (1991) *Educational Leadership*. London: Falmer Press.

Strong, J. (1989) 'Managing organisational change', *The Australian Way* (Australian Airlines).

Chapter 2

Creating Effective Schools through Site-Level Staff Development, Planning and Improvement of Organizational Culture

Daniel U. Levine

Much of the material in this chapter is an updated version of sections in a lengthy monograph (Levine and Lezotte, 1990) that summarized more than twenty years of United States research and analysis on unusually effective schools – that is, schools that have higher achievement than most other schools that enroll students who are comparable in social class. The first half of the monograph primarily discussed eight general 'correlates' of unusual effectiveness (for example, 'Productive school climate and culture' and 'Appropriate monitoring of student progress') and provided examples of policies and practices that analysts have reported help account for unusual effectiveness. For example, after identifying 'Effective instructional arrangements and implementation' as a key correlate (or characteristic) of unusually effective schools, the monograph cited numerous policies and practices involving 'Successful grouping and related organizational arrangements', 'Appropriate pacing and alignment', 'Active/enriched learning', and six other aspects of effective instructional arrangements. The remainder of the monograph was concerned primarily with research on the process of creating unusually effective schools and the results of projects and efforts that have been initiated to make schools more effective.

As indicated in the title of this chapter, I will emphasize aspects of the literature in the United States that deal with the creation of effective schools through site-level staff development and planning, and with issues involving modification of organizational cultures that impede effectiveness. Conclusions are derived largely from three types of analysis examined and summarized in the monograph:

1 descriptions of unusually effective schools;
2 descriptions of projects to enhance school effectiveness; and
3 more general analysis dealing with the change process in education, organizational behaviour and development in schools and other institutions, and related topics.

PRACTICE-ORIENTED STAFF DEVELOPMENT AT THE SCHOOL SITE

Descriptions of unusually effective schools indicate that in-service training and other forms of staff development generally are on-going activities which are carried out at the school site and are focused on practical considerations involving implementation of the instructional programme (for example, Fleigel, 1971; Lonoff, 1971; Glenn, 1981; Jackson, 1982; Jackson *et al.*, 1983; Hallinger and Murphy, 1985; Louis and Miles, 1990). Stedman (1987) has provided an excellent summary with examples of this emphasis on practice-oriented staff development as follows:

> Effective schools gave demonstration lessons to inexperienced teachers ... provided extra preparation periods for novices ... [to allow them to observe] experienced teachers ... videotaped teachers' performances to help improve instruction and evaluations ... and helped teachers make selections of materials and teaching techniques ... The emphasis throughout the inservice training was on the exchange of practical teaching techniques and on making training an integral part of a collaborative educational environment.
>
> (Stedman, 1987, p. 220)

Within this emphasis on practical, on-going, on-site, in-service training, much of the staff development at unusually effective elementary schools has taken the form of both intra- and cross-grade-level meetings and planning sessions at which teachers work together to improve co-ordination of instruction, select key learning objectives for a mastery-oriented approach to instruction, determine how to improve the performance of individual students, and otherwise work to attain important school-wide objectives (Levine and Stark, 1981; Ferguson, 1984). Although most of the schools described in the studies cited above were inner-city schools, Wick and Turnbaugh (1983) have described an intervention in middle-class elementary schools at which intra- and cross-grade-level meetings held to improve selection and assessment of skills emphasized in a mastery framework resulted in considerable improvement in student achievement.

On-going, practice-oriented staff development at the school site is the antithesis of traditional in-service training, which remains today the most common approach used for staff development in elementary and secondary schools. Traditional in-service training is characterized by 'one-shot' presentations which fill up all or part of a day devoted to presentations by outside 'experts'. Occasionally the participants in this activity are designated as 'trainers of trainers' who are expected to go back and teach their colleagues to use new methods and techniques effectively, even though they have not developed adequate skills for doing so and little, if any, time or other resources are subsequently devoted to follow-up and adaptation at the building or classroom levels. Traditional training of this kind is not just unproductive but is counterproductive, because it frequently manifests an 'informal covenant' in which teachers agree to listen to speakers for a few hours, in return for administrators' agreement to leave them fundamentally undisturbed in their classrooms (Parish, 1981). Faculty at unusually effective schools participate in this charade relatively little, or not at all; instead, they are heavily involved in regular staff development that focuses primarily on providing assistance to improve classroom teaching.

Guidelines for initiating and carrying on staff development to increase school effectiveness are identical to those which have been identified as desirable or necessary for significant school improvement efforts in general. As summarized by Fleming and Buckles (1987), staff development should incorporate the following emphases:

> Initial training should be just that: an introduction to the key features, approaches, and materials required ... [Later activities should] provide opportunities to discuss the plan and how to incorporate activities into daily teaching ... [and] time for teachers and administrators to reflect on desired practices and their impact on student performance. Programs that include classroom demonstrations, peer observation and feedback sessions, and other opportunities for personal reflection have more lasting impact than a flurry of initial activity with no follow-up.
>
> (Fleming and Buckles, 1987, p. 4)

Suggestions for assisting schools engaged in staff development designed to enhance instructional effectiveness also have been provided by members of the School Improvement Assistance Team sponsored by the Maine State Department of Education. (In general, these suggestions are similar to guidelines and recommendations provided in *The Empowered School* by Hargreaves and Hopkins (1991).) As summarized by Arbuckle (1986), suggestions offered by the Maine Improvement Assistance Team were as follows:

- Be patient.
- Provide staff with carefully selected reading material on relevant research before training or problem-solving sessions.
- Space training or problem-solving sessions over time, with enough time between to apply information.
- Use research on effective staff development practices as a guide in planning improvement activities. Be sure to model these practices.
- Recognize that building needs differ and capitalize on their diversity. Don't push for consistency if there isn't any.
- Think creatively! Don't let the 'yes buts' get in your way.
- Define and formalize collaborative mechanisms within schools to plan and manage continuing improvement activities.

(Arbuckle, 1986, pp. 4–5)

SCHOOL-SITE PLANNING AND DECISION-MAKING

Historically, most unusually effective schools in the United States were 'mavericks' created through the vigorous efforts of an outstanding principal who worked indefatigably to shape the inspired efforts of an assembled group of like-minded teachers (Stringfield and Teddlie, 1987). They were mavericks in the sense that their faculty frequently ignored or even violated rules and regulations that functioned to limit their effectiveness. Beginning in about 1980, however, numerous multi-school projects were launched to create unusually effective schools through site-based planning that reflects accumulating knowledge of the correlates of effectiveness. Descriptions and analysis of problems encountered in implementing effective schools projects that have emphasized site-based planning and decision-making led us

(Levine and Lezotte, 1990) to reach five major conclusions that are summarized below.

First, there is a real dilemma in moving to provide teachers with more decision-making authority at the same time that research clearly underlines the importance of administrative action and initiative in improving school effectiveness (Conley, 1989). This dilemma cannot be resolved successfully largely on the basis of flip ideological claims to the effect that empowering teachers by itself will somehow transform them into members of a cohesive faculty committed in practice to the extremely difficult work of reforming schools. Although decision-making in organizations is not a zero-sum game in which greater participation necessarily reduces the power of administrators (Tannenbaun, 1986; Pecheone and Shoemaker, 1984), simplistic movement towards teacher empowerment will not do much to improve school effectiveness (Conley, 1989; also see Wagner and Gooding, 1987, for somewhat discouraging data on the general effects of shared influence and decision-making in business and industry).

Our second conclusion, closely related to the first, was that from some points of view many actions required to make schools more effective may run counter to teachers' desires and/or self-perceived interests. For example, acquisition of new instructional techniques will be a painful task for many teachers, and delivery of active and enriched learning focused on higher-order skills necessitates a reduced emphasis on skills that are most easily taught. This argument can and should be turned around in pointing out that it is precisely the 'hardships' of change that may make participation a prerequisite for gaining teachers' commitment (Duffy, 1992; Presseisen, 1992), but the potentially counterproductive effects of teachers' perceived self-interest also suggest caution in moving toward radical increase in participation and empowerment.

Third, success of efforts to involve faculty in decision-making as part of effective schools projects or similar thrusts will depend on provision of appropriate and substantial training and related technical assistance for both teachers and administrators (Collins, 1988; Duttweiler, 1988; Harrison et al., 1989; Strusinski, 1989; David and Shields, 1991; Easton et al., 1991; Levine and Eubanks, 1992). The importance of training was emphasized as follows in a study of developments in a snowball sample of thirty-one school districts attempting to initiate one or another approach to school-based management (SBM):

> Increased training is an obvious response to the difficulty of the roles involved in SBM, and lack of training did surface as a problem. ... In schools or districts where very little training was provided, participants complained that they had been given inadequate orientation to the program.
>
> (Clune and White, 1988, pp. 28–9)

A fourth and closely related conclusion regarding the functioning of site planning committees or councils involves the necessity to provide their members with substantial amounts of time to develop and monitor both their planning procedures and their action plans for change (Dutweiler, 1988; Henderson and Lezotte, 1988; David, 1989; Mauriel and Lindquist, 1989; Saxl et al., 1989; Louis and Miles, 1990; Easton et al., 1991). As pointed out by Clune and White (1988), planning can be a 'very time-consuming process' for principals and teachers who are 'already burdened with time-consuming activities' and experience difficulty in devising and pursuing 'ideas which go against state laws or district policy' (Clune and White, 1988, p. 28). Absence of time allocated for participation can lead to what Firestone and Corbett (1988) have called 'mock' participation.

Fifth, a discretionary fund should be available so that planning committees and, indeed, entire faculties participating in school effectiveness projects can acquire early experience in aligning and realigning resources and educational goals, and can move quickly to initiate significant changes in instructional programming (David, 1989). The importance and utility of a significant discretionary fund have been stressed in evaluations of efforts to implement site-based planning in Chicago and New York City (Kelley and Willner, 1988; Easton *et al.*, 1991). Beyond provision of a discretionary fund, some school-based management projects are experimenting with possibilities for allowing faculties to overhaul their budgets systematically with little restraint imposed by state or district policies or by contracts negotiated with teacher organizations (David, 1989; David and Shields, 1991). It is too early to determine whether or how often and in what circumstances this approach is likely to succeed.

Planning components and emphases

Effective schools projects typically involve the establishment of building-level planning committees and subcommittees which prepare annual or longer-range improvement plans that deal, in one way or another, with various correlates of effectiveness. Many of the correlates of unusual effectiveness, such as site-level staff development, provision of substantial technical assistance, and orientation toward practical problem-solving, have clear implications concerning the preparation and implementation of improvement plans. Beyond such rather obvious implications, which I will not belabour here, little is known about how to shape and carry out the planning process. However, a few comments may be helpful regarding experiences reported by persons who have participated in projects to create unusually effective schools.

1   Planning in effective schools projects should be 'data-driven' in the sense that analysis and decisions should take account of data on key indicators such as the extent to which disadvantaged students attain satisfactory performance on central learning objectives. Experience in many successful improvement projects indicates that appropriate data provide a critically important resource in encouraging and redirecting faculty towards meaningful change in existing practices (Henderson and Lezotte, 1988; Bullard and Taylor, 1992). Examples of data which have been helpful in modifying attitudes and behaviour in order to focus on strategic equity and effectiveness goals include: peer observations in which teachers assess each others' interactions with low achievers; curriculum-alignment activities in which teachers analyse a variety of data in collaborating to select skills to emphasize and de-emphasize at and across grade levels (Levine and Stark, 1981, 1982; Neidermeyer and Yelon, 1981; Wick and Turnbaugh, 1983); analysis of Degrees of Reading Power data which in effect force teachers to consider possibilities for change when their text and other materials are mismatched with their students' current comprehension levels (Harris and Cooper, 1985; Levine and Eubanks, 1989; Levine and Sherk, 1989,

1990); and information on student and faculty 'time-on-task' which school improvement specialists help faculty collect and analyse as part of their participation in effective schools projects (Everson *et al.*, 1986).

2   A clear signal indicating that a school is concerned largely with 'organizational maintenance' and the 'politics of efficiency' (Fraatz, 1988) rather than fundamental improvement frequently is present when its plan specifies that most or all teachers or grades will participate to the same extent in the same intervention and/or will receive exactly the same resources. Since imperatives for improvement and needs for increased resources almost always vary from teacher to teacher and grade to grade, equivalence in interventions and/or parity in resources throughout a school usually indicate that faculty have seized on simplistic solutions that require minimal change in instruction. For example, plans that represent mostly an 'easy way out' with little or no modification of ineffective practice include the following:

- components specifying that every teacher receive exactly the same funding for supplementary materials;
- 'schoolwide' plans which redirect compensatory education resources to bring about slight reduction in the size of every elementary class, with no fundamental intervention in arrangements for delivering instruction:
- provision of the same fraction of a (fragmented) paraprofessional's time for every classroom teacher;
- provision of a few minutes a week of obviously meaningless time in a computer lab for every student in a given grade or subject;
- purchase of a computer lab without a teacher or aide to maintain it, or with too few computers to allow for effective utilization;
- purchase of truckloads of consumable workbooks and ditto sheets that keep students occupied in seatwork.

3   If they are to make much difference, school improvement plans generally will involve changes that some or many faculty will find distasteful, frequently because the modifications required will upset customary arrangements or interfere with faculty 'rights' and privileges. A few examples that occur with some frequency include the following:

- regrouping arrangements which reduce senior faculty privileges in deciding who they will teach;
- introduction of tutoring for low achievers before and after school, even though this may require teachers to work beyond their contractual obligations;
- agreement within a department, grade, or entire school to follow common testing practices, homework policies, and/or discipline rules, even though some or many faculty are satisfied with current idiosyncratic practices;
- reassignment of rooms, which may require senior teachers to forego space they have worked hard to customize and improve.

4   Persons responsible for the success of a school improvement committee or council should anticipate that the group will have to deal with and move beyond

predictable stages in the development and implementation of a plan for change. Differing skills and understandings and, in many cases, differing sources of external assistance will be required to help participants succeed in carrying out tasks that are most central at each stage (Sudlow, 1989; Miles, 1992). One useful formulation of the major overlapping stages generally encountered in developing a meaningful improvement plan has been provided by the Effective Schools Unit of the New York State Department of Education as follows:

Preparation Stage: concerned with membership, roles, functions and expectations.

Start-Up Stage: concerned with establishing trust, workable procedures, time commitments.

Group Problem Solving and Process Analysis Stage: concerned with how to handle disagreements, do data analysis, identify strengths and concerns.

Action-Planning Stage: concerned with priorities, funding, resources, activities, and communication with faculty.

Implementation and Evaluation Stage: concerned with school improvement plan, sustaining and documenting change, revising the plan and monitoring the effectiveness of the team.

(Effective Schools Unit, 1987)

ORGANIZATIONAL CULTURE ASPECTS AND ISSUES

While there are innumerable definitions of 'organizational culture', most authors who analyse this concept stress that it has to do with the 'way we do things around here'; that is, the beliefs and norms members of an organization tend to share concerning what they should or should not, can or cannot do in performing their roles (Deal, 1985; Schmuck and Runkel, 1985; Corbett and Rossman, 1989). Most authors also stress more specific aspects of organizational culture such as whether participants are relatively likely to resist or welcome innovations (Corbett *et al.*, 1987; Peterson, 1988), and are passive in the face of obstacles rather than exemplify a problem-solving, 'take care of business' orientation (Heckman, 1987; Miles, 1992). These aspects of organizational culture obviously are important in determining whether an effective schools project – like other school improvement efforts – will be likely to succeed and how it should be implemented to bring about substantial change.

One major issue regarding organizational culture involves the question of how it is influenced and shaped by leaders in the organization. In this regard, Schein (1985, p. 2) has speculated that the 'only thing of real importance that leaders do is to create and manage culture.' In recent years particular attention has been given to ways in which both leaders and non-leaders may influence organizational culture through stories, legends, myths, analogies, rituals, ceremonies, sagas, images, parables, and related symbolic interpretations in various kinds of organizations (for example, Deal and Kennedy, 1982; Taylor, 1984; Deal, 1985; Firestone and Wilson, 1989). Analysis by Peterson (1988) and Deal and Peterson (1989) also has drawn attention to a variety of means that principals use to develop an organizational culture that can facilitate greater school effectiveness. In addition to providing strong support for productive teachers, distributing 'material, social, and symbolic'

43

rewards to reinforce desired norms and roles, and recruiting a staff that supports the principal's vision of school improvement, effective cultural leadership involves 'modeling, teaching, and coaching' to support core goals such as professional development and enhanced teacher collegiality (Peterson, 1988).

A second major issue involves the extent to which fundamental, lasting improvement in organizational functioning can be brought about without systematic change and improvement in organizational culture, at least in the case of organizations which are functioning poorly in part because shared norms and beliefs are unproductive or dysfunctional. A closely related issue involves the reverse possibility that improvements in organization culture may be extremely difficult to bring about unless the organization is functioning at some minimum level of adequacy which allows participants to look beyond immediate, day-to-day problems and crises.

Unfortunately, little systematic research has been conducted to help leaders in schools or other organizations knowledgeably address issues and questions involving the extent to which change in organizational culture must take place very early in an effectiveness improvement project. As regards organizational culture and stages in school improvement, Taylor (1984) studied elementary schools engaged in effective schools projects and found that those which had made progress with respect to several aspects of organizational culture (that is, development of a 'working consensus' and 'negotiation of rubber duck areas') showed signs of continuing and lasting improvement in functioning, whereas those which had not improved these aspects of culture had 'plateaued' after registering some progress with respect to climate and achievement. In addition, Taylor concluded that progress in improving organizational culture in the schools she studied reflected principals' skills in using their 'knowledge-in-action' to enhance 'sensemaking processes' through 'strategic communication episodes' and 'units of strategic dialogue' (Taylor, 1984, p. 177).

Although the generalization that organizational culture should be improved or, at least, attended to early in a school improvement project cannot be viewed as well-established, it is reasonable to accept this conclusion as a working hypothesis given the many ways in which cultural considerations appear to be important in the development and implementation of such an effort. For example, the importance of a shared criterion of effectiveness stressing that all students can learn, of faculty input in decision-making, and of a general orientation toward problem-solving suggests that explicit attention should be given to these and other aspects of organizational culture early on in an effective schools project. Indeed, multi-school projects to improve effectiveness on a systematic basis typically do pay attention to various cultural considerations during the initial stages of implementation. Frequently utilized instruments such as the Connecticut School Effectiveness Questionnaire include items dealing with existence of a clearly articulated mission, the principal's role in developing shared understandings, the prevalence of high expectations for students, and other aspects of organizational culture, and much of the work of project facilitators usually focuses in one way or another on analysing and improving the organizational culture of participating schools.

However, despite the apparent centrality of cultural considerations in understanding and working to improve organizational effectiveness, it is somewhat uncertain whether and how knowledge of organizational culture and its dynamics can be used to improve outcomes in a planned, intentional fashion. In this regard,

Vaill (1989, pp. 162, 158, 157) has described the 'conceptual and semantic swamp' organizations tend to get mired in when members try to develop clarity in their mission, as well as tendencies for activities aimed at improving organizational culture to degenerate into 'off-site visioning seminars and spirituality workshops' that take the place of 'active pursuit and fulfillment of the mission and vision'. In general, he concludes, 'those who would "change the organizational culture" have a different and more difficult job than some of them seem to realize' (Vaill, 1989, p. 159). Similarly, Firestone and Wilson (1989, p. 283) have examined the literature on development of organizational culture in schools and concluded that 'Until there have been more studies of the professional culture of schools, judgement must be withheld about how susceptible they are to administrative influence.' Thus possibilities and approaches for modifying organizational culture should be viewed as constituting an important frontier deserving of considerable attention from practitioners and researchers who participate in future efforts to create unusually effective schools.

REFERENCES

Arbuckle, M. (1986) 'An update from Maine: some things we've learned about school improvement', *The Developer*, **1** (March), 3–5.

Bullard, P. and Taylor, B.O. (1992) *Keepers of the Dream*. Needham Heights, MA: Allyn & Bacon.

Clune, W.H. and White, P.A. (1988) *School-Based Management*. New Brunswick, NJ: Center for Policy Research in Education, Rutgers University.

Collins, R.A. (1988) *Interim Evaluation Report School-Based Managment/Shared Decision Making Project*. Miami, FL: Dade County Public Schools.

Conley, S.C. (1989) '"Who's on first?": School reform, teacher participation, and the decision-making process', Paper delivered at the annual meeting of the American Education Research Association, San Francisco, March.

Corbett, H.D., Firestone, W.A. and Rossman, G.B. (1987) 'Resistance to planned change and the sacred in school cultures', *Educational Administration Quarterly*, **23** (4), 36–59.

Corbett, H.D. and Rossman, G.B. (1989) 'Three paths to implementing change: a research note', *Curriculum Inquiry*, **19** (2), 164–90.

David, J.L. (1989) 'Synthesis of research on school-based management', *Educational Leadership*, **48** (8), 45–53.

David, J.L. and Shields, P.M. (1991) *Making Schools More Effective: A Literature Review from Effective Schools to Restructuring*. Menlo Park, CA: SRI International.

Deal, T.E. (1985) 'The symbolism of effective schools', *Elementary School Journal*, **85** (5), 601–20.

Deal, T.E. and Kennedy, A. (1982) *Corporate Cultures*. Reading, MA: Addison-Wesley.

Deal, T.E. and Peterson, K.D. (1989) *The Principal's Role in Shaping School Cultures*. Manuscript prepared for the US Department of Education (draft).

Duffy, G.G. (1992) 'The new school reform: implications for literacy instruction', Paper delivered at the annual meeting of the American Educational Research Association, San Francisco, April.

Dutweiler, P.C. (1988) *Organizing for Excellence*. Austin, TX: Southwest Educational Development Laboratory.

Effective Schools Unit (1987) *New York School Improvement Program Guidebook*. Albany: Effective Schools Unit.

Everson, S.T., Scollay, S.J., Fabert, B. and Garcia, M. (1986) 'An effective schools program and its results: initial district, school, teacher, and student outcomes in a participating district', *Journal of Research and Development in Education*, **19** (3), 35–49.

Ferguson, B. (1984) 'Overcoming the failure of an inner-city school', *Phi Delta Kappan*, **65** (9), 629–30.

Firestone, W.A. and Corbett, H.D. (1988) 'Planned organizational change', in Bogan, N.J. (ed.) *Handbook of Research on Educational Administration*, pp. 321–38. New York: Longman.

Firestone, W.A. and Wilson, B.L. (1989) 'Using bureaucratic and cultural linkages to improve instruction: the principal's contribution', in Burdin, J.L. (ed.) *School Leadership*, pp. 275–96. Beverly Hills, CA: Sage.

Fleigel, S. (1971) 'Practices that improve academic performance at an inner-city school', *Phi Delta Kappan*, **52** (6); 341–342.

Fleming, D.S. and Buckles, C. (1987) 'Implementing school improvement plans'. Andover, MA: Regional Laboratory for Educational Improvement of the Northeast and Islands.

Fraatz, J.M.B. (1988) 'Managed equality', Paper delivered at the annual meeting of the American Educational Research Association, New Orleans, April.

Glenn, B. (1981) *What Works? An Examination of Effective Schools for Poor Black Children*. Cambridge, MA: Harvard University of Law and Education.

Hallinger, P. and Murphy, J. (1985) 'Instructional leadership and school socio-economic status: a preliminary investigation', *Administrator's Notebook*, **31** (5), 1–4.

Hargreaves, D.H. and Hopkins, D. (1991) *The Empowered School: The Management and Practice of Development Planning*. London: Cassell.

Harris, T.L. and Cooper, E.J. (1985) *Reading, Thinking, and Concept Development*. New York: College Entrance Examination Board.

Harrison, C.R., Killion, J.P. and Mitchell, J.E. (1989) 'Site-based management: the realities of implementation', *Educational Leadership*, **46** (8), 55–8.

Heckman, P. (1987) 'Understanding school culture', in Goodlad, J.I. (ed.) *The Ecology of School Renewal*, pp. 63–78. Chicago: University of Chicago Press.

Henderson, A. and Lezotte, L. (1988) 'SBI and effective schools: a perfect match', *NETWORK for Public Schools*, **13** (5), 1, 3–5.

Jackson, S.C. (1982) Instructional leadership behaviors that characterize schools that are effective for low socioeconomic urban black students, unpublished Ed. D. dissertation, Catholic University of America, Washington, DC.

Jackson, S., Logsdon, D.M. and Taylor, N.E. (1983) 'Instructional leadership differentiating effective from ineffective low-income urban schools', *Urban Education*, **18** (1), 59–70.

Kelley, T. and Willner, R. (1988) *Small Change: The Comprehensive School Improvement Program*. Albany, NY: Educational Priorities Panel.

Levine, D.U. and Eubanks, E.E. (1989) 'Organizational arrangements at effective secondary schools', in Walberg, H.J. and Lane, J.J. (eds) *Organizing for Learning*, pp. 41–9. Reston, VA: National Association of Secondary School Principals.

Levine, D.U. and Eubanks, E.E. (1992) 'Site-based management: engine for reform or pipedream?', in Lane, J.J. and Epps, E.G. (eds) *Restructuring Schools: Problems and Prospects*, pp. 61–82. Berkeley, CA: McCutchan.

Levine, D.U. and Lezotte, L.W. (1990) *Unusually Effective Schools*. Madison, WI: National Centre for Effective Schools Research and Development.

Levine, D.U. and Sherk, J.K. (1989) 'Implementation of reforms to improve comprehension skills at an unusually effective inner city intermediate school', *Peabody Journal of Education*, **66** (4), 87–106.

Levine, D.U. and Sherk, J.K. (1990) *Effective Implementation of a Comprehension Development Approach in Secondary Schools*. Kansas City: University of Missouri–Kansas City.

Levine, D.U. and Stark, J.C. (1981) *Instructional and Organizational Arrangements and Processes for Improving Academic Achievement at Inner City Elementary Schools*. Kansas City: University of Missouri–Kansas City.

Levine, D.U. and Stark, J.C. (1982) 'Instructional and organizational arrangements that improve achievement in inner-city schools', *Educational Leadership*, **40** (3), 41–6.

Lonoff, R. (1971) 'Supervisory practices that promote academic achievement in a New York City school', *Phi Delta Kappan*, **52** (6), 338–40.

Louis, K.S. and Miles, M.B. (1990) *Improving Urban High Schools: What Works and Why*. New York: Teachers College Press.

Mauriel, J.J. and Lindquist, K.M. (1989) 'School-based management: doomed to failure?', Paper delivered at the annual meeting of the American Educational Research Association, San Francisco, March.

Miles, M.B. (1992) '40 years of change in schools: some personal reflections', Paper delivered at the annual meeting of the American Educational Research Association, San Francisco, April.

Niedermeyer, F. and Yelon, S. (1981) 'Los Angeles aligns instruction with basic skills', *Educational Leadership*, **38**, 618–20.

Parish, R. (1981) 'Discontinuation of innovative programs in Missouri schools', Unpublished PhD dissertation, University of Oregon, Eugene.

Pecheone, R. and Shoemaker, J. (1984) *An Evaluation of the School Effectiveness Program in Connecticut*. Hartford: Connecticut State Department of Education.

Peterson, K.D. (1988) 'Mechanisms of culture building and principal's work', *Educational and Urban Society*, **20** (3), 250–361.

Presseisen, B. (1992) 'Implementing thinking in the school's curriculum', Paper delivered at the Third Annual Meeting of the International Association for Cognitive Education, Riverside, CA, February.

Saxl, E.R., Kaplan, M., Robinson, J.J. and Springer, C.M. (1989) *Project BASICS in the Schools: There for the Long Haul*. New York: Center for Policy Research.

Schein, E.H. (1985) *Organizational Culture and Leadership: A Dynamic View*. San Francisco: Jossey-Bass.

Schmuck, R.A. and Runkel, P.J. (1985) *The Handbook of Organizational Development in Schools* (3rd edn). Prospect Heights, IL: Waveland Press.

Stedman, L.C. (1987) 'It's time we changed the effective schools formula', *Phi Delta Kappan*, **69** (3), 215–24.

Stringfield, S. and Teddlie, C. (1987) 'A time to summarize: six years and three phases of the Louisiana School Effectiveness Study', Paper delivered at the annual meeting of the American Educational Research Association, Washington, DC, April.

Strusinski, M. (1989) 'The provision of technical support for school-based evaluations: the researcher's perspective', Paper delivered at the annual meeting of the American Educational Research Association, San Francisco, March.

Sudlow, R.E. (1989) 'Implementing effective research in a K-12 suburban district: the Spencerport Model', in Lezotte, L.W. and Taylor, B.O. (eds) *Case Studies in Effective Schools Research*. Okemos, MI: National Center for Effective Schools.

Tannenbaum, A. (1986) *Control in Organizations*. New York: McGraw-Hill.

Taylor, B.O. (1984) 'Implementing what works: elementary principals and school improvement programs', unpublished PhD dissertation, Northwestern University, Evenston, IL.

Vaill, P. (1989) *Managing as a Performing Art*. San Francisco: Jossey-Bass.

Wagner, J.A. III and Gooding, R.Z. (1987) 'Shared influence and organizational behavior: a meta-analysis of situational variables expected to moderate participation–outcome relationships', *Academy of Management Journal*, **38** (3), 524–41.

White, P. (1988) *Resource Materials on School-Based Management*. New Brunswick, NJ: Center for Policy Research in Education, Rutgers University.

Wick, J.W. and Turnbaugh, R.C. (1983) 'A successful program to improve student performance', Paper published by the Northwestern University School of Education Division of Field Studies, Evanston, IL.

Chapter 3

The Contribution of Quality Assurance Reviews to Development in School Systems

Peter Cuttance

INTRODUCTION

The accountability and improvement of education has been an issue on the political agenda for most of the last two decades. Partly in response to this, schools and school systems have developed a range of approaches to review and improve their performance. These have been referred to under the rubric of school improvement programmes, school development plans, school-based review and self-evaluation, and, more recently, quality assurance and external review. These approaches all have one overriding aim, the improvement of the process of schooling and the raising of educational standards, but they derive from different traditions. The main developments in the 1970s and early 1980s were 'school improvement' programmes, which derived originally from attempts to rejuvenate inner-city schools in the USA, and school-based review and self-evaluation, which was a response from pressures for schools in various countries to be more accountable (Hopkins, 1985). External review approaches have their heritage in the United Kingdom schools Inspectorate, although there are now clear differences between the 'inspection' focus of United Kingdom school inspection methodologies and the 'quality assurance' orientation which characterizes recent developments in South Australia and New Zealand (Cuttance, 1992a).

Although school improvement programmes could be treated as a particular type of activity under school-based review, it is useful to treat them as different because the international literature for each has tended to ignore the other (Reynolds, 1992). The school effectiveness and school improvement literature is reviewed in Cuttance (1986), Levine (1992), Murphy (1992) and Reynolds (1992). Hopkins (1985) reviewed the school-based review and self-evaluation literature. The present chapter discusses key aspects of the experience with school review and evaluation in the United Kingdom that were important in the development of the framework for school review and development in South Australia. The discussion brings together the requirements of accountability and development within a framework of quality assurance.

The use of school-based reviews in the United Kingdom focused on the adoption by individual schools of self-evaluation schemes. In addition to this being a response to the perceived pressures for greater accountability, it was also a reflection of the growing professionalism of teachers (see Nuttall (1981) for further discussion of this point). In contrast to these internal[1] approaches to review and evaluation, Her

Majesty's Inspectors of Schools (HMI) have provided the main paradigm for *external* reviews and evaluations of schools.[2]

The systems of self-evaluation that were introduced in schools in the United Kingdom had certain weaknesses which were responsible for their failure to operate in the way that their proponents had initially expected. One of the reasons for this is the heavy demands that it makes on teachers' time. Another problem has been the lack of in-service training in the skills necessary to carry out analytical evaluations and reviews of school performance. In addition, school self-evaluation has been viewed in many cases as a process that involved only the teachers in a school, because it has been orientated towards the professional development needs of teachers. Its exclusion of other parties to schooling from the review process (pupils, parents, school counsellors, administrators, etc.) has meant that it has not satisfied external demands for accountability. Further, the strong focus of reviews and self-evaluations on professional development has tended to detract from the overall objective of improving schools, because the findings of reviews have not been translated into the appropriate action plans required for school development, or because of a lack of success in managing the process of change (Hopkins, 1989; Clift, 1987).

INTERNAL SCHOOL REVIEWS

The United Kingdom experience

Hopkins (1989) provided a prescriptive statement of the main characteristics of successful schemes of internal school-based review:

- they are based on a systematic review and evaluation process, and are not simply an exercise in reflection;
- their immediate goal is to obtain information about a school's condition, purposes, and products;
- they are meant to lead to action on an aspect of the school's organization or curriculum;
- they are a group activity that involves participants in a collegial process;
- optimally the process is 'owned' by the school;
- their purpose is school improvement and development, and their aspiration is to progress towards the ideal goal of a 'problem-solving' or 'relatively autonomous' school.

This list of characteristics has benefited from hindsight gained through the evaluation of school-based review schemes over the last decade. In reality, few schemes have conformed to this idealized set of characteristics, partly because there has been considerable variation in purpose among the schemes that have been in use. Following from this variation in purpose there has been variation in the way that schemes have been implemented. Nuttall (1981) listed a series of questions, developed out of the experiences of those involved in a group of school-based review projects, that addressed the key evaluation issues for school reviews:

Questions about context
- Who or what is the scheme for? Who is examining what and reporting it to whom?

- What balance is intended between professional development and rendering account?
- Who has taken the initiative?
- Is it to be mandatory?
- Who is to control the process? Is it specified in detail?
- Are the lines of communication and consultation such that the process of evaluation will be fully understood by all involved?
- Is it potentially threatening to schools, or teachers?

Questions about process
- Is it economical in terms of time and resources?
- Who is to be involved, both inside and outside the school, and what is their sense of involvement?
- What supports, skills or other resources will be available?
- How is trust being ensured or developed?
- What is the focus of attention of the evaluation?
- What methods, instruments or techniques are to be employed?
- Over what period of time will the scheme be conducted?
- How will the programme be sustained?
- How frequently will it occur?

Questions about reporting
- What guidance will be given in drafting the report?
- Who drafts the report? Who authorizes the final draft? What are the stages in this process?
- Who receives the report?
- What is the style of the report? Descriptive or judgemental; bland or blunt; what format; length; what tone; etc.?
- Are individuals to be named or otherwise identified?
- Is the report to be validated? If so, by whom and at what stage? Will this validation be recorded and reported?
- What part will the public media be expected to play?

Questions about action
- Is implementation built in to the process?
- Are advisers to be involved in implementation?
- How will implementation be managed?
- Is it expected that implementation will be continuous, part of a cyclical process of evaluation, planning, and action?

(Nuttall, 1981)

The Guidelines for Review and Internal Development in Schools (GRIDS) scheme was one of the most common United Kingdom approaches to school self-evaluation. This approach was intended for the 'whole school' rather than for individual teachers or small groups (McMahon *et al.*, 1984). However, this was not meant to imply that schools should tackle all issues simultaneously. The advice was to select one or two areas for development and focus on these before evaluating the process and moving on to new priority areas.

Another scheme of school-based review and evaluation was the Institutional

Development Programme. This scheme used a questionnaire survey to help diagnose problems affecting institutional functioning and performance.[3] The feedback of the information from the questionnaire to schools is employed as a strategy to generate a process of goal setting, planning and action. The assistance of a consultant is considered to be important in the process of interpreting the responses to the questionnaire and in assisting the school to establish its development plan. Various other schemes that use standardized schedules of items to assess school functioning and process were reviewed by Hopkins (1989).

How Successful Has Internal School Review Been?

Part of the failing of school-based internal self-evaluation and review schemes stems from changes in the prevailing view of the management of education. When school-based review schemes were introduced in the late 1970s the administrative orientation towards the conduct of public sector organizations was predominantly one in which accountability was referenced by the standards and traditions of professional institutions. Thus, school-based reviews invested primary responsibility for the development of schools in the professionals who were involved in schooling. However, even then there was concern that schooling was an activity that is directly funded by the treasury, and that this public responsibility requires some additional form of formal accountability.

This tension between public and professional accountability is apparent in several of the questions in Nuttall's list. Nuttall summed up the situation with respect to school self-evaluation schemes:

> Accountability and professional development are therefore not necessarily incompatible, but admittedly the tide is not running in favour of accountability procedures which appear to exclude the public or its representatives. Then, assuming that formal account has to be rendered to parents, governors and/or LEA, is there still a way that the exercise [of self-evaluation] can also be one that generates professional development?
>
> (Nuttall, 1981, p. 23)

Since that time the prevailing view has strengthened in terms of the requirement for schools, and other public sector organizations, to provide evidence that they are accountable for their activities. This, however, need not result in a weakening of the accountability of schools to professional standards and traditions. Indeed, paradoxically as it may seem, the more market-oriented the school system becomes, the weaker the argument for direct control through accountability mechanisms emanating solely from the treasury. The increased demand for accountability is not so much to the public as electors, and therefore providers of funds, but as the consumer of the services offered by schools.

The major problem with school-based reviews in the United Kingdom was their failure to construct analytically critical reviews and evaluations of the process of schooling (Clift, 1987; Hopkins, 1989; Hargreaves, 1988). Evaluations tended to be defensive and often did not tackle issues central to the process of learning and teaching critically (Hargreaves, 1988). In addition, the development that should follow an evaluation was often not managed successfully, and often did not result in the intended improvements (Hargreaves, 1988).

There are various reasons for these failures. Successful change in social organizations through a process of review, development and evaluation requires a high level of complex skills and management. It requires motivation (Clift, 1987) and access to training in skills of evaluation and the management of change (Clift, 1987; Hopkins, 1989). The significant investment of time required for successful school development means that all the participants must have a strong commitment to the changes needed, and be prepared to divert time and energy from other activities into the various phases of the programme (Hopkins, 1989). The lack of experience in planned change and in managing the commitment and time required to redeploy resources have also been significant reasons for the failure of school self-evaluation systems to lead to successful school development (Clift, 1987).

Other failings of school-based reviews have been:

- they have rarely involved all stakeholders – their focus has often been that of professional development for school staff, and therefore pupils, parents, school councillors, community members, and administrators have not always been included in the review process;
- they have tended to be too time-consuming and exhausting of the energies of those involved;
- they have often attempted to be all-encompassing and have tackled too large a task;
- the period between reviews has often been too long to make a timely and significant impact on the development process in schools.

In addition, the programmes of change and development that have followed from such reviews have tended to fail because:

- of the substantial investment of time required and the high level of motivation necessary in order to translate review recommendations into development processes;
- the participants have not had access to the requisite skills for managing and monitoring the change process, and this has resulted in:
  - the change and development process not being tailored to the resources available
  - a failure to analyse and source the appropriate resources to successfully carry out the change process.

In the systems where school-based review has been institutionalized in an attempt to establish system-wide evaluation it has tended to fail in all but the most committed schools. This has meant that it has been difficult in a school-based system of review to obtain the information necessary to assess the performance of the system as a whole, and to develop and implement change strategies in the weaker schools. For this reason there has been a strong move towards the incorporation of at least some elements of external review in system-wide review structures. In some cases these review structures are entirely external to schools, but in others they have resulted in combined internal–external review systems.

EXTERNAL SCHOOL REVIEW

HMI inspections of schools are the foremost example of *external* assessment of whether a school is performing at acceptable levels in terms of professional standards. However, the traditional inspection programme is not as well-suited to the demands of development as it is to those of accountability.

In recent years HMI have carried out a series of survey reviews through short visits to gather information on particular aspects of schooling. These exercises have provided the basis for national reports on the condition of certain aspects of schooling (for example, Department of Education and Science, 1979, 1982, 1985). The number of schools visited in any one year is relatively small, and the system as it stands at present is not suitable as a basis for regular and timely reporting on every school.

In terms of its potential contribution to school development, another problem with the traditional Inspectorate system is the length of the reporting cycle. The relatively long time-lag between the inspection and the report back to schools makes it unsuitable as a basis for school development programmes. Further, the Inspectorate system has not provided an adequate basis for locating the under-performing schools in the system.[4]

In brief the HMI approach has certain weaknesses in terms of current thinking on the purposes for reviewing schools:

- it provides for only a sparse sampling of schools;
- it is very labour-intensive and expensive;
- it generally does not provide sufficient overview information on the performance of the system as a whole – although the system of shorter reviews which were introduced have done much to address this issue;
- it has been criticized for not being sufficiently explicit about the criteria for reviewing schools;
- the length of the reporting cycle and of the review process itself is not conducive to making a significant contribution to school development;
- it does not systematically locate the under-performing schools in the system or those whose performance is declining.

Combined internal–external review systems

The former Inner London Education Authority (ILEA) attempted to overcome the weaknesses of the self-evaluation approach and of external review methods while building on their strengths in developing a new system of school review and development. In particular, the ILEA set out to:

- explicitly link the review process to development processes within schools;
- involve all stakeholders in both the review and development process;
- revise the role of inspectors and advisers in the review process to provide schools with a more substantial stake in the ownership of the review:
  - inspectors and advisers were employed to assist principally in areas in which schools felt that they did not have all the necessary skills and knowledge – particularly in relation to subject reviews in secondary schools;

- provide a clear statement of the objectives for individual reviews.

The ILEA system was based on quinquennial reviews of schools, and it contained a significant school-directed component. As with most school self-evaluation schemes this was principally in the hands of school heads and their senior staff. Principals were expected to do most of the monitoring and assessment and suggest future development for their schools. The Inspectorate role was to assist schools in the review process, to either endorse the development proposals or supplement schools' own findings, and to assist them to achieve the objectives set out in the development proposals.

The role of the Inspectorate was found to be valuable in the review phase, especially when it addressed inadequacies in the school's own self-report. But such co-ordination between the various parties did not always occur. Because of the differences in time frame between Inspectorate visits and a school's self-evaluation timetable, there was often a lack of integration between the contributions of the Inspectorate and schools to the review process.

The main area of failing in relation to the Inspectorate role, however, appears to have been in the contribution of the subject inspectors.[5] Although the main role of subject inspectors was to validate the self-evaluation reports from subject departments, there was confusion about their involvement in supporting the review process itself. The subject inspectors tended to see the school's needs through the lens of their own subject and, as a consequence, their reports and contributions to reviews were not always in line with those of general inspectors, who had a 'whole-school' remit. After some time the subject inspectors' remit was withdrawn.

There were also structural problems with the coherency and co-ordination of the review process. The guidelines were not internally consistent and schools tended to select the elements that suited their preference at the time. Further, the five-year period between major evaluation exercises in each school was found to be too long to provide support to a process of continuous development. This failing would have been alleviated if the original proposals for quinquennial reviews to be supplemented by brief annual reviews in the intervening period had been implemented.

In addition to the above problems, the quinquennial review system continued to suffer from some of the significant failings of earlier school self-evaluation approaches. The ILEA's own review of the quinquennial review system found that:

- it failed to involve consistently all the relevant stakeholders in the review process;
- the reports from the school self-evaluation component were often too long and descriptive, lacked critical self-assessment, and were open to the challenge of self-justification;
- the reports from schools rarely tackled the quality of learning in classrooms.

In addition, the review found that:

- little provision was made for training in evaluative skills;
- the validation of school self-evaluation reports by the Inspectorate did not act as a corrective to the failings of the school's contributions;
- the process often failed to evaluate the working relationships of

> schools with external agencies, such as welfare and special education services;
>
> • the review process did not provide the systemic information required for the system's management to adjust on-going policy implementation and develop new policy in response to emerging issues.

The ILEA revised its system of internal–external reviews to provide for a stronger assessment role for the Inspectorate and introduced a new system of Inspectors Based in Schools (IBIS) to assist development in the weaker schools. Further, the review cycle was revamped to provide a sharper focus and a major review in each school every three years.

SCHOOL AND SYSTEM DEVELOPMENT

As discussed earlier, review systems have a dual focus: accountability and development. Internal review approaches have traditionally been directed more at development and external review approaches have tended to have a sharper accountability focus. The combined internal–external approach developed by the ILEA explicitly attempted to marry the requirements of accountability and development. It did this by building a collaborative review process on the foundation of school development plans.

Lessons from earlier attempts at school development and change

The idea of the development of schools as organizations themselves derives from earlier work in the field of professional development. School-based professional development activities in the 1970s led to a realization that the development of individuals depends upon the health of the organization in which they work. This led to the conceptualization of organizations themselves as being capable of development.

In North America, research-led school improvement programmes emerged during the 1970s. Although the lack of a rigorous review component in these programmes was evident, a substantial body of research literature indicates that certain factors in the development of schools as organizations are important for their success.

A recent review of this literature by Levine and Lezotte (1990) found that the most consistent correlates of effective schools are:

- *productive school climate and culture*
  - orderly environment
  - staff commitment to a shared and articulated mission focused on achievement
  - problem-solving orientation
  - staff cohesion, collaboration, consensus, communications and collegiality
  - staff input into decision-making
  - school-wide emphasis on recognizing positive performance;
- *focus on student acquisition of central learning skills*
  - maximum availability and use of time for learning
  - emphasis on mastery of central learning skills;

- *appropriate monitoring of student progress;*
- *practice-oriented staff development at the school site;*
- *outstanding leadership*
  - vigorous selection and replacement of teachers
  - maverick orientation and buffering
  - frequent, personal monitoring of school activities, and sense-making
  - high expenditure of time and energy for school improvement actions
  - support for teachers
  - acquisition of resources
  - superior instructional leadership
  - availability and effective utilization of instructional support personnel;
- *salient parent involvement;*
- *effective instructional arrangements and implementation*
  - successful grouping and related organizational arrangements
  - appropriate pacing and alignment
  - active/enriched learning
  - effective teaching practices
  - emphasis on higher-order learning in assessing instructional outcomes
  - co-ordination in curriculum and instruction
  - easy availability of abundant, appropriate instructional materials
  - classroom adaptation
  - stealing time for reading, language and maths;
- *high operationalized expectations and requirements for students;*
- *other possible correlates*
  - student sense of efficacy/futility
  - multicultural instruction and sensitivity
  - personal development of students
  - rigorous and equitable student promotions policies and practices.

Another important feature of most successful school improvement programmes has been their focus on a limited number of change strategies at any one time (Levine, 1992). The concept of focused change as encapsulated in more recent proposals for *school development plans* takes on board several lessons from school improvement programmes (Department of Education and Science, 1991; Hargreaves *et al.*, 1989; Hargreaves and Hopkins, 1991; Hopkins, 1989). It also provides an interface to the best features of both the internal and external review systems which emerged during the last decade or so.

Systemic change

Schools are only one component part of education systems. The performance of schools is dependent upon the support and the materials that are delivered to them by other parts of the system. Schools are responsible for the performance of individual programmes and policies within the resource constraints and support that is provided to them.

The structure of relationships between the various levels in the system is sometimes referred to as *nested*. The activities of the operational directorates are nested within the framework of policies and programmes provided by central directorates and systemic functions. The operation of schools is nested within the structure provided by regional directorates. This makes it clear that the performance of the system as a whole is dependent upon the articulation of support structures between the various organizational levels of the system. For the system to be maximally effective, support for the delivery of a programme or policy to schools must be cumulative through each level of the organization. Therefore, the support structure for schools must be an integral component in the review of systemic performance.

The support structure for schools consists of at least three parts. The first component is the curriculum and other materials which are developed for each programme or policy. The second is the allocation of resources to support the programmes and policies implemented in schools. The third is training and development in the required skills within schools for the implementation of particular programmes and policies in the teacher–learning context. All three parts of this delivery system must be well co-ordinated to maximize the effectiveness of programmes and policies for student learning.

Change in successful organizations

The research by Peters and Waterman on America's best-run companies found that certain attributes characterized development and change in the most successful of them. These attributes have since been described as applicable to schools as follows (Clark *et al.*, 1984):

- *Commitment*
  The collective staff agreed behaviours and outcomes are sufficiently specific to control the behaviours of veteran members and integrate new members into the organization.
- *Expectations*
  Successful schools are staffed by confident teachers who expect others to perform to their level of quality. Students also know what they are expected to achieve.
- *Action*
  Successful schools have a bias for action and a sense of opportunism. Challenges are promoted and strengths are exploited.
- *Leadership*
  Effective schools promote primary work groups and the talents of their staff. Leaders emerge at all levels of the system to create an environment that supports experimentation and innovation.
- *Focus*
  Effective schools pay close attention to their learning–based tasks. Classroom time is targeted towards academic learning and teachers strive to maximize the engagement of students in learning activities. Staff development activities focus on instructional skills and under-standings.

- *Climate*
  Successful schools maintain an orderly and safe environment for staff and students. They are good places to work and stimulating learning environments for all participants in the education process.
- *Slack*
  Successful schools have a reasonable level of human resources and are able to organize their activities and schedules to create some slack time. There is time for staff to participate in developmental activities and to incorporate new practices into their busy schedules. Challenges are valued and there is a tolerance of failure arising from experimentation and innovation.

The research on successful organizations has found that success depends on the interaction between process and organizational factors. Organizational-structural factors are a prerequisite for success – they provide the framework for change. Process factors empower innovations and provide the drive required to make change happen.

School development in South Australia

Strategic development plans have now become commonplace in many school systems. They have been introduced in most Australian state systems over the last three years or so and are also being widely introduced in the United Kingdom. The discussion below focuses on the purposes and form of these plans, known as *school development plans* (SDPs), in South Australia. The developments elsewhere are broadly similar, although there are also interesting variations from system to system.

The introduction of SDPs in South Australia was announced in 1989. SDPs are the focus of a substantial part of the review activity of the Education Review Unit. All schools are expected to have a SDP that sets out their proposed development for the next three years. This plan is rolled forward each year after an internal review of the progress that has been made in terms of its stated objectives and outcomes. That is, each school undertakes an annual internal review of its planning and development. To facilitate these internal reviews the outcomes indicated in the SDP should be stated in a way which allows them to be verified without the need to go to a great deal of effort to investigate whether or not they have been achieved.

SDPs are set within the context of a school's statement of purpose, or vision statement. They provide a statement of how the school is attempting to address the overarching goals contained in their statement of purpose. SDPs must encompass the core of the development and change activity in schools. Therefore, they must incorporate all of the major changes and developments which a school wishes to undertake during the life of the plan. However, SDPs should omit the day-to-day maintenance activities that are not part of the core development activity. The major themes for change and development in schools arise from two sources. First, there are the programmes and policies which the government of the day wishes to implement in schools. Second, there are areas of change and development which emanate directly from the needs and aspirations of school communities.

Schools are encouraged to limit the number of major themes of change that they address simultaneously. Experience with successful organizational change suggests that only a small number of major changes can be satisfactorily undertaken at the same time. Although it is often tempting to view half a dozen objectives as being a relatively small task to manage, these objectives give rise to a larger number of strategies which must all be handled simultaneously. It is at this operational, or action, level that many of the difficulties in controlling change are experienced.

In large schools with more complex organizational structures it is also necessary to develop *action plans* at the faculty, or sub-school, level. In this situation the number of change strategies that are being actioned simultaneously can be quite large. For example, if there are six objectives being addressed in a particular year of the SDP and these are implemented through three strategies each, then the school will be simultaneously actioning eighteen change strategies. This will expand out further if several curriculum departments or sub-schools then develop their own action plans. The number of simultaneous change strategies that are in effect at any one time could be as high as about fifty. In small schools the action plan required to operationalize the change strategies may be integrated directly into the SDP. That is, the SDP itself may spell out the action plan strategies.

The strategies which schools specify in their SDP are the driving force through which innovation is introduced into the system. They provide the basis on which professional practice is developed in the context of a systemic framework for schooling. The ownership of the change process itself, through the choice of strategies chosen to implement changes, must rest squarely with the professional staff of schools and the partnerships which they have with their communities.

The action plans which schools develop in order to implement their change strategies are easier to monitor if the school also establishes a set of performance or success indicators to indicate whether or not the change strategy has been implemented and produced the desired effect. Thus, performance indicators in this context should be related directly to the individual action strategies which the school is using to implement change. These action plans require that individual teachers address the particular actions necessary to implement development in the school. One of the pervasive problems in many earlier attempts at school change, particularly in the context of school-based self-evaluation exercises, was confusion over whether it was necessary for teachers to individually and consistently implement the action strategies agreed in schools.

In South Australia the introduction of SDPs and the establishment of the review programme – that is, both internal and external review – took place over a two-year period. Regional directors were responsible for the approval of each school's plan, and all schools were expected to have had their SDPs approval by the end of the first year. The approval was based upon an assessment of whether or not the plan met published guidelines. These guidelines dealt essentially with the form of objectives, strategies and outcomes expected in SDPs. Further, the approval process briefly assessed the appropriateness of the process used to develop the plan.

The Education Department provided guidelines which indicated a number of basic principles for developing a plan (Education Department of South Australia, 1990). They indicated that plans should:

- be based on consideration of the expressed needs and priorities of students, the parent community and school staff;

- provide opportunities for students, parents and school staff to partic-ipate in planning and decision-making;
- be economical in terms of time, energy, resources and outcomes;
- take full account of system priorities.

The guidelines reaffirmed that principals as managers of schools were formally responsible for development in their schools and therefore should ensure that the school community is prepared for, and actively involved in, school development planning. Principals were encouraged to consider the processes necessary for staff, parents, students and school councils to work towards:

- the establishment of agreed priorities for school development;
- translating these priorities for development into objectives and strategies to achieve specific outcomes for student learning.

The appropriateness of the level of performance that a school is expected to aim for depends upon both the context of the school and its prevailing level or stage of development. That is, schools are expected to make progress according to where they are at the time, given their circumstances. This allows all schools to maximize the advantage to be gained from planning and to set their plans according to the particular context in which their development is taking place. The primary consid-eration is not the level of performance of other schools, but rather the appropriate rate of progress for an individual school. Individual schools are expected to set themselves targets that stretch their capacity, but nevertheless are achievable.

The effectiveness of implementation

A review of support for school development planning conducted a year after its introduction in South Australia found that:

> most schools had successfully formulated a plan but require[d] support and assistance . . . to ensure that:

- the plan identifies and prioritises school needs and system priorities;
- it clearly identifies outcomes for students;
- action plans that involve and commit all staff to a range of practices to improve student learning are drawn up;
- the school community can define indicators of the outcomes to be achieved;
- monitoring and review processes to assist the implementation of the plan and sustain ongoing development are in place;
- all groups in the school community – school management, teachers, ancillary staff, students, parents and the school council – are involved and have a commitment to the ongoing development of their school.

> (Education Department of South Australia, 1991, p. 26)

The review found that at that time schools could be identified as being at one of four stages in their development planning:

Stage 1

Some commitment to school development planning by the principal and staff, but with minimal involvement of parents and students. Schools in this stage tended to have limited decision-making procedures and communication structures. The school had a development plan which required further work to clarify objectives, strategies and intended outcomes.

None of the principals surveyed considered their school to be at this stage. However, the school reviews conducted during the year found that a significant proportion of schools were experiencing difficulties with fundamental aspects of school development planning. Either, schools in the survey at the end of the year had overcome these difficulties and made sufficient progress to move beyond this stage of development, or they have tended to overestimate their progress in establishing effective development planning.

Stage 2

The school had a development plan which indicated objectives, strategies and outcomes. Further work was required to develop an action plan which took into account the specific roles of staff, students and parents in implementing the plan. The action plan did not indicate when things were to be done, how they were to be done, or the resources required, or include indicators of success.

Principals of schools at Stage 2 appeared to gain more from workshops than cluster meetings. They were least likely of all principals to attend cluster meetings. Thirty-three per cent of the schools surveyed indicated that they were at this stage.

Stage 3

The school had a development plan and action plans, and was progressing with the implementation of the strategies in the plan. All groups in the school community had been involved in the development of the plan – although some to only a very limited extent. There was limited monitoring of the plan to ensure that the strategies were achieving the planned outcomes.

Principals of schools at Stage 3 indicated that they gained most from sharing ideas with other principals through cluster meetings or district groups. Forty-five per cent of the schools surveyed indicated that they were at this stage.

Stage 4

The school had a well-constructed development plan and effective action plans and monitoring processes. The school had conducted an internal review to assess the success of each objective and rolled the plan forward to provide a new three-year horizon for school development. All groups in the school community had been involved to some extent in the school development process.

Twenty-two per cent of schools surveyed indicated that they were at this stage.

Principals of schools in Stage 4 were more likely to indicate that they made effective use of the full range of options available to them for supporting school development. Principals in these schools made effective use of resources available to them from within the region as well as those available centrally, in addition to services available from outside the system.

Education Review Unit external reviews conducted during the last term of the year found that 76 per cent of schools had reached, or with assistance from normal support services would be able to establish the structures and processes necessary for sustainable development. Schools assessed as having already attained, or in the near future were expected to attain, a state of sustainable development had reached Stage 3 or 4 in the above classification.

The reviews in the last term of the year found that 24 per cent of schools had not established the structures and processes necessary for sustainable development. Such schools were still at Stage 1 or 2 in the above classification.

External reviews of 203 schools were conducted during the year following the above review of the implementation of SDPs. The reviews assessed the planning and management processes associated with the development and implementation of school development plans, and the effectiveness of the strategies adopted by schools to achieve their particular objectives. They found that 36 per cent of the schools reviewed were well advanced in school development planning and were able to effectively manage and sustain their own development. A further 39 per cent were likely to be able to establish the necessary structures and processes for sustainable development with the normal assistance and support provided by regional and system programmes. Nineteen per cent were assessed as requiring early and continuing support to establish the necessary structures and processes for sustainable development. Six per cent of the schools reviewed required substantial support over a prolonged period in order to establish the structures and processes for sustainable development. Significant leadership and organizational change was thought to be necessary for effective development in this latter group of schools.

DISCUSSION

The school self-evaluation approaches that were introduced over the last two decades had shortcomings which hindered the realization of the aspirations that were held for them. Where they were used voluntarily or by highly motivated school staff who were able to command the experience and skills to manage change they served their purpose well. However, where they became embedded in formal evaluation and assessment systems they tended to fail. Their reports were too defensive, they lacked rigour, and they were insufficiently critical, in an analytical sense. Further, they rarely tackled the important issues that related directly to the conditions of learning in classrooms, and were not particularly successful as a means of establishing a basis for continuing school development.

There has been a growing demand for greater accountability in school systems. Further, the management of public institutions now devolves responsibility for many of the day-to-day decisions to the operational units of the systems. These two factors have resulted in increased demands for an effective system for improving and monitoring the performance of schools.

School development

Perhaps the primary problem of planned change in schools is the control of the implementation of development so that it achieves the objectives that are set for it. This requires that plans for development specify clear objectives and that schools are therefore clear about the particular outcomes which they wish to achieve. For this reason it is recommended that the outcome statements in SDPs be written in a form that allows them to be readily verified. Monitoring is required in order to assess whether or not strategies are being implemented appropriately and to determine whether they are having the level of impact required in order to achieve the desired outcomes. In most cases operational adjustments in the implementation of strategies will amount to fine-tuning, although special circumstances may also generate the need to depart significantly from the plan.

Function of review

Review serves two functions in relation to change in schools. First, it provides information and support for the development process itself, and second it provides information for accountability purposes. Accountability is both a process and an outcome. It must assure the quality of outcomes, but it must also assure that the process required for the continuing achievement of outcomes is capable of doing so.

Internal review and assessment for development primarily serves a development purpose. However, the practice of internal review itself is part of the effective management of development in schools, and therefore contributes to a demonstration of accountability. It contributes to accountability through the assessment of progress towards stated objectives. The approval of SDPs is a further check in the system which primarily serves an accountability purpose. Monitoring the implementation of strategies is primarily development orientated, but because it involves the assessment of whether professional standards of practice are being upheld it contributes also to a demonstration of accountability.

Periodic external reviews of individual schools should be development-orientated in that their task is to support the progress of schools towards the attainment of their stated objectives. However, they also contribute directly to the accountability of the system, particularly when they have a degree of independence from the operational structures of the system, conduct their work openly and report publicly.

External reviews of schools are an essential component in the evaluation of the systemic performance of programmes and policies. They provide an assessment of the success of the system in meeting its publicly stated objectives.

Where reviews are conducted according to publicly stated criteria they serve accountability purposes, in addition to their contribution to development through the identification of factors responsible for the effectiveness of programmes and policies. It is this dual focus on accountability and development that gives some recently developed review systems an explicit 'quality assurance' perspective beyond the 'inspection' focus of earlier external assessment functions in education (Cuttance, 1992a).

Internal review

Internal school reviews must raise awareness of the process of development and of progress and attainments in relation to the plan. They must strive for a critical and analytical perspective of progress and of the needs of the school. In addition to assessing the progress that the school has made, internal reviews must determine the development priorities for the school as its plan is rolled forward. That is, internal reviews are essentially formative in nature – they assess how far the development of the school has gone, and they analyse what is required for the next stage of development. Internal school reviews must address the fundamental processes and organizational structures most important to learning. In particular, they must address the issue of how development can achieve a direct impact on the quality of student learning. All other aspects of school activity and practice should be assessed primarily according to the support they provide for the quality of learning in the school.

Internal reviews must uncover the least effective practices of schools. This can be viewed from a perspective of the revision of priorities in a school. In many cases the least effective activities, in terms of the support they provide for learning, have become so, not because they have changed or are less capably carried out, but because they have become less relevant in the prevailing learning situation. Effective schools recognize their ineffective practices and take positive steps to discontinue them and free up resources to support more effective practices and activities in the school.

School development requires specific professional skills: some related to the planning and management of change, and others determined by the substance of the strategies to be implemented. Schools need to review their training needs in their context and to provide those responsible for supporting and servicing them with information on their requirements. Training which is teacher–teacher based has been shown to be more effective than that centred around experts. The key to effective training is to involve individuals who are closely in touch with the day-to-day activities of schools. Effective classroom teachers, advisory teachers and district superintendents in the present system fit this model, but even wider use of cluster-groups of teachers may be profitable. This form of training and dissemination of knowledge is particularly appropriate to most activities associated with SDPs.

External review

The cycle of external reviews must be timed to facilitate the development and change processes in schools. A five-year cycle has been found to be too long for this purpose. It is considered that three years is probably optimal in terms of the effective utilization of resources, and in terms of its contribution to school development. The task of external review is to assess progress in terms of schools' plans, to review the effectiveness of their consultative and planning processes and the management of development. Because the implementation of change itself impacts on the development process, external reviews must take account of the fact that objectives and implementation strategies will be adapted to local needs and conditions. Adaptation to local needs and conditions is important as it increases the probability of acceptance and the success of system-wide programmes and policies.

The task of external review, however, is not just to review individual schools, but also to provide information for evaluating the performance of the system as a whole. As indicated earlier, schools themselves work with the services and resources that are provided to them. It is, therefore, necessary to review the support structures for schooling and the effectiveness with which programmes and policies are delivered to schools in order to evaluate the performance of the system.

The reports from external reviews of schools should be formulated through a process and written in a style that involves schools and contributes directly to their development. The information contained in a school report should parallel effective practice in pupil assessment. That is, it should contain summative information, diagnostic information and formative information. Certain types of comparative information are also informative for development purposes.

Reviews of schools should be summative in the sense that they should assess the extent to which developments have achieved the stated objectives. Summative information provides a backdrop against which it is possible to compare the success of different strategies for development across schools.

The analysis of information in school reports must also be diagnostic. It should discuss aspects of school performance that require attention and suggest areas that require reassessment in terms of both objectives and strategies. The diagnosis should also provide a basis for assessing the support that schools require for their development. Reports must also indicate where the development process in schools accords with effective management practice.

School reports should provide formative information which is constructive and helpful in relation to individual school plans. They should focus on the particular development aims of schools and indicate areas of process and functioning that schools need to address in the next stage of their development. Reports may also indicate appropriate targets for development.

Comparative information in school reports may be of two types. First, as indicated above, it may provide information on the success of different strategies for development across schools. Second, it may provide self-referenced information on the performance of individual schools. That is, the performance of schools in the present may be compared with their previous performance.

Comparative analyses across schools can also be useful provided they take account of the different circumstances of individual schools. For example, over the past decade a methodology has been developed for the comparative assessment of secondary schools in terms of student attainment in public examinations in the United Kingdom (Audit Commission, 1991; Cuttance, 1992b). These assessments should aim to take account of differences in the extent of social disadvantage in school intakes and of differences in the entry level attainments of students.

Reports from external reviews of schools must consider the audience for which they are written. In addition to the school community generally this will include those with formal responsibilities for the school – school staff, school councils, regional directors, etc. The report must be written in an accessible language and in a positive tone in order to maximize the effectiveness of its contribution to development. It should convey the expectation of high achievement within the context of local conditions.

Reports from external school reviews provide an independent record based on criterion-referenced assessment of the performance and functioning of schools. Therefore, they provide a primary statement of the accountability of schools and of the system.

NOTES

[1] The term 'internal' is used here to describe approaches to review and evaluation that are controlled and initiated by schools themselves, and the term 'external' is used to refer to approaches in which all stakeholders have some say in the way the review or evaluation is conducted.

[2] The function of the Inspectorate in the United Kingdom is to assess and evaluate the effectiveness of teaching and learning, and not, as in some systems, the inspection of teachers for accreditation and promotion purposes.

[3] The questionnaire covers aspects of values and goals, school objectives, staff relationships, school climate, leadership and management, decision-making, communications, assessment and evaluation, teaching methods, and teacher activities (Dalin and Rust, 1983).

[4] The Conservative Government in the United Kingdom introduced legislation to change the role of HMI radically. The legislation proposes that schools will be reviewed every four years, with an increased emphasis on quality assurance and standards.

[5] This section draws on internal ILEA documents which reported reviews of the quinquennial review system.

REFERENCES

Audit Commission (1991) *Assuring Quality in Education*. London: HMSO.

Clark, D.L., Lotto, C.S. and Astuto, T.A. (1984) 'Effective schools and school improvement: a comparative analysis of two lines of inquiry', *Educational Administration Quarterly*, **20** (3), 41–68.

Clift, P. (1987) 'School-based review: a response from the UK perspective', in Hopkins, D. (ed.) *Improving the Quality of Schooling: Lessons from the OECD International School Improvement Project*. Lewes: Falmer Press.

Cuttance, P. (1986) *Effective Schooling: A Report to the Scottish Education Department*. Edinburgh: Centre for Educational Sociology, University of Edinburgh.

Cuttance, P. (1992a) 'Quality assurance and quality management in education', Keynote paper presented to the National Seminar on Education Review and Evaluation, 27–8 February 1992, Adelaide.

Cuttance, P. (1992b) 'Evaluating the effectiveness of schools', in Reynolds, D. and Cuttance, P.F. (eds) *School Effectiveness: Research, Policy and Practice*, pp. 71–95. London: Cassell.

Dalin, P. and Rust, V. (1983) *Can Schools Learn?* Windsor: NFER–Nelson.

Department of Education and Science (1979) *Aspects of Secondary Education in England*. London: Department of Educational Science/HMSO.

Department of Education and Science (1982) *Education 5 to 9: An Illustrative Survey*. London: Department of Education and Science/HMSO.

Department of Education and Science (1985) *The Curriculum from 5 to 16* (Curriculum Matters 2). London: Department of Education and Science/HMSO.

Department of Education and Science (1988) *Education Reform Act: Local Management of Schools*, Circular 7/88. London: Department of Education and Science/HMSO.

Department of Education and Science (1991) *Development Planning – A Practical Guide – Advice to Governors, Headteachers and Teachers*. London: Department of Education and Science/HMSO.

Education Department of South Australia (1990) *Guidelines for School Development Planning*. Adelaide: Education Department of South Australia.

Education Department of South Australia (1991) *A Review of Support for School Development Planning,* Education Review Report. Adelaide: Education Department of South Australia.

Hargreaves, D. (1988) 'Assessment and performance indicators: the English experience', in Ruby, A. and Wyatt, T. (eds) *Indicators in Education*. Sydney: Australian Conference of Directors-General of Education.

Hargreaves, D. and Hopkins, D. (1991) *The Empowered School: The Management and Practice of Development Planning*. London: Cassell.

Hargreaves, D.H., Hopkins, D., Leask, M., Connolly, J. and Robinson, P. (1989) *Planning for School Development: Advice to Governors, Headteachers and Teachers*. London: Department of Education and Science/HMSO.

Hopkins, D. (1985) *School Based Review for School Improvement*. Leuven, Belgium: ACCO.

Hopkins, D. (1989) *Evaluation for School Development*. Milton Keynes: Open University Press.

Levine, D. (1992) 'An interpretive view of effective US research and practice dealing with unusually effective schools', in Reynolds, D. and Cuttance, P.F. (eds) *School Effectiveness: Research, Policy and Practice*, pp. 25–47. London: Cassell.

Levine, D. and Lezotte, L. (1990) *Unusually Effective Schools: A Review and Analysis of Research and Practice*. Madison, WI: National Center for Effective Schools Research and Development.

McMahon, A., Bolam, R., Abbot, R. and Holly, P. (1984) *Guidelines for Review and Internal Development in Schools*. Primary and Secondary School Handbooks. Harlow: Longman for the Schools Council.

Murphy, J. (1992) 'Effective schools: legacy and future', in Reynolds, D. and Cuttance, P.F. (eds) *School Effectiveness: Research, Policy and Practice*, pp.164–70. London: Cassell.

Nuttall, D. (1981) *School Self-Evaluation: Accountability with a Human Face?* London: Schools Council.

Reynolds, D. (1992) 'School effectiveness and improvement', in Reynolds, D. and Cuttance, P.F. (eds) *School Effectiveness: Research, Policy and Practice*, pp. 1–24. London: Cassell.

Chapter 4

The Centrality of the Autonomy–Accountability Dilemma in School and Professional Development

Viviane Robinson

When schools themselves are required, as in New Zealand, to manage their own development and evaluation activities, school leaders are faced with a series of human problems which they could avoid while these functions were centrally administered. These human problems arise from the dual requirement for them to be accountable to the State and the local community for the quality of teaching and learning, while simultaneously fostering collegiality and the professional autonomy of their staff. The tension between professional autonomy and accountability is now played out in every local school rather than between the professional body and the national and regional agencies that represent the interests of the State. School leaders can no longer ignore or play down the accountability aspects of their role; they must accept that they are both colleagues and managers of their staff. A few examples serve to illustrate the human problems involved. The requirement to develop and report on a programme of staff appraisal means that it is now much harder to ignore or cover up the poor performance of a Head of Department. Conflict between staff about how to spend development funds must be resolved if a school-based development programme is to gain approval. The push from a school's business-oriented governing body to adopt the appraisal checklist used in the insurance industry must be resisted in the interests of fostering staff creativity and professional autonomy.

Preliminary evidence on the New Zealand school self-management experience suggests that school leaders feel unprepared, and in some cases unwilling, to accept the more formal accountability responsibilities that arise from the devolution of these previously centralized personnel functions. Six months after the implementation of the self-management reforms (New Zealand Department of Education, 1988) a task force was set up to review progress and identify areas where further help was needed. The resulting report (Education Reform Implementation Process Review Team, 1990) identified the personnel management area as one where little progress had been made, possibly due to lack of relevant skills on the part of principals and school trustees. Similar conclusions were drawn by two other researchers in independent reports about the way principals were implementing the new policies (Alcorn, 1990, p. 10; Battersby, 1991, p. 15). While it may be true that lack of skills, role conflict and vague guidelines are hampering implementation, such analyses do not go far enough. Precisely what skills are lacking? What exactly is the nature of the role conflict? What guidelines are compatible with an educationally sound development and appraisal process?

The position taken in this chapter is that the answers to these questions are centrally concerned with how school leaders understand and act to resolve the tension between the two principles of accountability and autonomy. This position will be defended by explaining how this tension arises, what research shows about how it is typically resolved, and the implications of various resolution strategies for the effectiveness of school and teacher development programmes. A case study of a professional programme in a large secondary school illustrates the argument by showing how failure to resolve the tension between accountability and autonomy jeopardized the programme's effectiveness despite generous resourcing and superb organization.

Before proceeding further I should explain why I see the issue of accountability and evaluation as relevant to a volume whose central theme is that of development and not that of evaluation. In brief, I see evaluation, no matter how informal, as a necessary condition of development since to describe a state of affairs as a development or improvement is to evaluate it as more desirable than a comparison condition (Kelly, 1987; Scriven, 1989, 1991). The conceptual point can also be made practically. Development resources are wasted when they are not linked to an evaluation or audit of a school's programme, and when the outcomes of the development effort are not carefully monitored (Hargreaves and Hopkins, 1991).

THE TENSION BETWEEN AUTONOMY AND ACCOUNTABILITY

I take accountability to be the rendering of an account to others so that they may make a judgement about the worth, quality or adequacy of the activities so described (Scriven, 1989, p. 94; Sockett, 1976). Exactly which groups constitute the 'others' is a matter of some debate as Strike makes clear in his discussion of three different models of accountability (Strike, 1990). His model of bureaucratic democracy recognizes the right of the state to hold teachers and schools accountable for the carrying out of the policy of elected officials. The communitarian model treats the whole-school community as the primary point of accountability, while the professional model sees teachers and schools as accountable to a largely autonomous professional association.

Regardless of which group is given priority, all three models of accountability recognize that the work of schools and teachers should be open to the critical scrutiny of others.

I take the principle of autonomy to mean that teachers should be free, within constraints set by other competing principles such as that of accountability, to make their own decisions about the conduct of their work, including about how it should be evaluated. The autonomy principle recognizes that the intellectual independence of teachers is critical to the performance of their work. The principle does not deny the right of other constituencies to seek to influence the judgements of teachers; rather it requires that such influence be exercised in ways that enhance rather than diminish teachers' intellectual independence.

In theory, the two principles of autonomy and accountability are reconcilable because evaluation by others does not rule out self-evaluation. In practice, however, there is frequently a considerable tension between them because the principles govern not just the process of making an evaluation but the locus of control over the educational and managerial decisions that are contingent upon them. Those who stress the importance of accountability are interested in more than just making judgements about teachers; they also seek to exercise some control over the way teachers practise. The tension between autonomy and accountability is brought into sharp relief when interested parties disagree, because in such cases the two principles legitimize different degrees of external influence. Reconciling the two principles in the context of school-based development activities makes major demands on the analytic and interpersonal skills of school leaders.

RESEARCH ON THE AUTONOMY–ACCOUNTABILITY DILEMMA

When appraisal and development schemes are designed and managed at the local level, staff have to implement and live with the consequences of the decisions that they themselves, rather than some external agency, have made about how to evaluate and improve their practice. There is considerable evidence that under these conditions, teachers and administrators give far greater weight to the principle of professional autonomy than to that of accountability. McLaughlin and Pfeifer (1988) conducted intensive case studies in four Californian school districts chosen for their 'commitment to installing meaningful teacher evaluation programs based on accountability and improvement objectives' (p. 89). They asked teachers about their views of the principal's role in teacher evaluation. On the whole, teachers 'acknowledge that evaluation generally is not something that most principals do easily or well. Respondents in all our districts used the same word to describe the usual principal role in teacher evaluation: "gutless"' (p. 38).

Bridges (1986) reports an empirical study of the way administrators deal with the problem of perceived teacher incompetence in the state of California. The most common response is to tolerate, protect, and avoid direct confrontation of the ineffective subordinate. Transfer to another school system or redesign of the teacher's job are also common responses. Rivzi's (1990) evidence from an Australian experiment in federally funded school development shows that issues of accountability are avoided by professional peers as well as by administrators. When teachers from neighbouring schools met to review each other's school development plans they were reluctant to engage in critical evaluation, with some groups adopting a 'you scratch my back, I'll scratch yours' attitude (p. 315). To the extent that teachers and administrators sacrifice issues of accountability when dealing face-to-face with professional colleagues, programmes of staff and school development and evaluation are going to be less efficient and effective than is desirable. What do we know about the basis of this avoidance and about how to overcome it?

UNDERSTANDING THE NEGLECT OF ACCOUNTABILITY

Bridges' research suggests that the neglect of issues of accountability can be attributed to the 'deeply-seated human desire to avoid the conflict and unpleasantness which often accompany criticism of others' (1986, p. 20). Given the centrality of the work role to most people's self-esteem, the possibility of threat accompanies many aspects of teacher supervision, evaluation and professional development. To criticize

71

others is to run the risk of perpetrating such threat and of being threatened in turn by the reactions of the other. When we hold others we work with accountable, we may not only fail to solve any problems we perceive in their performance, but we may also create additional ones by damaging the relationship between us. The avoidance of evaluation and of in-depth inquiry into school-based problems can be understood, therefore, as a defence against the pain and embarrassment which are frequently associated with such situations. Like any defensive strategy, such avoidance brings the price of failing to acknowledge publicly and resolve the situation that is the cause of the original concern (Argyris, 1985, p. 3).

To label such withdrawal as a defensive strategy and to treat the appeal to professional autonomy as, in part, a rationalization of such behaviour is to leave unresolved, however, the question of why such a response to the autonomy–accountability dilemma is so prevalent. In theory at least, the resolution of the dilemma does not require the actor to choose between either holding others accountable and risking unpleasantness, or protecting professional autonomy and risking ineffectiveness. There are other possible responses which avoid both horns of the dilemma by construing autonomy and accountability as equally important principles which must be resolved by the relevant parties within a context of collegial dialogue. This involves disclosure by the colleague, supervisor or evaluator of their judgements about the other's practice, in a way that encourages reciprocal disclosure and mutual uncoerced examination of the merits of both parties' views. In such a dialogue, the principle of autonomy is respected by the absence of any form of subtle or direct coercion, and the accountability principle is respected through public examination of the teacher's practice (Haller and Strike, 1986, p. 328). If the autonomy–accountability dilemma can be transcended in this way, why is such practice so rare? In short, because such a response requires interpersonal skills and understandings which are incompatible with those which people typically use when they anticipate or experience threat and embarrassment.

The collegial dialogue outlined above presupposes that participants act from a value base of openness and mutual respect. While most people, including school principals, espouse such an interpersonal style, they are perceived by others and judged by analysts of their actual conversations to be employing a quite different style and to be unaware that they are doing so (Argyris, 1982, pp. 41–81; Bifano, 1989). This style, which Argyris calls Model 1, reflects two central values of winning and avoidance of unpleasantness. The main concern in such a style is how to gain acceptance of one's view without upsetting the other person. This can be achieved relatively easily if, as in the majority of encounters, taken-for-granted assumptions are shared or if nothing much is at stake. This requirement is more difficult to satisfy, however, where there is actual or anticipated disagreement. In such cases, it is difficult to both gain acceptance of one's view and to do so in ways that avoid unpleasantness. Argyris's analysis of hundreds of simulated and actual work-place interactions has shown that people attempt to resolve this dilemma by conveying their views in indirect and subtle ways (Argyris, 1982). While such easing-in strategies may reduce unpleasantness, their cost is that the other party does not hear the message or can choose to ignore it (Beer, 1987). If these costs are judged to be too high the actor may sacrifice the attempt to reduce unpleasantness and switch to a more direct forthright communication, involving language that is highly generalized, judgemental and closed to correction or inquiry.

There is a high degree of match between Argyris's description of these easing-in and forthright styles and Bridges' independently generated analysis of the way administrators dealt with actual cases of teacher incompetence. The majority of their responses fell into the easing-in, indirect category because they involved under-statement or distortion. For example, administrators' reports included highly generalized positive comments about such teachers' performance (a strategy which Bridges calls 'ceremonial congratulations'), and double-talk (criticisms couched as suggestions for change). Teacher ratings were inflated so that even those who were eventually induced to resign were initially rated as 'satisfactory'. As a result, the early reports on these teachers seldom included any negative feedback. Bridges' research also showed, however, that when these strategies proved ineffective and there was pressure on administrators to take further action, they would move into a much more direct 'salvage' phase.

> During the salvage stage administrators abandon the practices of the earlier period. They no longer sprinkle their observation reports with glowing generalities. They no longer cloak their criticisms in the guise of constructive suggestions. They no longer inflate the evaluations of the incompetent teacher. Straight talk replaces double-talk.
>
> (Bridges, 1986, pp. 48–9)

Teachers who have perhaps experienced years of double-talk and ceremonial con-gratulation, predictably react defensively to this 'out-of-the-blue' negative feedback.

Bridges' findings parallel those reported in research on evaluation processes in non-educational organizations where a similar pattern of avoidance and positive distortion of negative feedback is prevalent, with less frequent switches to a more direct punitive approach (Beer, 1987).

THE APPARENT IRRESOLVABILITY OF THE AUTONOMY–ACCOUNTABILITY DILEMMA

Argyris's theory about the centrality of the values of winning and protection from unpleasantness goes a long way towards explaining the difficulty of resolving the autonomy–accountability dilemma. If developers and evaluators believe their views are right, are closed to testing their views, but wish to avoid unpleasantness, they will design diplomatic pleasant ways of communicating their 'correct views'. If this strategy fails and they feel compelled to take further action they will sacrifice the value of avoidance of unpleasantness in the interest of finally 'getting the message across'.

Neither of these strategies provides a satisfying and effective resolution of the dilemma. Anyone who takes for granted the validity of their own views is violating the autonomy of the recipient in their explicit or implicit expectation of acceptance. In these terms, there is little difference between the easing-in and the direct communicative strategies; both discourage the type of dialogue where both parties are open to examination of the basis of their views and committed to bilateral rather than unilateral resolution of any differences. On the other hand, both strategies also fail to satisfy the accountability requirement. In the case of the indirect strategy, there is considerable evidence that such feedback is either misunderstood or ignored by its recipient (Beer, 1987). While more direct feedback is less likely to be misunderstood, it is more likely to produce defensive rebuttals and denial, and to be ineffective in resolving disagreements between the parties.

Given these arguments, one can speculate that administrators frequently avoid supervisory and evaluative roles because they sense that they are in a 'no win' situation. Their indirect approach, while more pleasant, is ineffectual. The direct approach may make a bad situation worse by producing a defensive and adversarial relationship between the parties.

PROFESSIONAL DEVELOPMENT AT WESTERN COLLEGE: A CASE ILLUSTRATION

The centrality of the autonomy–accountability dilemma to the effectiveness of school and professional development is illustrated in the following case study of professional development at Western College. This large co-educational college in an ethnically mixed Auckland suburb had taken considerable responsibility for school and teacher development and appraisal, even before it was required by the Tomorrow's Schools reforms in educational administration. During her time as deputy principal, Carol had established a programme of staff and school development that was comprehensive, well organized and generously resourced. The programme's objectives were to integrate staff and school development so that the school remained responsive to the changing needs of its various constituent groups. These objectives were pursued through an extensive menu of professional development opportunities for staff, and through a more formal process of professional development consultation (PDC) in which a member of the executive team met regularly with staff who held positions of responsibility (Stewart and Prebble, 1985).

The research contract and methodology

Six months after her appointment as principal, Carol invited me to investigate her concerns about the impact of the programme, and about the persistent resistance of a few staff. After extensive negotiation, a colleague and I developed a contract with her that sought to test her perception that there was a problem, to investigate the cause of any such problem, and to discover why Carol and her management team had so far been unable to resolve their concerns about the programme. The inclusion of the last question reflected our conviction that effective school development pre-supposes effective management and problem-solving practices (Hargreaves and Hopkins, 1991, p. 14).

Once the existence of a problem was confirmed by a series of individual staff interviews, a problem-based methodology was used to investigate the links between those problems and the assumptions and strategies that informed the school's approach to professional development (Robinson, 1993). The result was a causal account whose accuracy was negotiated through critical dialogue with those whose actions it purported to describe (Robinson, 1992). The data for this analysis were gathered over a six-month period, and comprised interviews with the principal, and with staff chosen to reflect a range of views on the programme, and analyses of relevant shcool documents. Data on actual professional development practices were gathered from tape recordings of PDC sessions, from relevant staff meetings and from field notes made at professional development activities. A fuller account of the case methodology and analysis is reported in Robinson (1993).

Explaining the problems in the programme

Figure 4.1 explains the problems of staff resistance and low impact by showing how they are unintended consequences of the way the principal and senior staff understood the problem of how to design and implement an effective programme of school and professional development. They believed an effective programme had to satisfy two key constraints. First, as Carol explained, the programme had to be collegial, supportive and non-threatening to gain the enthusiastic participation of staff.

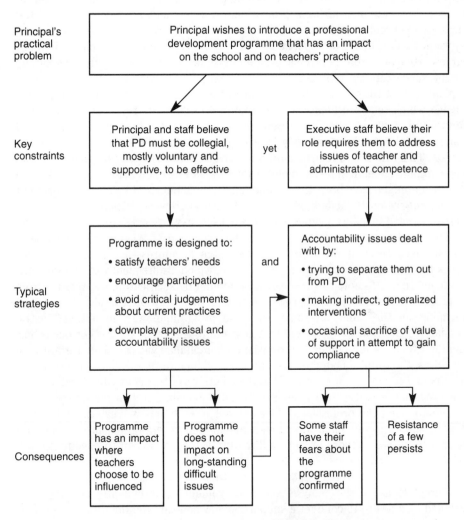

Figure 4.1 *Analysis of problems associated with a professional development programme.*

Carol: I haven't really identified some of the metaphors and things we use, but certainly it's ... I think you'll find people are culturally very comfortable [with it]. It's not seen as a threat to their competence, they're not given PD because they can't do something; it's not remedial or

a skill deficiency that we're pointing out. It's very much a stimulation,
enthusiasm building kind of attitude to PD.

At the same time, the programme had to be able to make an impact on tough issues
of administrator and teacher competence.

The tension between the collegiality and voluntarism of the first constraint and
the accountability thrust of the second was never adequately resolved. The first
constraint led to a focus on the participation of staff and a playing down of the
critical judgements that are an inevitable component of any effort to improve current
practices. For example, during a professional development activity for deans, staff
addressed the problem of the increasing number of students being sent out of class.
Two years earlier, heads of departments had found the referral of such students by
their own teachers too disruptive of their own work, so a procedure was set up
whereby such students reported to a duty dean. Now it was the deans who were
complaining that they were overloaded with referrals. A new set of procedures were
designed which required heads of departments to take more responsibility for such
referrals and to provide support to their own teachers. At no stage in this sequence of
problem-solving was there an analysis of *why* some teachers were making so many
referrals. This preventive focus would have involved discussion of teachers' instructional and management skills, and of the support they were currently receiving. Such
a discussion might have been threatening for the teachers and heads of department
involved, but the cost of avoiding it is probably another cycle of short-term solutions
to the problem of teachers sending students out of class.

The need to avoid threat presented the executive of Western College with a
dilemma, because their roles also required them to address accountability issues
such as teacher and administrator competence, which are frequently threat-inducing.
Sometimes they attempted to resolve the dilemma by segregating such issues from
the professional development programme, but this solution carried the cost of
confirming, in the minds of some, that the programme was an optional extra,
secondary to the real job of teaching and running the school. On other occasions,
when the executive felt compelled to insist on compliance with particular evaluation
procedures, the values of support and threat avoidance were forsaken. This response
strengthened some staff members' belief that there was an 'accountability rat' lurking
in the programme, and strengthened their resolve to maintain their resistance.

In summary, the professional development programme at Western College did
not have the expected impact on management and teaching, because it was not
designed to influence those processes directly. Instead, it sought to encourage staff
participation in a wide range of professional development activities, which they could
use as opportunities to reflect upon and alter their own and the school's practices. A
more direct focus on the analysis and improvement of problematic practices was
precluded by a desire to conduct a supportive and non-threatening programme. This
meant that critical discussion of teacher and school practices was difficult, and that
the executive were unable to address accountability issues while remaining consistent
with the ethos of the programme.

Explaining the persistence of the problems

Given the increased emphasis on school-based management of professional development and evaluation, it is important to answer the third question about why the principal had not been able to resolve the problems she perceived in the programme. In short, she was unable to do so because her acceptance of the professional development culture of supportiveness and threat avoidance placed her in the same bind as characterized the programme as a whole. She was caught between trying to gently persuade her staff to participate in the programme she had developed, and insisting on compliance with procedures, such as writing job descriptions and holding PDC conferences, which she believed were essential to effective performance. Figure 4.2 illustrates Carol's dilemma in the context of trying to resolve a problem with one of her department heads.

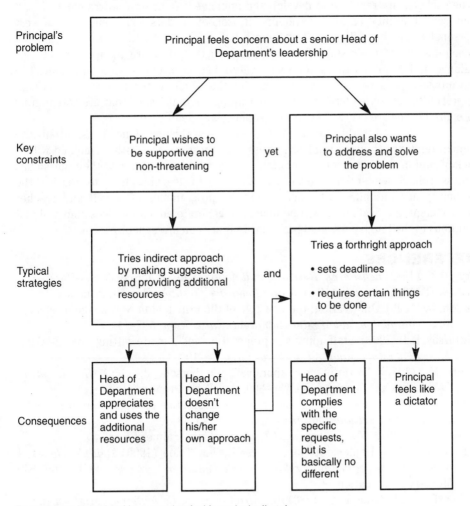

Figure 4.2 *Analysis of problems associated with a principal's style.*

In addition, Carol's leadership and problem-solving style prevented her from engaging in the type of dialogue with staff that would enable her to resolve the autonomy–accountability dilemma. While she took for granted the adequacy of her own conception of professional development and of how to foster it, she could only deal with staff who disagreed by leaving them alone, or by persuading them that she was right. It was only after an intensive period of training in the theory and practice of critical dialogue (Robinson, 1993) that Carol and her senior staff learned that the accountability–autonomy dilemma was resolvable by publicly recognizing and testing the assumptions that informed their practice of staff and school development and evaluation.

CONCLUSION

When schools are required to develop and implement their own programmes of staff and school evaluation and development, school leaders experience, on a very personal level, the difficulty of striking a balance between the autonomy and the accountability of their staff. Research suggests that they are likely to strike this balance, unless forced to do otherwise, very much in favour of staff autonomy. The advantage of this response is avoidance of the worst features of a managerialist approach to school leadership. The disadvantage is that issues that are threatening or embarrassing are overlooked or only superficially dealt with.

I have argued in this chapter that the cause of this imbalance is essentially the human tendency to avoid unpleasantness with those we live with, combined with a lack of skill in holding others accountable in ways that do not violate their autonomy. Unless school leaders are given assistance with learning how to resolve the autonomy–accountability dilemma effectively, programmes of school and teacher development and evaluation will be unable to generate educationally sound and just solutions to the tough personnel problems that arise in any school system.

REFERENCES

Argyris, C. (1982) *Reasoning, Learning and Action*. San Francisco: Jossey-Bass.

Argyris, C. (1985) *Strategy, Change and Defensive Routines*. Boston: Pitman.

Alcorn, N. (1990) 'One year on: the new role of the principal in New Zealand schools', *New Zealand Journal of Educational Administration*, **5**, 7–14.

Battersby, E.J. (1991) 'Staff appraisal: preparation and climate setting', *New Zealand Journal of Educational Administration*, **6**, 15–19.

Beer, M. (1987) 'Performance appraisal', in Lorsch, J. (ed.) *Handbook of Organizational Behavior*, pp. 286–300. New York: Prentice-Hall.

Bifano, S.L. (1989) 'Researching the professional practice of elementary principals', *Journal of Educational Administration*, **27** (1), 58–70.

Bridges, E.M. (1986) *The Incompetent Teacher*. Lewes: Falmer Press.

Education Reform Implementation Process Review Team (1990) *Today's schools: A review of the education reform implementation process*. Wellington NZ: Ministry of Education.

Haller, E.J. and Strike, K.A. (1986) *An Introduction to Educational Administration: Social, Legal and Ethical Perspectives*. New York: Longman.

Hargreaves, D.H. and Hopkins, D. (1991) *The Empowered School: The Management and Practice of Development Planning*. London: Cassell.

Kelly, A.V. (1987) *Knowledge and Curriculum Planning*. London: Harper & Row.

McLaughlin, M.W. and Pfeifer, R.S. (1988) *Teacher Evaluation: Improvement, Accountability and Effective Learning*. New York: Teachers College Press.

New Zealand Department of Education (1988) *Tomorrow's Schools: The Reform of Education Administration in New Zealand*. Wellington: Government Printer.

Rivzi, F. (1990) 'Horizontal accountability', in Chapman, J. (ed.), *School-Based Decision-Making and Management*, pp. 299–324. London: Falmer Press.

Robinson, V.M.J. (1992) 'Doing critical social science: dilemmas of control', *International Journal of Qualitative Studies in Education*, **5** (4), 345–9.

Robinson, V.M.J. (1993) *Problem-Based Methodology: Research for the Improvement of Practice*. Oxford: Pergamon Press.

Scriven, M. (1989) 'The state of the art in teacher evaluation', in Lokan, J. and McKenzie, P. (eds) *Teacher Appraisal: Issues and Approaches*, pp. 92–136. Hawthorn, Victoria: Australian Council for Educational Research.

Scriven, M. (1991) 'Beyond formative and summative evaluation', in McLaughlin, M.W. and Phillips, D.C. (eds) *Evaluation and Education: At Quarter Century*, National Society for the Study of Education, pp. 19–64. Chicago: Chicago University Press.

Sockett, H. (1976) 'Teacher accountability', *Proceedings of the Philosophy of Education Society of Great Britain*, **10**, 34–57.

Stewart, D. and Prebble, T. (1985) *Making It Happen: A School Development Process*. Palmerston North, NZ: Dunmore Press.

Strike, K. (1990) 'The ethics of educational evaluation', in Millman, J. and Darling-Hammond, L. *The New Handbook of Teacher Evaluation*, pp. 356–73. London: Sage.

Chapter 5

Written Planning and School Development: Biding Time or Making Time

Colin Biott, Patrick Easen and Madeleine Atkins

INTRODUCTION

This chapter sets out to explore the implications of formal school development planning for our understanding of organizational culture and professional collegiality. When school development planning was first introduced on a wide scale in 1991 most headteachers, but few class teachers, saw it as a worthwhile requirement. One of the main things that distinguished the responses of the different schools to the obligation was whether they were making time for a whole-hearted effort on written planning or biding their time before making such a commitment. What seemed to matter most was not their immediate response to an imposed demand but the strength of the relationship between real school development and written planning.

The chapter is based on a study of school development planning processes (and products) in fifty-seven schools in nine local education authorities (LEAs) in the north of England during 1991, the first year in which schools were required to submit written school development plans (SDPs) to their LEAs. The sample was drawn from all phases of schooling. Data were collected through 132 semi-structured interviews which focused on perceptions of SDPs, the process behind the construction of a plan, the use subsequently made of it and the contributions of different staff within school hierarchies. In each school the interviewees included the headteacher, a middle manager (where appropriate) and a 'main professional grade' teacher.

Identifying and defining 'quality' management processes in schools has been a recurring theme in school effectiveness and school improvement literatures. Hopkins (1991) argues that the inherent limitations of both can only be overcome with a strategy that affects the culture of the school. In particular, he advocates school development planning as a means to 'deliver significant curriculum and teaching innovations, whilst at the same time adjusting the schools' organisational character-istics or management arrangements' (p. 63). This argument relates to other work, pointing to the concepts of collegiality and collaboration as a means of supporting professional learning and therefore enhancing the development of practice (Little, 1982; Nias *et al.*, 1989, 1992). Such studies were conducted before the implementation of the Education Reform Act (ERA), but government demands in the United Kingdom would appear to emphasize, even further, the need for 'whole-school thinking'. For instance, the National Curriculum has meant that individual teachers are no longer expected to plan their teaching in isolation, while Local Management of Schools (LMS) has apparently opened up opportunities for teachers to be involved in decision-making beyond the traditional domain of their classroom.

Advocates of strategic planning see school development plans as a key to the successful management of the complexities inherent in multiple innovation and change (Hargreaves and Hopkins, 1991; HMI, 1991). One popular metaphor for the Plan is the 'tray' enabling the numerous and diverse plates, which teachers claim to be spinning, to be carried with ease. School development planning offers a rich area for research. For example, the ways in which plans are conceived, constructed and used may or may not reveal new roles for teachers and new ways for them to influence decision-making in their schools. The processes of school development planning may enhance collegiality and collaboration. Alternatively, they may reinforce existing patterns of interaction or conceal new forms of control.

One particularly interesting finding emerged from our study. Where many or all of the staff had been involved in discussion about the school development plan the headteacher regarded this in itself as beneficial; indeed this participation was seen as probably more important than the finished document and self-evidently a 'good thing'. Table 5.1 shows the extent of staff participation in the construction of the school development plans. The table itself does not convey the subtlety of what was actually happening. The extent of staff participation may not necessarily be a reflection of the overall management style or of the professional culture of the schools. For example, most of the primary headteachers who wrote the plans themselves spoke in the interviews about how they were 'shielding colleagues' at a time of excessive external demands upon their time, but this did not mean that the staff were not working together on other aspects of school life.

Table 5.1. *Staff participation in the construction of school development plans.*

Type of school	Headteacher	Headteacher + senior management team	Headteacher + senior management team + Middle managers	Headteacher + senior management team + Staff	Headteacher + senior management team + Staff + Others
Primary	9	4	0	9	2
Secondary*	0	10	6	2	1
Special	1	3	1	3	0
Middle	2	2	0	2	0

*Secondary (includes the one sixth form college included in the survey)

Even in those schools where most staff participation was reported, it did not follow that the middle managers and classroom teachers necessarily valued this or shared the headteacher's view of the worthwhileness of the plans. Some of those who had participated regarded their involvement as unimportant. Crude attempts to quantify participation, or indeed simplistic notions of the concept itself, may not, therefore, reflect the nature of the school culture and particularly of staff working relationships.

THE DIVERSITY OF SCHOOL DEVELOPMENT PLANNING: SOME KEY DIMENSIONS

The project generated a considerable amount of data about both school development plans and the practices adopted in schools for their construction. It became very clear that the concept of school development planning meant very different things to the various people engaged in the activity. Local education authorities (LEAs) varied in both their expectations of how plans should be set out, and in their approaches to providing support for schools. Even within the same LEA we still found considerable diversity across schools. In some schools, for example, the planning process seemed to involve the accumulation of policies relating to various aspects of school life. In other schools it seemed to involve a highly structured, analytical, evidence-based process from which was drawn a detailed and closely argued set of targets and action plans. In yet other schools, it involved drawing up a brief checklist for action in the near future. According to the image that was held of a school development plan in a school, further implications followed for the process of construction and for subsequent use of the plan.

In an attempt to convey the diversity, complexity and subtlety of what was happening we created a set of dimensions to plot variations between schools. The dimensions were:

1   *the construction relationship dimension* concerned with how those involved in the construction of a school's plan interacted during the process;

2   *the managing planning dimension* concerned with the extent to which the production of a SDP was integrated into the normal processes of management of the school;

3   *the quality assurance dimension* concerned with the extent to which success criteria were used in the review process;

4   *the content dimension* concerned with the comprehensiveness and internal coherence of the plan;

5   *the change dimension* concerned with the extent to which school development planning was used to support change or to maintain existing policies and practices;

6   *the participation and control dimension* concerned with the extent to which control of the agenda, discussions and decisions related to the plan was retained by the head/senior managers or exercised as a partnership with other staff.

Each dimension has a number of points against which a school might be located. (See, for example, Figure 5.1, which shows the points on the 'construction relationship' dimension. In most, but not all, cases these positions seemed to represent an order. Although neither the continua nor the positions upon each should be regarded as definitive, their contribution is as an analytical tool for examining patterns and relationships which are neither immediately obvious nor visible. They have been used subsequently to stimulate discussion, both within and across schools, about current practices and future aspirations.

The implications of this form of analysis may be seen through a detailed consideration of the 'construction relationship' dimension. Any school development

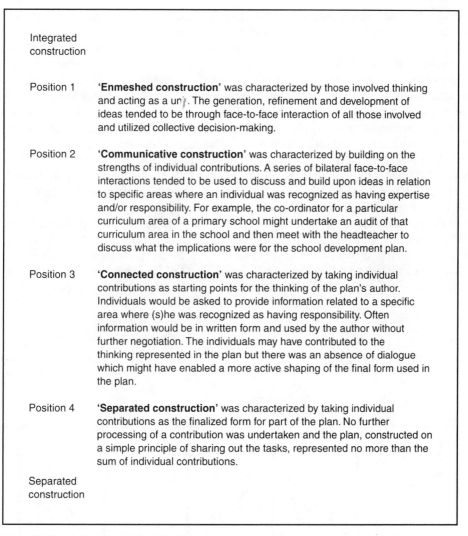

Integrated
construction

Position 1   **'Enmeshed construction'** was characterized by those involved thinking and acting as a un/. The generation, refinement and development of ideas tended to be through face-to-face interaction of all those involved and utilized collective decision-making.

Position 2   **'Communicative construction'** was characterized by building on the strengths of individual contributions. A series of bilateral face-to-face interactions tended to be used to discuss and build upon ideas in relation to specific areas where an individual was recognized as having expertise and/or responsibility. For example, the co-ordinator for a particular curriculum area of a primary school might undertake an audit of that curriculum area in the school and then meet with the headteacher to discuss what the implications were for the school development plan.

Position 3   **'Connected construction'** was characterized by taking individual contributions as starting points for the thinking of the plan's author. Individuals would be asked to provide information related to a specific area where (s)he was recognized as having responsibility. Often information would be in written form and used by the author without further negotiation. The individuals may have contributed to the thinking represented in the plan but there was an absence of dialogue which might have enabled a more active shaping of the final form used in the plan.

Position 4   **'Separated construction'** was characterized by taking individual contributions as the finalized form for part of the plan. No further processing of a contribution was undertaken and the plan, constructed on a simple principle of sharing out the tasks, represented no more than the sum of individual contributions.

Separated
construction

Figure 5.1 *The construction relationship dimension.*

plan represents the knowledge and understanding that its author(s) has of the school itself, of the planning process and of the way in which the latter may contribute to the development of the former. How that knowledge and understanding is created, therefore, and the extent to which it is shared by those involved in the plan's construction, may be a useful indicator of the nature of professional social interaction within a school. In other words, it may offer pointers to a school's professional culture and its potential for development and change if it is accepted that, in essence, these depend upon teachers learning together about what the whole school is, and might be.

Although two primary schools may have involved all teaching staff in the construction of a plan, they may have used very different processes in order to do so. In one school, formal planning may have been a whole-staff interactive learning activity through which everyone developed a shared set of meanings about the school. In another school, it may have been merely an administrative exercise undertaken by a set of individuals and organized by the plan's author. In terms of the learning of the constructors of the plan, these are qualitatively different types of involvement. This suggests, then, that knowing who is involved in the construction of a plan is insufficient without some consideration of this dimension. How the involvement happens, the nature and quality of interaction, its contribution to the thinking encapsulated in the plan, and the extent to which the thinking is shared by those involved are all features that need to be taken into account.

The project team felt that the use of these dimensions not only added a further level of explanation about development planning in the schools but also helped pinpoint further questions. For example, by profiling two primary schools in the same LEA (see Figure 5.2), we can see the interplay between school development planning and deeper social processes. Although the schools were at the same point on three dimensions (and this may have been related to local training), they varied on others. The most significant variations concerned the extent to which school development planning was integrated into the overall management of the school and how far it was used to support change. In one of the schools, writing the school development plan was seen as an event confirming the status quo, while in the other it was prepared by existing working groups and it lead to developments within the school.

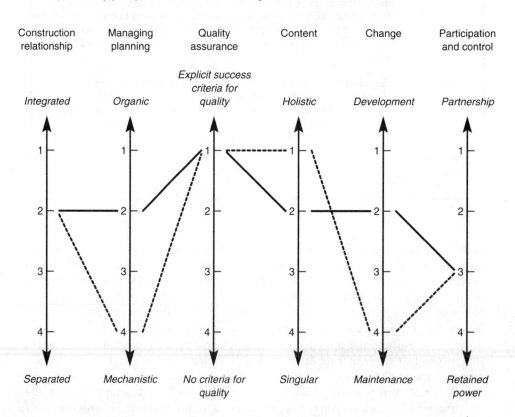

Figure 5.2 *Profiling two primary schools on the dimensions.*

THE SUBTLETY OF PARTICIPATION IN SCHOOLS

The project cast doubts upon some common assumptions about the relationship between school improvement and teacher participation in school management. The interviews indicated that whilst formal school development planning was meaningful for most headteachers of primary schools and for senior management teams in secondary schools, this was not so for the main professional grade teachers. Even where there had been an attempt to involve the whole staff in democratic decision-making, the teachers we interviewed had not felt that the activity was a significant aspect of their work. Its processes had not excited them nor had its values been internalized like cherished teaching beliefs and practices. This questions the extent to which teachers' involvement in formal whole-school planning and democratic decision-making might be 'empowering' for them.

One clue to this heretical suggestion is provided by Louden (1991), who found that Australian teachers tended to contest the legitimacy of school management reform while accepting curriculum reform. The recent Australian management reform, known as the 'Better Schools Project', aimed for a system of 'self-determining schools' which would provide more democratic workplaces for teachers. As a result of their involvement teachers certainly had their workloads increased but they found the outcomes to be unconvincing because these had more to do with school management than with the curriculum. In contrast, a parallel curriculum reform project, 'First Steps,' was accepted by the teachers. Its values and aspirations to improve teaching and learning were considered to be legitimate.

Many of the headteachers we interviewed were, in fact, reluctant to impose school development planning on all teachers at this time, and Louden reports similar views from a group of Australian secondary school principals:

> teachers have to do so much committee work now that they do not have enough time to teach. School development planning often takes teachers away from teaching.
>
> (Western Australian Secondary Principals' Association, 1990)

This is not so much a rejection of the value of participation but more of a recognition of the importance of context and of the meanings which the teachers make of working together. Lunden, for instance, argues that a collegial culture in schools is still a powerful force in supporting educational improvement when it has a curriculum focus. What is essential is 'establishing the legitimacy, clarity and practicability of the changes' (Louden, 1991, p. 370). On the other hand, a management focus for working together seems to be deplored by some teachers as an inappropriate intensification of their labour.

Acker has also raised a similar question of whether 'attempts to impose collegiality contain control features not necessarily in teachers' best interests' (Acker, 1991, p. 302). The imposition she refers to is the 1988 Education Reform Act in the United Kingdom with its drive towards National Curriculum and assessment frameworks, formal planning and the production of written policies. She, too, considers how these imposed demands might affect the ways that teachers talk and work together. Drawing on studies of schools as workplaces, which pre-dated the 1988 Reform Act in the United Kingdom, she argued that distinctions between collegiality and individualism have not been clear cut. For instance, in the negotiated order of secondary schools, groups and individuals with vested interests might compete for resources, territory and career advantage. As a result any collegiality which does exist is likely to flourish only in sub-groups and subject departments. In the micro-politics of the school these competing groups can be manipulated by managers.

In the different context of collegial primary schools she found that teachers' sense of membership and belonging was sustained by a range of shared social events, work routines and rituals which also sustained school values. There headteachers were pivotal in building and maintaining a culture of collaboration which was essentially about personal relationships. Significantly, at that time the schools had 'oral cultures with little reference to written documentation' (Acker, 1991, p. 305).

It is too early to draw any firm conclusions about lasting effects of the Education Reform Act on teachers' working relationships, but we can already begin to see the significance of some issues emerging from Acker's study. She does not mention school development planning specifically, but she does refer to the great deal of time which was spent, prior to the legislation, in meetings and conversations. The meetings were mainly about 'domestic' and 'curriculum' matters. Since the Act, she reports that staff meetings have become more serious and academic with more concern about having to write policies and keep records. She has observed that the schools had become no less collaborative but 'the preoccupations were shifting, with the division of labour becoming more pronounced' (Acker, 1991, p. 310). She recognizes the potentially manipulative function of the recent encouragement to be collegial in order to implement the ideas of others. However, concluding from her own work and from two other recent studies (Osborn and Broadfoot, 1991; Ball and Bone, 1991), she suggests that teachers are striving to interpret the demands of the ERA collectively to help each other to cope creatively and to develop sensible ways of doing what is now expected of them.

To turn specifically to school development planning, then, it is perhaps to be expected that because it is congruent with what they do, we should find that it was meaningful to headteachers and senior management teams. In many cases, headteachers told us that they were arranging their own informal self-help groups as well as using the telephone 'grapevine' to talk over the task of writing the school development plan. It was also the headteachers themselves who were most keen on training opportunities to refine their planning skills, mainly for writing policies, establishing success criteria and involving staff. Most of the headteachers thought that school development planning should eventually generate high staff involvement, but in many cases they were biding their time and holding back from making extra demands upon their staff. The reasons given were that the imposed time-scale was unrealistic, that there were too many unknown factors at this stage (especially about finance and staffing), that they needed to learn more about development planning themselves before involving others and that teachers needed protecting from yet another chore.

Some headteachers, then, were aware of the lack of congruence between formalized whole-school planning and what teachers currently do. This was substantiated by the teachers themselves. Many had been involved minimally in the formal planning and were content with this detachment. Some knew little, or even nothing, about the existence of the plan, and even among those 'middle managers' who had participated in drawing up the plan few saw it as a key part of their work.

This should not be taken to mean that teachers do not want to be part of the whole school or that they do not want to plan. Perhaps the problem is that the ideology of the school management reform movement, which is translated into the requirement to produce annual written school development plans, does not match the way that teachers currently conceptualize 'whole school' or 'planning' or the way that schools function as organizations. Recent research in primary schools in the United Kingdom (Nias *et al.*, 1992) has suggested that there is much development but it is seldom sequential, rational and systematic. The authors' description of the nature of primary schools as organizations catches the active membership of the staff in ways that a study of the formal processes of school development planning would probably miss. Like Acker, they convey the strength of teachers' existing approaches to collaboration and development. This is not so much to do with written policies but it is essentially about action that is rooted in beliefs and values. Real development is slow moving and involves teachers learning to be likeminded. They learn key beliefs collectively in processes that are embedded in the everyday life of schools, such as in assemblies, through displays and in various interconnected and simultaneous events and occasions for working together, observing, talking, and sharing.

Perhaps, then, the term 'participation' may serve to fudge rather than clarify the nature of the ways staff work together in developing schools. In some schools, participation may merely hold connotations of routinized and ritual involvement with opinions being solicited and 'inputs' being made in response. Even when head-teachers assume that the best management style means involving others in the construction of a school development plan, in practice many maintained a strong, if subtle, control over both the planning and the plan. Their strategies of control may have presented problems for the growth of collegiality and collaboration. Leithwood and Jantzi (1990), for instance, suggest that a more equitable distribution of power for decision-making among staff is a *sine qua non* of a truly collaborative professional culture in a school.

However, participation, control and school development can take many forms. Nias *et al.* (1992) have taken a new look at the role of headteachers in 'whole schools' in which teachers do work and learn together for development and change. They found that headteachers were central, powerful figures who exercised a controlling influence upon school developments in ways which they formerly assumed to be incompatible with collegiality and democratic decision-making. For this reason, they distinguish between 'whole schools' and collegial ones. In 'whole schools' it is acceptable to both heads and teachers that the head has a powerful and pivotal role. Nias *et al.*, conclude that 'whole schools' are characterized by a high degree of complex professional and personal interaction which is not to be mistaken for straightforward notions of collegiality or teacher democracy.

Like Acker and Louden, Nias *et al.* take a positive view of teachers' capacity to work together for change when the focus is directly on what they believe to be important, when it involves their own learning and when it is based mainly upon their own informal patterns of interaction. In different ways all three studies have cast serious doubts on school development reforms which propose that teachers will necessarily find it empowering to produce formal, written school development plans on a pre-arranged time-scale, and even in some LEAS to a standard proforma.

One of the main observations arising from our study also confirms the centrality of the headteachers' role. Many said they were judging how to incorporate the imposed requirement to produce a school development plan into the range of legitimate and competing demands upon their own time and that of their staff. Most of the headteachers we interviewed were, at least for the time being, purposely restricting the scope and scale of the task. As well as protecting staff from additional burdens, most were not attending to the full set of development headings which had been provided: curriculum, staff development, fabric, community, and finance. There was a tendency for what Cyert and March (1963) have called 'uncertainty avoidance' and the 'quasi-resolution of conflict', where strain is reduced by limiting decisions to the familiar and more certain aspects about which 'local rationality' has already been established. We found that many schools avoided uncertainty by concentrating mainly upon curriculum planning (see Table 5.2) with some links to staff development and, less commonly, to finance. Even then, in many primary schools, the subjects were being dealt with sequentially for the purposes of formal planning.

Table 5.2. *Content of school development plans.*

Type of school	Curriculum		Staff development		Fabric		Community		Finance		No plan	
Primary	23	(96)	20	(83)	11	(46)	11	(46)	10	(42)	1	(4)
Secondary	19	(100)	18	(95)	11	(58)	9	(47)	10	(53)	0	(0)
Special	6	(75)	3	(98)	1	(13)	0	(0)	0	(0)	0	(0)
Middle	6	(100)	6	(100)	3	(50)	2	(33)	1	(17)	0	(0)
Total	54		47		26		22		21		1	
Percentage of full sample		(95)*		(82)		(46)		(39)		(37)		(2)

Note: All figures in parentheses are approximate percentages

CONCLUSION

Evidence from the project suggests that school development planning is regarded favourably by primary headteachers and also by senior management teams in secondary schools, but that they also felt that the task should be accomplished in a realistic way. In many schools the mandate to produce written plans was not being translated readily into an urgent whole-school priority. In the main, the headteachers were taking a central role in limiting the scope and scale of the involvement of staff and of the content of the plan. In this sense, the heads were acting as a 'critical screen' (Fullan, 1988) for their staff in response to what they perceived as a constant bombardment of external change.

For this reason, the planning practices of these schools reflected the judgement of the heads about the place of formal written plans in the overall development of the school, and about the relative priority of different demands upon staff time and energies. Looking forward, most of the headteachers anticipated that, in the longer term, they may pay more attention to formal written planning and in those circumstances might create more opportunities for staff involvement in the construction of the plans.

We found that the requirement to produce written school development plans was not immediately meaningful to teachers. In some cases they had been protected from the task, and most of those who had been involved had felt it to be neither significant nor a burden. In the few cases where the process had been seen as worthwhile, the focus was seen as most practicable when it was on the curriculum and domestic matters, such as procedures for dealing with 'wet playtimes'. Most were, in any case, preoccupied with the immediate and pressing demands of teaching the National Curriculum and working with new assessment requirements. Nevertheless, recent studies in primary schools (Acker, 1991; Nias *et al.*, 1992) have suggested that teachers are highly involved in real school development. They are working and learning together as active leaders and members to create 'whole schools' which are driven by shared values and beliefs.

The central issue, of course, is what impact school development planning may have on what is at the heart of school effectiveness and improvement, namely pupil learning. After all, Tomlinson (1981) suggested that effective schools are merely schools organized to pursue learning consistently. Such consistency derives from coherence in the individual and collective practices of teachers. The question is whether this is best done through strategic planning or the more embedded interaction, dialogue and communication built up through working together over time.

At the time of the study, formal school development planning was a new and under-researched concept. We still await further studies which investigate the relationship between the externally imposed mandate to produce written development plans and the processes of actual whole-school development. What are the effects of the attempt to introduce systematic and written whole-school development planning into what have previously been oral and action-orientated cultures? As yet there is little understanding of this issue.

REFERENCES

Acker, S. (1991) 'Teacher relationships and educational reform in England and Wales', *Curriculum Journal*, **2** (3), 301–16.

Ball, S.J. and Bone, R. (1991) 'Subject to change? Subject departments and the implementation of National Curriculum policy: an overview of the issues', unpublished paper, King's College, London (forthcoming in *Journal of Curriculum Studies*).

Cyert, R.M. and March, J.G. (1963) *The Behavioral Theory of the Firm*. Englewood Cliffs, NJ: Prentice-Hall.

Fullan, M. (1988) *What's Worth Fighting For in the Principalship?* Toronto: Ontario Public School Teachers' Federation.

Hargreaves, D. and Hopkins, D. (1991) *The Empowered School: The Management and Practice of Development Planning*. London: Cassell.

HMI (1991) *Management of Educational Resources: 5. The Role of School Development Plans in Managing School Effectiveness*. Edinburgh: Scottish Office Education Department/HMSO.

Hopkins, D. (1991) 'Changing school culture through development planning', in Riddell, S. and Brown, S. (eds) *School Effectiveness Research: Its Messages for School Improvement*, pp. 249–80 Edinburgh: The Scottish Office Education Department/HMSO.

Leithwood, K. and Jantzi, D. (1990) 'Transformational leadership: how principals can help reform school cultures', *School Effectiveness and School Improvement*, **1** (4), 249–80.

Little, J.W. (1982) 'Norms of collegiality and experimentation: workplace conditions of school success', *American Educational Research Journal*, **19**, 325–40.

Louden, W. (1991) 'Collegiality, curriculum and education change', *Curriculum Journal*, **2** (3), 361–73.

Nias, J., Southworth, G. and Yeomans, R. (1989) *Staff Relationships in the Primary School. A Study of Organizational Cultures*. London: Cassell.

Nias, J., Southworth, G. and Campbell, P. (1992) *Whole School Curriculum Development in the Primary School*. London: Falmer Press.

Osborn, M. and Broadfoot, P. (1991) 'The impact of current changes in English primary schools on teacher professionalism', Paper presented at the annual meeting of the American Educational Research Association, Chicago, April.

Pava, C. (1986) 'New strategies of systems change: reclaiming non-synoptic methods', *Human Relations*, **39** (7), 615–33.

Tomlinson, T. (1981) 'The troubled years: an interpretive analysis of public schooling since 1950', *Phi Delta Kappan*, **62**, 373–6.

Western Australian Secondary Principals' Association (1990) 'Second Draft of a Report prepared by WASPA Action Learning Working Party', Mimeo, Perth, Australia.

Chapter 6

Three Arenas of Tension: Teachers' Experience of Participation in School Development Planning

Hilary Constable

SCHOOL DEVELOPMENT PLANNING

School development planning is now part of the annual cycle of work in schools in England and Wales. Although few schools may be able to achieve the ideal expressed in the School Development Plans Project of a plan which 'captures the long term vision for the school within which manageable short term goals are set' (Hargreaves *et al.*, 1989, p. 4), some progress and achievements can be detected (Wallace, 1991; Hall and Wallace, 1992; McMahon and Wallace, 1992; Constable *et al.*, 1991; Constable, 1992). The School Development Plans Project makes a point of arguing that it is the very fact that there is so much externally imposed change which demands that schools take charge of their own development: 'A development plan helps to relieve the stress on teachers caused by the pace of change. Teachers come to exercise greater control over change rather than feeling controlled by it' (Hargreaves *et al.*, 1989, p. 4).

PARTICIPATIVE PRACTICES

This chapter reports on the actual, experienced practice of school development planning. It is unusual in that it draws on the perceptions of 'ordinary' teachers rather than headteachers, who, it is freely acknowledged, would very likely have had quite a different view. For those unfamiliar with the system of education in England and Wales, the management processes referred to are within school processes and the headteacher is roughly equivalent to the school principal in North America. The words 'pupil' and 'student' are used interchangeably and the schools referred to cater for various age ranges of student, mainly 5 to 11 and 11 to 16.

SCHOOL DEVELOPMENT PLANNING IN PRACTICE

School development planning is where, in practice, different constructions of teachers' work, management of schools and educational policies are worked out. Participative practices have been selected as a focus because they are sensitive to underlying themes.

In the work reported here teachers were asked to report on their experience of school development and the construction of school development plans. In line with the definition in the earlier study of the implementation of Guidelines for Review and Internal Development in Schools (GRIDS) (Constable *et al.*, 1988), teachers were asked to discriminate between participation and involvement. Participation was to include the practical activities in which individuals took part such as making a response to a questionnaire, writing a document, or organizing a working party or being a member of one, whereas involvement was a positive feeling associated or not with any of these activities.

High-quality pupil learning must be one intended purpose of schooling, and school development planning in general and participation in particular are far from trivial with respect to this. The effect of schools on pupils is mediated through the context of human relations in which they find themselves. In organizations with purposes different from schools it may be possible to argue that development work is merely a management issue. In schools this argument does not stand up. The processes and procedures of school development, the expectations held for teachers and by teachers are the context of the work of pupils and students. Joyce and Showers (1988) argue for collective approaches to development and change, and link these explicitly with student or pupil experience and achievement:

> The school has its impact in three ways: one what is taught, the second is in how it is taught, and the third is its social environment. Teachers and administrators need to be engaged in the continuous study of all three, continually increasing knowledge of academic content, models of teaching, and models for school environments and how to create them.
>
> (Joyce and Showers, 1988, p. 4)

They remind us:

> While the most familiar image of teachers and administrators is at work as individuals, the improvement of the school requires collective work. The social climate of the school and the attitudes and patterns of behaviour it promotes greatly influence the process of education.
>
> (Joyce and Showers, 1988, p. 6)

As stated earlier, it is in practices and procedures such as school development planning that views about different aspects of schooling and organization have their expression. First some examples from the case studies – in the first two extracts the plan is made available but it is hard to see what contribution is being made to the development of the school or even to informing staff of their goals by the arrangements:

> The current SDP is the third plan the school or, perhaps more accurately, the head has produced. The 1991–92 plan seems to have been more widely publicized and made more accessible to the teaching staff than either of the others – the staff being told at a morning briefing meeting to call in if they wanted a copy. I was not killed in the rush! The head confided that I was the third to take one and that the other copies printed would probably sit on his shelf until next year.

> Until I requested a copy of the Development Plan for this work I had not been privy to it. Only the head and deputy [head] (and possibly the governors although I am not sure of this) had seen it.

In the latter case the writer also raised the entirely pertinent question: 'How then were we as staff to know of the goals and time scale in it?' It is worth adding that several teachers at first denied the existence of any such plan and were not keen on asking to see it.

Picture an arrangement like the one reported here:

> At the present moment the head, two deputies and the three senior teachers have a copy of the SDP. The other staff have been told there is a copy for them *but* that they must request one from the deputy head personally.

Teachers can hardly be expected to pursue goals that have not been communicated to them. Even assuming the most managerial stance, the potential for communication has been lost. As one of the teachers put it: 'If this plan is to be utilized . . . staff need to see it.' Unless of course the plan does not have any goals or targets which can be made use of – more designed to avoid decisions about priorities than to make them: 'On reading it, it appears to be very general, not committing the school . . .'

Another possibility is to argue that the finished document was merely the summary of processes in which teachers had participated or about which they were informed. Further, it could be argued that it was the processes rather than the document which were important and that teachers had internalized common understandings and shared goals rendering the document superfluous. This may well be the case, sometimes. In the following cases such an argument would be hard to sustain:

> Following this work I was asked to prepare a science document for inclusion in the three-year development plan. The language co-ordinator was asked to do the same . . . As far as I am able to tell, no one else on the staff was asked to contribute and largely they were unaware that the plan was being drawn up.

This next teacher raised another kind of question, whether or not to support a participative practice:

> I was asked to write a new school policy for science within the school. I was advised to do this without consultation with staff (I had suggested that we meet together to discuss the policy) as this would save time and the staff would receive a finished policy.

The headteacher's reasons for advising against participation may have been both pragmatic and benign. Whatever the case, the communicative function has been reduced by the tactic adopted.

Teachers showed a sophisticated appreciation of the issues in generating shared understandings, commitment and ownership. The problem of achieving the optimum balance between time spent and potential benefits is as evident to this teacher as to any head (even though one might wish to quibble about the conflation of ownership and authorship):

> I participated in the writing of the document and the head was involved as she looked over each component when it was completed. As far as staff involvement was concerned, none were involved at its inception as they

only saw it after it had been drafted – no part of the writing – no ownership. People's feelings on the issue of involvement indicated that most staff at this particular time were overloaded with work and therefore quite relieved that the document was written for them. However, whether it will be consulted or adhered to is difficult to assess.

Teachers were sometimes asked to contribute to school development plans without being told the purpose or scope of the task they had been asked to perform. I find this amazing. At the very least and taking an unproblematic view, it cannot be easy to fulfil the brief to prepare a school development plan if you do not know that is what you're doing:

> By careful questioning it became apparent that the new deputy head and myself were indeed in the process of collating and developing the SDP.

There is plenty of scope for headteachers to claim (sincerely or otherwise) that there has been consultation or even participation when teachers themselves remain unaware of any such events or processes. Some teachers found themselves asked for their opinion in the course of a casual chat over a cup of coffee in the staff room. Consider the extent to which reactive remarks in such circumstances can be taken as a considered response. Consider also the position the questioners have allowed themselves to be put in:

> Members of the senior management team were asked to identify areas of concern. This consultation process was informal to the point that discussion was often held over coffee. Perhaps the only time staff had to talk.

> At this point none of us realized we were being consulted or involved in an audit and I was certainly unaware that I was actually writing any part of the SDP.

It becomes increasingly hard to sustain the view that these crypto-participative events were the accidental products of shortage of time:

> Curriculum co-ordinators were involved in curriculum audit whether they were aware of it or not.

Even where the headteacher can sustain such an argument, the position of surveillance which staff have been put in is, to say the least, uneasy:

> I was given two days to visit each class teacher and observe their children working. . . . This was a very informal visit after which my observations were to be divulged to the head. I was not aware at the time that what I was involved in was an 'audit'.

Underlying issues

A wider exploration of the case studies in general shows school development planning in a reasonably good light (Constable *et al.*, 1991; Constable, 1992). There is some evidence of development from year to year, although it should by no means be assumed that simple repetition leads to improved practices, for dysfunctional practices can be built in as well as productive ones. Inevitably there are some difficulties and sometimes a loss of potential. Teachers are by no means naive; they appreciate the conflicting pressures on heads between, say, careful consideration and the need to act at speed. Few teachers argue for a radical form of participation and involvement, but they do dislike attempts to deceive them into believing that a practice is participative when it is not. Further, it should be recalled that each school exists in its own history (see also Sanday, 1990). Destructive experiences may cause permanent harm in that they become part of the organizational climate.

Headteachers are shown through the extracts above apparently doing some rather strange things. Whether these actions represent an unbridged gap between aspiration and practice or whether they are an effort to disguise an unpalatable form of management or even to fail to acknowledge the management style of preference is not altogether clear. Certainly headteachers find themselves negotiating tricky terrain here, caught, even torn, by a number of dilemmas; for instance, at a practical level, needing to act in real time but also needing to consider actions carefully. At another level they may be caught between the pulls of collegiality on the one hand, and a managerial stance on the other, or merely unclear about the purpose of any participation.

The activities reported above offered insight into the processes of school development planning. The practices are various and best not lumped together as if they were one thing. There is instead a range of participations, each with different intentions and different key features. There are difficulties and while a few may be somewhat intractable, this is not necessarily true of them all.

SCHOOL DEVELOPMENT PLANNING AS AN INNOVATION

Three arenas have been identified as possible sources of the discontinuities and tensions evident in the extracts above. The first source of potential difficulty is school development planning as an innovation. It may not be obvious that school development planning needs to be treated as an innovation in the same way as innovations of a more substantive sort. Fullan has offered a useful analysis of educational change as generally occupying three phases:

> Most researchers now see three broad phases to the change process. Phase I – variously labelled initiation, mobilization, or adoption – consists of the process that leads up to and includes a decision to adopt or proceed with a change. Phase II – implementation or initial use (usually the first two or three years of use) – involves the first experiences of attempting to put an idea or reform into practice. Phase III – called continuation, incorporation, routinization or institutionalization – refers to whether a change gets built in as an ongoing part of the system or disappears by way of a decision to discard or through attrition.
>
> (Fullan with Stiegelbauer, 1991, p. 47)

He goes on to say that schools give much the most attention to the earliest stage of initiation and successively less to the following stages. In this respect, school development planning is an innovation like any other. It needs not only to be initiated, but also implemented and finally incorporated – to reach the stage of 'this is how we do things round here'. In other respects, of course, school development planning is a different kind of innovation in that it is essentially content-free and the means by which other innovations are handled, prioritized, implemented and so on. Arising from this analysis it is clear that attention needs to be paid to the implementation and incorporation of school development planning as an innovation. In other words as in any innovation, routine difficulties of implementation must be expected to occur. Indeed the very existence of difficulties may be taken as positive indication that something is happening. It would seem unconvincing to claim that real change is taking place without any difficulty whatsoever. For school leaders such difficulties should not be a source of worry, but neither should they be ignored; with attention these problems should be curable. In practice, the difficulties of implementation are associated with other issues which are more intractable.

MODELS OF SCHOOL DEVELOPMENT AS PRESCRIPTION AND AS DESCRIPTION

The second possible source of underlying tension comes from the status of portrayals of school development planning. There is a tension between acting and understanding, and between portrayals of school development planning designed for one or the other. This is the distinction between management theories and organization theories. Hoyle summarizes this well:

> We can thus make a broad distinction between organization theory which is theory for understanding and management theory which is practical theory and hence has a narrower focus. However the distinction cannot be pressed too hard since management theory is grounded in, and the research which it generates contributes to, organisation theory. On the other hand organisation theories frequently display a tendency to be normative and at least to contain an implicit commitment to improving life in organisations.
>
> (Hoyle, 1986, p. 1)

Another way of putting this is as a tension between imposing order and generating complexity. In the traditions of school improvement and management literatures, ways of thinking are devised to guide actions. Here conceptual order is imposed. At one level everyone who takes part recognizes that real life is not going to be like the diagrams in school improvement and development booklets. Indeed, that is part of the attraction. This is exactly the advantage such guidance has: order is imposed and a coherence offered. From this order actions can be recommended and a sequence offered. In determining actions this can be helpful but in understanding or even apprehending what is happening it can distract attention from critical incidents. The development and management literatures rest on an implied ordering of the world of the school which is over-simple and can be misleading.

Work on understanding organizations shows another picture, not a unitary vision of organizations but rather a heap of partial understandings and contrasting perspectives. The writing on organizations emphasizes complexity and draws attention to the fractured and fragmentary nature of understandings and the lack of an overarching theory of organizations.

In action, heads and teachers find themselves caught between understandings which, while meaningful, can give only limited guidance on one hand and on the other recommendations for action not well grounded in understanding schools. It is easy to see that this position is open to drift, and the need to impose order in order to act becomes confused with the existence of order – if the organization cannot be fully described in some particular way, it ought to be. This is the second source of difficulty: the blurring of the boundary between descriptions of differing status. An uncritical view of organizations arising from school development planning guidance may leave heads and teachers blunted in their apprehension of their own experience and therefore hampered in their learning and action.

VALUES IN SCHOOL DEVELOPMENT PLANNING

In the third arena are contrasting views about the values embodied in school development planning. Teacher participation in school development planning is sometimes portrayed as not only valuable but an appropriate form of organizational behaviour in a democratic society. In contrast is the view of school development planning as a tool of management, as portrayed, in this case, by the Audit Commission:

> Although final decisions on a school's development plan rest with the governing body, the headteacher will take the lead in the preparation of the plan. The headteacher should involve all the staff who will implement it in order to maximise their commitment to its success.
>
> (Audit Commission, 1991, p. 20)

Here as Ball argues:

> Teacher participation relates not to involvement for its own sake, as a collegial professional or democratic concern, but for the purposes of the management of motivation. The SDP signifies and celebrates the exclusion of the teacher.
>
> (Ball, 1992, p. 18)

Hargreaves (1992) adds to this that apparent autonomy can be seen as merely the separation of groups with like interests into competing factions, and that apparent delegation of responsibility is better seen as a process of balkanization. Together all these views accept that school development planning may be content-free but that it can hardly be value-free. It is instead the arena for the struggle between competing power groups. These arguments are a far cry from any idea that the processes (not content) of school development planning can be seen as outside or immune from value and power-laden positions as is sometimes suggested in portrayals of collegial development. School development planning does not lie outside the world of values and conflict. Nevertheless it is sometimes represented as if it did. Ideas such as the self-managing school, the developing school or the learning school are from a Mary Poppins 'value free world of consensus, collaboration and self control' (Ball, 1992, p. 17). Further, he argues, value-free portrayals of school development planning may be professionally acceptable but do not represent reality. Rather, the use of such ideas is not always entirely benign. They can be used to ease the acceptance of an overt imposition of management based on a culture of market and budget rather than professionalism. He captures this vividly with the image of the self-managing spoonful of sugar which helps the managerial medicine go down (Ball, 1992).

The implication for school leaders is then that they may be caught, even torn, between a professionally acceptable but sanitized view of school development, and another which acknowledges values and power but seems characterized by unresolvable conflict. They may also find their preferred style of management in conflict with various aspects of their context such as the local education authority or governors or the Audit Commission.

CONCLUSION

School development planning is a piece of real life with all that that entails. In other words, it is not going to be possible to sort out school development planning quickly with one analysis. Nevertheless, the difficulties are indicative of unresolved underlying tensions and greater clarity about these, while not offering instant solutions, may help to prevent headteachers shooting themselves in the foot.

The imperatives driving different participations may be very different, ranging from a managerial need to inform teachers of decisions which alter their working practices, through the need to harness the creativity of staff, to an appropriate characteristic for organizations in a democratic society. Teachers are as much actors in school development planning as heads and have as much need to be as clear about what is supposed to be going on, not least because they can hardly otherwise comply with heads' requests.

School development is important not merely from a management or a motivation point of view, but because schools contain pupils and the work of schools is *with* and *for* pupils. Some of the difficulties experienced in school development, while not necessarily easy to solve, are relatively unproblematic. However, there are also some complex underlying issues and ignoring these is likely to lead to increasing frustration and further practical problems.

Problems are likely to arise from three main arenas. Difficulties arising from the first of these, school development planning as an innovation, can be seen as good news: these are to be expected and indicate that something is happening. The second arena, the gap between understanding organizations and the need to act, is likely to hamper the ability of school leaders to learn from their experience. However, difficulties arising from conflicting value priorities, the third arena, are more intractable and may not be open to easy resolution. This is not to suggest that it would be desirable, even if it were possible, for the procedures of a school to be uniformly consistent in this respect. Indeed, it can be argued that the presence of alternative views is what provides the creative cutting edge necessary for educational development.

The case studies show much promising work in school development. However they also show teachers exposed to and taking part in some activities which are so bizarre that they seem unlikely to fulfil management intentions however argued. These activities appear to arise from a mosaic of imperatives. Teachers are tolerant of a wide range of management styles and practices. If there is anything likely to turn off their general goodwill and motivation, it is attempts to disguise unpalatable management practices as something more attractive. For these reasons school leaders wishing to improve their practice could do worse than search their intended participations for critical revelations.

REFERENCES

Audit Commission (1991) *The Management of Primary Schools*. London: Audit Commission.

Ball, S.J. (1992) 'The worst of three worlds: policy, power relations and teachers' work', Paper given at the British Educational Management and Administration Society Research Conference, Nottingham, April.

Constable, H., Brown, R. and Williams, R. (1988) 'An evaluation of the implementation of GRIDS in a local education authority', *Educational Management and Administration Society*, **16**, 43–58.

Constable, H., Norton, J. and Abbott, I. (1991) *Case Studies in School Development Planning*, Sunderland: School of Education, Sunderland Polytechnic.

Constable, H. (1992) 'Four dead trees will be felled: participation and involvement in school development planning', Paper given at the British Educational Management and Administration Society Research Conference, Nottingham, April.

Fullan, M.G., with Stiegelbauer, S. (1991) *The New Meaning of Educational Change*. London: Cassell.

Hall, V. and Wallace, M. (1992) 'Team approaches to strategic planning in secondary schools', Paper given at the British Educational Management and Administration Society Research Conference, Nottingham, UK, April.

Hargreaves, A. (1992) 'Curriculum reform and the teacher', *The Curriculum Journal*, **2** (3), 249–58.

Hargreaves, D.H., Hopkins, D., Leask, M., Connolly, J. and Robinson, P. (1989) *Planning for School Development: Advice to Governors, Headteachers and Teachers*. London: Department of Education and Science/HMSO.

Holly, P. and Southworth, G. (1989) *The Developing School*. London: Falmer Press.

Hoyle, E. (1986) *The Politics of School Management*. London: Hodder & Stoughton.

Joyce, B. and Showers, B. (1988) *Student Achievement through Staff Development*. New York: Longman.

McMahon, A. and Wallace, M. (1992) 'Development planning in a turbulent environment: the case of multiracial primary schools', Paper given at the British Educational Management and Administration Society Research Conference, Nottingham, April.

Sanday, A. (1990) *Making Schools More Effective*. Warwick: CEDAR, University of Warwick.

Wallace, M. (1991) 'Coping with multiple innovations in schools: an exploratory study', *School Organization*, **11** (2).

Chapter 7

Observing Primary School Change: Through Conflict to Whole-School Collaboration?

Elizabeth Newman and Andrew Pollard

INTRODUCTION

The concept of school development planning, in itself, derives a good deal of its attractiveness and ideological power through the sense of benevolent, progressive and rational management which it conveys. To the extent that this can be turned into a reality, such ideas must, of course, be applauded. And yet, one of the main contributions which researchers can make to such developments is to point out the contradictions, complications and challenges which are associated with the practical implementation of such rhetorics.

This chapter raises such issues using the case of developments in one English primary school. In so doing, it focuses on the associated concern of many primary school headteachers with the development of collaborative staff cultures as an integral element of planned whole-school provision.

As Woods (1987, p. 121) and many others have suggested, English primary schools have a long-term reputation for generating a 'family atmosphere'. This is thought to lend itself to staff collegiality and to the provision of an ethos which is appropriate for the education of young children. However, although such commitments have been part of the stated intentions of primary school teachers for a very long time, it is arguably the case that it is only in recent years that headteachers have sought to achieve such cultures in deliberative and managed ways. The new emphasis is, of course, associated with the new educational legislation of the late 1980s and early 1990s which, particularly with the introduction of local management, the National Curriculum and increased requirements for accountability, has meant that headteachers now face an inescapable imperative to develop the coherence and consistency of policy and practice within their schools. The achievement of coherence is now a structural necessity and this is most commonly sought through the adoption of some form of school development planning.

However, given the history of commitment to strong interpersonal relations in English primary schools, actions which could be construed as 'managerialist' have been treated with suspicion by many primary school headteachers. Instead, and directly meeting the needs of the time, a strong argument has developed which suggests that it is possible to achieve coherent school practice through the development of cultures of collaboration among school staffs. Change is thus brought about through teamwork as colleagues contribute towards shared goals. The work of

Jennifer Nias, Geoff Southworth and their colleagues at the Cambridge University Institute of Education has been particularly significant in this whole area and it is on this work which we have focused the present chapter.

We begin with a brief description of the work of the Nias team and, in the main parts of the chapter which then follow, we present the detail of our case study. In the conclusion we will return to the themes raised in this introduction.

THE WORK OF NIAS AND HER COLLEAGUES

Jennifer Nias and her colleagues have made many unique contributions and provided much insight in specifying and elaborating the nature of staff relationships and of whole-school curriculum development in primary schools. The research on which these insights were based derived from detailed case-study work on a total of eleven primary schools in which the headteachers had been in post for between eighteen months and eighteen years. The schools studied had, in other words, relatively established relationships between their headteachers and teaching staff. Thus, for instance, Nias *et al.* were able to talk about 'developing and maintaining a culture of collaboration' in terms such as:

> The 'culture of collaboration' began when the first leadership acts of openness, sensitivity, tolerance and flexibility were reciprocated by other members of the staff group. From then on, it was sustained whenever members behaved consistently with the collaborative norms which the group was developing. In other words, once the culture of collaboration was established, it tended to become self-perpetuating.
>
> (Nias *et al.*, 1989, p. 75)

In their 1992 book, Nias, Southworth and Campbell report teachers' perception of a 'whole school' as:

> having a strong sense of community
> [sharing] educational beliefs and aims [and] interpretations of these in
>   their actions
> [having] autonomy within their classrooms but [feeling] able to play an
>   individual role within the school and call upon one another's expertise
> members related well to one another
> they worked together
> their knowledge of the school encompassed the concerns, practice and
>   classes of their colleagues
> they valued the leadership of the headteacher
>
> (Nias *et al.*, 1992, p. 108)

There is, we feel, a degree of idealization here in the tendency to highlight the consensual, developmental and organic features of primary school life. In a sense, then, the perspective may be viewed as articulating with child-centred ideologies and, like them, may be vulnerable to the critique of maintaining an unrealistic sentimentality in forms of practice and views of primary education (Alexander, 1984, 1991).

Of course, the Cambridge team are well aware of these issues. For instance, there are important qualifications in the first quotation above in that self-perpetuation is deemed to occur only *once* the culture of collaboration is established. Similarly the 'difficult enterprise' of developing a 'whole school' is acknowledged and three reasons for this are given. First, working together might lead to the emergence of 'fundamental differences in value and practice'. Second, there is a tension between classroom autonomy and whole-school policies. Third, primary schools are 'constantly changing' with subsequent effects on the 'nature as well as the dynamic of the staff group' (Nias *et al.*, 1992, pp. 109–11).

However, having acknowledged such qualifications, we pursue the suggestion of idealization in the Cambridge team's work. This is well seen in the summary of their qualifications where it is claimed that:

> developing a sense that the school was 'whole' was therefore: slow in pace; delicate, requiring differences, when they emerged, to be treated with care and sensitivity and individuality to be balanced against interdependence; and vulnerable to organisational disturbance.
>
> (Nias *et al.*, 1992, p. 111)

'Wholeness' for the school is thus associated with slow development, delicacy, sensitivity and vulnerability, just as, as we saw above, the 'culture of collaboration' is associated with openness, sensitivity, tolerance and flexibility.

Attractive and caring though this organic sensitivity may be, there remains a question over the extent to which it actually reflects the nature of organizations such as primary schools in the 1990s – despite the strong commitment of primary school teachers to fostering good interpersonal relationships in their work.

In the argument which follows, we present a qualification of the organic assumption which tends to underpin the work of the Cambridge teams. Our analysis is based on an ethnographic study of planned developments in one English primary school following the appointment of a new headteacher. This case study shows overt conflict and the use of power to reshape a school staff, while, at the same time, the rhetoric of attempting to build a whole-school culture of collaboration was used by the headteacher and a number of the staff. However, the initial phase of the headteacher's attempt to develop a culture of collaboration in the school resulted in a power struggle which, though in many senses positive, also proved to be both problematic and painful for the teachers concerned.

Perhaps the import of the argument which we generate is simply that there are probably several phases in the development of staff relationships, and that these stages may tend to be characterized by different degrees of conflict or consensus. On the other hand, it could also be that the values, research design and methods of the Cambridge team may have produced a particular type of result which future work will qualify further.

THE CASE-STUDY SCHOOL AND THE RESTRUCTURING OF STAFF RESPONSIBILITIES

The data for this case-study were collected over an eight-month period by means of a series of semi-structured interviews conducted with the headteacher and the teaching staff in one primary school. Data were also collected using participant observation at staff meetings, and observation in classrooms and by referring to school documents (brochures, institutional development plans, job descriptions, etc.).

The school was a maintained county primary in an urban location. It had a staff of head, 7.5 teachers, a secretary and a caretaker. Parents helped in the school and there was a steady stream of visitors. The atmosphere was of warmth and welcome. The initial staffing of the school is shown in Table 7.1. At the time the research began, the headteacher, Mrs Dawson, had been in post for one term, succeeding a retiring head of fourteen years standing. The school was judged, by a local authority adviser, to be in need of considerable attention. As he put it, 'That school hasn't had any leadership for years!' The new head was positive, enthusiastic and a self-confessed workaholic emphasizing the 'Plowden values' that are well documented as being important to primary school teachers.

Table 7.1 *The initial staffing allocation – showing curriculum and other responsibilities and salary allowances additional to the Main Professional Grade (MPG).*

	Initial staff allocation
Mrs Dawson	Headteacher
Mrs Jones	Deputy Headteacher
Mrs Munn	English MPG and B-allowance (Temporary)
Miss Jamieson	Science MPG and B-allowance (Temporary)
Mr Cowdrey	Maths MPG and A-allowance (Temporary)
Mrs Sammons	History/Geography MPG
Mrs Attwell	Information Technology MPG
Mrs Hume	Music MPG
Miss Lawson	SEN MPG (Part-time post)

Having taken stock of the situation during her first term and with the strong support of the chair of the school governors, Mrs Dawson then wanted to change the school culture in three major ways. These were to:

- replace what she saw as the ineffective 'old regime' with its lack of management structure;
- create the conditions in which a collaborative culture could develop, with teamwork among the staff, parents and governors;
- raise awareness of equal opportunity issues.

Unlike her predecessor, whom many staff regarded as having been autocratic, Mrs Dawson aimed to create a collaborative management team which would support her and share in decision-making. This, she envisaged, would be made up of herself, the deputy head and two B-allowance post-holders.

Thus, the headteacher had a coherent plan which, in common professional judgement, might well be regarded as a model of good practice and as entirely appropriate in the circumstances which were faced. However, as we shall see, the creation of this team turned out to cause considerable stress among some staff and to require Mrs Dawson to act with more decisive and overt resolve than she would perhaps have wished.

As can be seen in Table 7.1, when Mrs Dawson took up her posts there were two temporary B-allowances for English and Science and one temporary A-allowance for Mathematics. She felt, and was firmly told by the LEA adviser, that this was not good practice. It was thus necessary to make new permanent appointments – a move which, in itself, provided the opportunity to begin to create the new management team.

The English and Maths posts were advertised internally, and open and rigorous procedures for appointment were introduced. These procedures included 'counselling sessions' to discuss the job specifications before the main interview. The interview panel of the head, deputy head, chair of governors and a parent-governor conducted the interviews with great care, using LEA guidelines. Regarding the English post, Mrs Munn, who had previously held the post, was not reappointed because it was felt that Mrs Sammons had simply performed better at the interview and had shown that she had more to offer. On the Maths post the interviewing panel felt that Mr Cowdrey, who had held the temporary position, had 'interviewed badly' and could not be offered the permanent allowance. He was offered a one-year temporary allowance to be combined with staff development work on Maths with the headteacher. However, having considered this he declined. Mrs Dawson acknowledged that, in such circumstances, she had 'found the post difficult to fill' among the staff of a small school. In the event, Mrs Attwell, who had a Maths degree, enquired about the post and, after interview, she was appointed. However, Mrs Attwell reported that she was not keen on assuming this responsibility but agreed to take it on the understanding that it could be undertaken on a temporary basis. The Science allowance remained unallocated at this point as the previous post-holder had recently been appointed to a deputy headship.

Having introduced and followed professional appointment procedures in as careful a way as they could, both Mrs Dawson and her deputy felt that they had done everything possible to make the creation of an appropriate management team a painless and constructive one for the school. However, Mrs Dawson was concerned about the morale and interpersonal relationships of staff who were not included in, or were no longer a part of, the management team. She hoped that those teachers had the capacity to rise above the difficulties which their re-allocation presented and she explicitly planned to offer her support so that they might become involved in other curriculum areas in which they might gain new expertise.

Table 7.2 summarizes the outcome of these changes in terms of the allocation of staff responsibilities and salary allowances above the Main Professional Grade.

Table 7.2. *Changes in staff responsibilities following restructuring.*

	Initial staff allocation	Staff allocation after restructuring
Mrs Dawson	Headteacher	Headteacher
Mrs Jones	Deputy Headteacher	Deputy Headteacher
Mrs Munn	English B-allowance (Temporary)	Humanities MPG
Miss Jamieson	Science B-allowance (Temporary)	Left school for new post (B-allowance unallocated)
Mr Cowdrey	Maths A-allowance (Temporary)	Physical Education MPG
Mrs Sammons	History/Geography MPG	English B-allowance (Permanent)
Mrs Attwell	Information Technology MPG	Mathematics A-allowance (Temporary)
Mrs Hume	Music MPG	Music MPG
Miss Lawson	SEN MPG (Part-time post)	SEN MPG (Part-time post)

In reviewing the teachers' perspectives of these new rules, we can begin with the deputy, who was a universally trusted member of staff both personally and professionally. She described her role as that of a 'go-between who was able to move things forward' – a description that bears a striking resemblance to the discussion of the role of the deputy in the Nias *et al.* (1989) study. Thus, in spite of their short relationship, Mrs Dawson and her deputy were very positive about each other. Mrs Dawson saw the deputy as a superb classroom teacher who was particularly valuable because she had a sense of the school's history. Similarly, since the arrival of her new colleague, the deputy had been included in the decision-making process – an involvement she had not enjoyed under the previous head. This made her feel 'liberated'. The deputy head was also particularly concerned about equal opportunities, but expressed concern about the level of commitment of some staff.

The new English post-holder, Mrs Sammons, had a strong interest in issues of equal opportunity, a history of disagreement with the previous head and a great deal of confidence in the new one.

The two former post-holders, Mrs Munn and Mr Cowdrey, were given new responsibilities in areas of established interest or confidence. Mr Cowdrey, the ex-maths post-holder and the only male on the staff, certainly retained his interest in Physical Education, to which he had been allocated, but he was very negative about many aspects of school life. In particular, he was bitter about the whole process of restructuring: 'I saw £2,000 taken away from Mrs Munn, for whom I have a lot of respect. I lost £1,000. It was how it was done too. It was a bad management decision.'

The two remaining Main Professional Grade teachers presented further diversity in perspectives. Miss Lawson was a well-established and highly regarded special needs teacher who was committed to issues of equal opportunities. The other original MPG teacher, Mrs Hume, was a young, unambitious music specialist in her third year of teaching. Mrs Hume was positive about the previous head, but unhappy about the increased curriculum pressure which she was experiencing. She attributed this to Mrs Dawson, the new headteacher, rather than to any external requirements in relation to the implementation of the National Curriculum. She was largely indifferent to issues of equal opportunities and there was evidence of considerable friction between her and Mrs Dawson.

School development through INSET

Having completed the staff restructuring, the next period of change instigated by Mrs Dawson was associated with the attempt to create a collaborative culture and an awareness of issues of equal opportunities. For this, Mrs Dawson and the deputy head wanted to introduce a collaborative form of INSET that provided flexibility, would involve the whole staff and was not too expensive. The teaching staff did not have a history of collaborative working. Indeed, under the previous headteacher they had tended to focus almost exclusively on their own classrooms. However, Mrs Dawson noted that they 'got on well' with each other and seemed to accept that more whole-school planning was necessary.

The change agents used (distance learning materials) were designed to be used collaboratively by all members of a school staff and to support work towards consistency, progression and continuity. The specific materials, 'School Development Programmes', had been produced by the Faculty of Education of the University of the West of England and mirrored the recommendations of the School Management Task Force (1990). In particular, this had argued that the provision of INSET should be targeted on the needs of whole schools rather than individuals. The model for these materials was also underpinned by a process model of reflective teaching and classroom-based action research and a social constructivist model of learning. As well
as having a cyclical element, the School Development Programme was structured so that staff were able to select an appropriate route through the set of activities provided. Figure 7.1 illustrates the principle of these features.

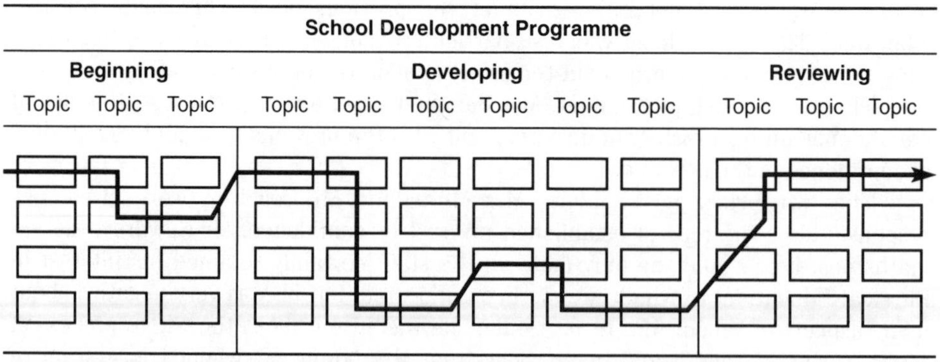

Figure 7.1 *The model for structured choice through a School Development Programme.*

Mrs Dawson and Mrs Jones, her deputy, felt that use of the School Development Programme in equal opportunities would provide a good start to development work by ensuring that the staff examined their own feelings about their teaching, their beliefs and practices relating to equal opportunities. Mrs Dawson thought that use of the School Development Programme would assist the staff in formulating a school policy on equal opportunities which had been part of her brief, set by school governors, on her appointment. In addition, it would enable the staff to work together as a team to begin to establish a common set of values. Working with the School Development Programme would, therefore, help to develop a culture of collaboration and would produce a positive climate which would enhance school effectiveness. Mrs Jones led the initiative though, as we shall see, other staff tended to attribute responsibility to Mrs Dawson.

The School Development Programme on equal opportunities was introduced with three initial meetings for teachers and governors. These were chaired and structured by Mrs Jones and they focused on gender.

A video, *Towards Equality*, was presented and considerable discussion took place, largely focused on the experiences of the staff and governors who were present. The dominant topic was the career difficulties of women and girls. Mr Cowdrey, as the sole male teacher, gave the appearance of slightly amused, but silent, disapproval. When asked for his views by Mrs Dawson, he replied: 'A lot of sexist comments have been made here today.' He did not elaborate or substantiate this statement, though invited to do so, and the discussion moved on without resolution of the apparent tension.

The group then decided to look at their own practice by focusing on selected gender-related activities. They aimed to work on these in their own classrooms and to report back to the group as a whole.

At the end of November, each member of staff reported action research findings from one of their selected activities. In all cases, except the observation of children in the playground, the data collected were relatively 'hard' rather than qualitative and the consensus largely appeared to be that the boys dominated both the classroom and playground. There was considerable discussion as to why this should be the case. There was also a general agreement that the boys were censured far more than the girls, but there was no conclusion on whether this was related to gender or personality factors.

Evidence collected also suggested that groups of girls generally worked co-operatively together, while groups of boys generally did not and in mixed groups the boys dominated. Friendship groups, except among the youngest children, were gender related.

A curriculum preference activity was attempted by Mrs Munn and Mrs Hume, the two teachers of young children. Mrs Jones reported gender-related choice – boys choosing Lego, and girls the home corner (unless it was converted into a 'cafe' or 'hospital', where mixing was greater). However, in the hospital situation the boys still wanted to be the doctors, girls the nurses. However, Mrs Hume, the somewhat disenchanted music specialist, felt that there were no differences in her activity (how children grouped themselves when sitting on the carpet) between boys and girls.

The other contribution which stood out was that of Mr Cowdrey, who had chosen to monitor teacher interaction with boys and girls. Unfortunately, he misunderstood how the activity should have been approached and, instead of interacting normally with his class and allowing an observer to monitor interactions, he had grouped the children by gender and recorded feedback from each individual in each group. Since there were significantly more girls than boys in the class it was inevitable that girls answered more questions than boys.

In the staff feedback sessions, each teacher contributed and at times quite heated discussion took place. These concerned the findings that emerged from the activities themselves, how they would be reflected in school policy and the value of classroom research. The majority were not greatly surprised by their findings, which largely mirrored their 'gut feelings' as class teachers. However, as we have seen, the two sets of results that were 'out of step' were from the two staff whose relationships with Mrs Dawson were already showing signs of strain.

At the end of this meeting the staff decided to monitor sanctions used to control behaviour, to see whether boys and girls were being treated evenly, and to report back to the group at the beginning of the new year.

In addition to the work on equal opportunities Mrs Dawson and the deputy had planned an INSET day which focused on the development of a positive behaviour policy. This was itself part of a wider initiative by the local cluster of schools. The behaviour policy was also intended to be closely linked to equal opportunities issues because it pivoted around the notion of equal and positive responses to all. All members of the school community were invited to the INSET day. Indeed, this involvement was a feature of the new head's explicit attempt to encourage collegiality and teamwork across the school.

During the INSET day it was unfortunate that some further conflict with Mrs Dawson emerged. Mrs Dawson again sought to achieve acceptance of a co-ordinated whole-school approach which, at the same time, required her to challenge some of the more individual practices which had previously existed. This emerged over the introduction of an element of 'assertive discipline' for implementation across the school. However, two of the infant staff, Mrs Munn and Mrs Hume, argued that a policy with such features was unsuitable for infants. This was a deeply felt issue which, in their eyes, took the form of the infant teachers trying to protect the younger children from an inflexible set of rules which they felt young children would not understand. The deputy head, an infant teacher herself, remained largely silent and later expressed the view that she had experienced a conflict of values.

This impasse remained even when, some weeks later, a policy document on behaviour, incorporating some assertive discipline procedures, had been written. Mrs Dawson had both led her staff in making the case for the new policy and used her authority in maintaining that a whole-school policy had to be adopted. The policy for discipline was thus formally agreed but, for the moment, it was left to individual teachers to implement and evaluate. The issues raised by Mrs Munn and Mrs Hume, the infant teachers, remained unresolved at that point.

Mrs Dawson's management of the school's development had thus become delicate at this point. She was attempting the difficult synthesis of articulating her belief in a collaborative style while, at the same time, purposefully offering the strong leadership to 'pull the school together' which she felt was necessary at this formative period of her headship. Indeed, regarding low-level organizational matters, she was observed to invite the opinion of other staff members constantly and she would frequently modify her own views. However, staff noted that she was very reluctant to concede ground on issues that she felt were important.

Early the next term, the staff shared their observations on monitoring behavioural sanctions, thus combining their work on positive discipline with that on equal opportunities. At this point the governors requested the production of the equal opportunities policy. Mrs Dawson was concerned about this, as work in this area had not progressed as fast as she and the staff had hoped. Nevertheless, she reluctantly bowed to pressure with the proviso that 'the policy' was presented as a draft working document which was likely to be developed further.

Teacher perceptions of the understanding they had gained during the use of the distance learning materials unsurprisingly related very closely to their experience of the restructuring. This in turn related to their views on equal opportunities. For instance, the deputy headteacher reported:

> There are lots of changes for the better, attitudes have shifted. We have become more of a unit. We are now going in the right direction no longer standing still as we were. As a staff becoming much more informed. Parents especially now see the school as more efficient.

Several teachers talked positively about their experiences and their comments showed the first signs of what may become a more collaborative culture. For instance, Miss Lawson, the special needs co-ordinator, commented:

> It has continued to crystallize my existing beliefs; hopefully this will be borne out in my attitudes. There has been more open discussion about equal opportunities, discussions have caused staff to address the issues ... in terms of staff attitudes both programmes have been significant for Special Educational Needs.

Another teacher, Mrs Sammons, felt that:

> Action research supports your own thinking, modifies it, encourages discussion; there is an increase in understanding amongst the staff, increased shared meaning and consensus.

Another, Mrs Attwell, added:

> We work more as a team, we are becoming less inhibited with each other. The action research that we do validates our work, we are more honest with each other. I don't mind bringing problems to the whole staff. I suppose it means we have confidence in each other.

In contrast, referring to equal opportunities, Mrs Munn, who had lost her B-allowance for English, said:

> In terms of examining our beliefs I don't feel we've got very far.

In summary, following the completion of the interim equal opportunities policy, at a point where Mrs Dawson had been in post almost a year, the position of most staff had changed and, with this, their perceptions.

Mrs Munn, the ex-English post-holder, had assumed responsibility for Humanities, thus gaining a welcome entrée into work at KS2. She had developed a stance which could be described as a form of 'situational adjustment' (Lacey, 1977):

> My job has changed. Initially I found it demoralizing but I didn't want the [English] job as it stood. I did not want a management responsibility. [When I lost the allowance for English] I was determined that it would not make any difference to me, determined not to be snide. I can now see it as a positive thing. I don't want promotion to be a head or a deputy.

Mr Cowdrey grew very discontented through the year as a result of both government initiatives which were impacting at the time and losing his A-allowance for Maths. He had planned to leave at the end of the academic year, but instead left in a very unhappy state, without completing his period of notice at the end of the spring term. As he put it: 'I am coming out of teaching ... going where I can earn some real dosh.'

The new maths post holder, Mrs Attwell, had a period in which she tried to adjust to her new position as a junior member of the management structure. However, she reported that she felt uneasy about the changes which had taken place. She was particularly aware of the unhappiness that these had caused to Mrs Munn and Mr Cowdrey. Towards the end of the year, this unease was combined with the pressure of other changes that were taking place in primary schools and also with family concerns. Eventually, she decided to resign:

> The pressure has just become too great in recent months. I am going to apply for jobs abroad – teach in a prep school where it is easy. If I can't get a job teaching I shall just leave the profession. I know it's giving in, I know I'm a failure but the pressure and the time it takes to do the job properly is just too great. The way I'd like to be teaching I just can't do it ... What are you doing is so important. I need to get a balance in my life; my husband doesn't like the time it all takes.

Of the remaining two teachers, the special needs teacher, Miss Lawson, had not been involved in structural change and seemed relatively content with her continuing work responsibility for children with special educational needs. Mrs Hume was openly critical of the new head, particularly her initiative on equal opportunities. At the end of the research period she announced her pregnancy and her intention to leave teaching temporarily.

Table 7.3 summarizes these perspectives and outcomes.

Reviewing the changes

Nias *et al.* maintain that a change of head in a school is analogous to a change of ownership (1989, p. 132). The major influence here is the new head's feelings of ownership, accompanied by his or her attendant vision and sense of mission.

In the case-study school, Mrs Dawson's sense of mission manifested itself in actions which, even during the relatively short period of the research, shifted the culture and established her as a new culture founder.

Shifting the school culture involved:

- recruitment and selection of staff to create a new management team supportive of her vision and commitments;
- adopting strategies which aimed to create unity and clarified management structures, for example, introducing job descriptions;

Table 7.3. *Staff perspectives and outcomes of change.*

Initial staff allocation	Staff allocation after restructuring	Perspectives and outcomes	
Mrs Dawson	Headteacher	Headteacher	Crucial changes made to form the basis of a new management team and co-ordinated, whole-school policies
Mrs Jones	Deputy Headteacher	Deputy Headteacher	Felt positive progress was being made towards openness and collegiality
Mrs Munn	English B-allowance (temporary)	Humanities MPG	Philosophical and resigned to the changes
Miss Jamieson	Science B-allowance (temporary)	Left school for new post	N/A
Mr Cowdrey	Maths A-allowance (temporary)	Physical Ed. MPG	Distressed, left teaching
Mrs Sammons	History/ Geography MPG	English B-allowance (permanent)	Felt positive progress was being made towards openness and collegiality
Mrs Attwell	Information Technology MPG	Mathematics A-allowance (temporary)	Concerned at the pressure of job and at restructuring. Left country
Mrs Hume	Music MPG	Music MPG	Openly critical, left teaching on maternity leave
Miss Lawson	SEN MPG (part-time post)	SEN MPG (part-time post)	Supported collaborative strategy and felt positive about equal opportunities developments

- emphasizing the importance of being in a team by her personal interactions with staff;
- providing a major focus for change in the form of INSET work through a School Development Programme.

The recruitment of new staff is an aspect of considerable significance for heads in changing the culture of the school. As Southworth says:

> Amongst heads there is a belief that the ideal state of school leadership is when the headteacher has selected all of his or her own staff.
>
> (1987, p. 64)

Mrs Dawson, as a new headteacher, clearly exercised her leadership function – using, in Etzioni's terms, her remunerative and normative power (1961, p. 61). From a staff that presented a wide range of stances and values, she began to establish a staff group which was more committed to the directions in which, enacting the governors' policies, she sought to develop the school. While consistently and sincerely speaking about the benefits of collegiality, she supported staff who shared her goals and this, perhaps inevitably, led to the displacement of those who did not.

Those teachers from the original school staff who formed the new management team – the deputy head and Mrs Sammons, the new English post-holder – were people for whom situational adjustment, caused by a change of headteacher, presented no difficulty. Indeed, as a result of the restructuring, both the deputy and the new English post-holder spoke of their increased confidence and their intention to seek promotion.

Those displaced in the process of change lost for a number of reasons. First, they had what Nias describes as a 'self-referential' view of teaching. This meant that they could not fully endorse a collaborative way of working. This was exemplified by an incident involving Mrs Munn, the ex-English post-holder, who was a dedicated teacher of infants. She had strongly resisted Mrs Dawson's attempt to introduce 'colour teams' for motivating pupil behaviour. The episode illustrated both how deeply concerned she was about the context in which her children learned and also how, in keeping with many other teachers (Burgess *et al.*, 1994), she found it difficult to sacrifice some of her autonomy to support a whole-school policy.

Second, they could not come to terms with Mrs Dawson's emphasis on the new, contractually prescribed professional duties of a Main Professional Grade member of staff. Thus, Mrs Hume found it very difficult to adapt to the increasing pressures and expectations to which she was subject, and, indeed, to distinguish between those emanating from Mrs Dawson and other external requirements. She too was self-referential in her view of her teaching and found it difficult to act as a full member of the staff group.

Third, they were not as committed as Mrs Dawson to equal opportunities. Mr Cowdrey, for instance, found this particularly difficult since he did not fundamentally recognize the basis of concern about the issue. Ultimately too, he felt that he could not fulfil the job description constructed for the post he had previously held. Further, from evidence provided by other members of staff, it was apparent that Mr Cowdrey found it hard to work collaboratively. For a while following the restructuring, he struggled to redefine himself. Eventually, however, feeling a lack of support from other staff and aware of his limited skill and opportunity to press his point of view, he too felt he had to go. After his resignation the deputy, talking about the staff as a whole, commented: 'He didn't fit in – we had to find someone who did.'

The role of the School Development Programme is interesting in this process of transition for it offered an explicit way of exploring and testing the extent of shared meaning and values. Such programmes attempt to address the issues of classroom pressure and teacher isolation by highlighting the importance of a collaborative culture and teamwork, encouraging teachers to become involved in decision-making processes, developing the shared ownership of common goals, a coherent philosophy and priorities in school development. Although as indicated earlier some teachers at the case-study school had reservations about the emphasis of equal opportunities there was no such difficulty with the notion of following a School Development Programme itself.

However, in spite of apparent staff confidence in the model, the School Development Programme exposed conflicts of interests and of values which three members of staff could not accommodate. In Mr Cowdrey's case, the School Development Programme may have proved to be the final straw. He made discoveries about himself and his colleagues which forced him to consider his position – made him, perhaps, realize that he did not understand what was happening around him. Similarly, Mrs Hume, the third member of staff who planned to resign, ostensibly because of her pregnancy, was made aware of values to which she did not wish to subscribe or regarded as a time-wasting and in addition, she felt, took her away from teaching.

Many writers have pinpointed the dichotomies that often arise between rhetoric and practice. In this case study there was a complex tension between the steps which Mrs Dawson felt she had to take in the short term and her longer-term goals and beliefs. In a sense, as in many other schools in this period (Pollard *et al.*, 1994), she might be seen as having taken advantage of the turbulence caused by the implementation of the Education Reform Act to implement other policies for school development. While, from her perspective, she was acting to create a culture of collaboration, several other staff perceived both her and her deputy to be superimposing their own priorities.

The School Development Progamme contributed to the popularization of the staff because it made overt both shared values and value differences. In a sense then 'collegiality', if that is what one could call the relative value agreement which resulted, was established through a degree of conflict. Indeed, given the context which was inherited in the school, perhaps such conflict was both valuable and inevitable?

The most appropriate model of school organization for this case study, rather than that of a whole-school culture of collaboration, would seem to be much more closely related to the conflict models of Ball (1987), Hoyle (1986) and Pollard (1985).

CONCLUSION

In the introduction of this chapter we suggested that the recent work of the Cambridge team centred on Nias and Southworth (Nias *et al.*, 1989, 1992) may, despite its qualities, suffer from a degree of idealization of organizational and interpersonal processes between primary school staffs. We suggested that, despite some qualifications, their work tends to highlight consensual, developmental and organic features of primary school life. Nias and her colleagues use some powerful concepts which have more than a little ideological power – 'collaboration', 'whole', 'development' to name but a few – and the question remains whether such concepts ultimately illuminate or mask the realities of organizational processes in schools. Additionally, the relationship between such concepts and those deployed within child-centred ideologies deserves further consideration. The case study on which we have reported in this chapter is an inadequate base for making categoric statements but it does suggest that further qualifications to the major findings of the Cambridge projects may be necessary.

In particular, the question of the processes by which degrees of value agreement are reached needs further elaboration and this may, in itself, produce further insights into the maintenance and decay of school cultures. Perhaps, indeed, they should be seen in phases, with an initial phase with considerable scope for conflict as new understandings between a new headteacher and her staff are contested and settled, followed by a longer and relatively stable phase in which a collaborative culture holds and can sustain itself. Finally, we might posit a third stage in which, through inertia or incapacity in the face of external change or staff movement, the collaborative school culture gradually disintegrates. In such circumstances headteacher authority may be legitimated more by hierarchy than by recognition of the capacity to lead the whole-school team.

In this context we might note that one year after the events described in this chapter there were many indications of more coherent and collegial practices in the case-study school. It may well have moved through an initial phase of relative tension to a more stable era of collaboration.

If we are to investigate the possibilities of such phasing then we need many more studies of the sort that Nias and her colleagues have conducted. However, we may need to look again at both the sampling and at some aspects of the method.

In terms of sampling, the tendency of the Cambridge work seems to have been to cover the middle, and relatively stable, phase of primary school development. We know, too, that schools were selected very carefully 'in the light of extensive knowledge and contact' of the Cambridge University Institute of Education (Nias *et al.*, 1992, p. 4) – an institution with a strong and deserved reputation for promoting exactly the kinds of interpersonal and whole-school relationships which these projects have recorded. It would be valuable to have more studies of the initial period of new headteachers' work and, indeed, to document the characteristics of schools where leadership was poor or unstable and, perhaps, conflict and dissent were apparent.

This would probably have some methodological implications, for one of the reasons for the quality of the work which Nias, Southworth, Yeomans and Campbell have been able to produce has undoubtedly been their clear and consistent articulation of an ethical code in which participating teachers could have great trust. This gave respondents the right to veto the use of interview or observational material in which they had participated, and indeed one school which was studied for the project reported in Nias *et al.* (1989) withdrew permission and was omitted.

However, there may be a dilemma here regarding the validity of data for different types of sample. Where research results support and reflect teacher self-image and teacher ideologies, permission may be much easier to obtain than when research findings are less affirmative – and yet the latter are arguably just as significant. We do still need to know what happens in circumstances of conflict, and we need to know the extent to which such circumstances occur and vary in schools across the country. These are very important issues.

It is possible, for instance, that a time of great pressure following the ebb and flow of new national policies on education may call for so many rapid and tough-minded decisions that collaborative cultures cannot be created and operated successfully. On the other hand, such forms of staff relationship also offer both team-based solutions to new circumstances and challenges and a source of personal and inter-personal fulfilment. In producing educationally effective schools, what exactly are the best management strategies for such circumstances?

The work of Nias and her colleagues has led the way in developing an understanding of the qualities of primary school organizations, and it is to be hoped that others will follow to build on, elaborate and extend their analyses.

For proponents of whole-school development planning, or even for those who may be attracted to the concept, the case study and the argument which we have mounted around it simply flag a warning. All organizational change, seen socio-logically, must involve challenge to the interests, perceptions and practices of established practitioners. The use of power is very probably unavoidable and is certainly part of the responsibility of management. The fascination, judgement and skill of creating constructive strategies for the management of change remain – but we cannot pretend that conflict can always be avoided, however rational planning processes may be.

ACKNOWLEDGEMENTS

We gratefully acknowledge the time and commitment of the headteacher and staff of this case-study school. Without their generous participation this chapter could not have been written.

REFERENCES

Alexander, R. (1984) *Primary Teaching*. London: Cassell.

Alexander, R. (1991) *Policy and Practice in Primary Education*. London: Routledge.

Ball, S. (1987) *The Micropolitics of the School*. London: Methuen.

Burgess, H., Southworth, G. and Webb, R. (1994) 'Whole school planning in the primary school', in Pollard, A. (ed.) *Look Before You Leap? Research Evidence for the Curriculum at Key Stage 2*. London: Tufnell Press.

Etzioni, A. (1961) 'A basis for comparative analysis of complex organizations', in *A Sociological Reader on Complex Organizations*. New York: Holt, Rinehart & Winston.

Hoyle, E. (1986) *The Politics of School Management*. Sevenoaks: Hodder & Stoughton.

Lacey, C. (1977) *The Socialisation of Teachers*. London: Methuen.

Newman, E. and Triggs, P. (eds) (1991) *Equal Opportunities in the Primary School: A School Development Programme*. Redland Centre for Primary Education: Bristol Polytechnic.

Nias, J., Southworth, G. and Yeomans, R. (1989) *Staff Relations in the Primary School*. London: Cassell.

Nias, J., Southworth, G. and Campbell, J. (1992) *Whole School Curriculum Development in the Primary School*. London: Falmer Press.

Pollard, A. (1985) *The Social World of the Primary School*. London: Cassell.

Pollard, A., Broadfoot, P., Croll, P., Osborn, M. and Abbott, D. (1994) *Changing English Primary Schools?* London: Cassell.

School Management Task Force (1990) *Developing School Management: The Way Forward*. London: Department of Education and Science/HMSO.

Southworth, G. (1987) 'Primary school teachers and collegiality', in Southworth, G. (ed.) *Readings in Primary School Management*. Lewes: Falmer Press.

Woods, P. (1987) 'Managing the primary teachers' role', in Delamont, S. (ed.) *The Primary School Teacher*. London: Falmer Press.

Chapter 8

School Development Planning: A Place for Partnership?

Janet Hodgson, Pat Broadhead and John Dunford

For beleaguered schools the processes of school development planning can be powerful tools for use in the control and management of externally imposed initiatives and demands. However, recent anecdotal evidence suggests that such processes and procedures are not sufficiently well established, in primary schools at least, for their essential features to survive in the battle waged between internal review and development and the perceived short-term demands of the Office for Standards in Education (OFSTED) inspection.

Having participated in a local project specifically designed to support individual schools in developing evaluative procedures in relation to the school development plan, we found ourselves considering the role to be played by the outsider in the formation and implementation of such plans. How can schools be helped to resist the present temptation to turn to short-term expediency and thereby run the risk of neither satisfying inspection nor contributing to the curriculum and organizational practices in the school?

Helping them to use systematic and focused evaluation in the cycle of review and development seemed one way forward. In 1993 the authors, three tutors from the School of Education at the University of Leeds, conducted a small-scale project on school development planning. This chapter describes and examines this project from the perspective of the current context for continuing professional development, looking particularly at the potential for partnership between schools and higher education (HE).

The past seven years have seen immense change in the educational system in the United Kingdom. Legislation since 1986 has gradually moved power and responsibility away from the local education authorities (LEAs) to the reconstituted governing bodies, but at the same time has also put power into the hands of the centre especially in terms of the funding of specific projects. The first changes in this type of funding happened in 1985 with the TVEI Related In-Service Training Scheme (TRIST) of the Manpower Services Commission. The importance of this was that it laid the foundations for changes in specific grant funding provided by the then Department of Education and Science (DES) which has continued until the present time. The new feature of the grants was that they were not funded at 100 per cent, but were at different rates according to their priorities. While the DES laid down the areas it was prepared to support, not every LEA was given grants for all the areas.

One of the implications of this change in funding was that it increased the amount of INSET money which was under the control of the LEA and now the school. School governors now control most of the finance, so many LEAs are having to come up with schemes whereby schools can opt to buy into LEA INSET programmes using this money. Governors are required to agree on a school development plan. The training needs of teachers as identified by the appraisal exercise will need to be considered in the terms of the development plan.

Schools need to evaluate the success of their development plans and decide how this will influence their policy on INSET. In many cases they will need to decide between the development of individual teachers and the organizational needs of the school. In some cases this will mean that most of the INSET funds will be spent on whole-school training, often during the five statutory INSET days. In some small primary schools these will absorb all the finance available.

Who then will be the major providers of INSET? In many cases schools will rely on in-house provision, while in others they will subscribe to LEA packages for their INSET requirements. Increasingly, Training and Enterprise Councils (TECs) will see it as their role to become involved in the training of school-based personnel – not only teachers – through schemes such as the Management Charter Initiative.

A great deal of professional expertise lies in the HE institutions, especially those that are involved in Initial Teacher Training. For decades they have also been involved in INSET courses of all types. How can these institutions compete in the new world of INSET? They are having to consider new ways of marketing the expertise they have. An example of an initiative that suggests one model for HE–school partnership is now described.

BACKGROUND

The nine-month project involved primary schools, all of which felt that they would benefit from engagement in an initiative of this kind. The six were selected by LEA advisory personnel from a group of volunteer schools. The criteria for selection were unknown to the university team. The LEA–project link person had agreed the project aims with the joint funding body, the local TEC. The LEA representative attended whole project meetings and facilitated administrative arrangements, but did not play a role in the work carried out in school. The whole project was evaluated with a view to eventually expanding the work to a wider range of schools. Participants were given the opportunity to give evaluative comments both orally and in documentary form. In addition each school was asked to submit a report of its work in the project. Naturally, the aims of the project were the basis for the whole project evaluation.

The project was designed to guide six primary schools through a cycle of review and development; to initiate each school into a process to be utilized beyond the life of the project. The project recognized from the outset that the school development plan is dynamic, a catalyst rather than an outcome. The process of review and development will not only focus on a specific aspect of the plan; it will ultimately re-configure the plan. It was also recognized that the schools concerned were at different stages in the review and development cycle, and that the project would need to be sufficiently flexible to accommodate the differences.

The overall aims of the project were:

- to develop an understanding of evaluation processes in all school staff members;
- to use evaluation processes in the review and development of a selected area of the school development plan;
- to strengthen teamwork within the school;
- to improve the quality of teaching and learning in the schools.

Three key areas from the literature informed the design and development of the whole project. Further to this, each area became an integral feature of the insider–outsider partnership in relation to individual schools.

First, the management of innovation. It was clear that across schools, head-teachers would have key, although not necessarily identical, roles. This needed to be borne in mind. Alongside this, familiarity with evaluation procedures should enhance staff effectiveness (Constable *et al.*, 1988). However, this implies a time element and making the best of the time, in developmental terms. The role of the head would seem to be a key factor in the context of primary schools, where the head maintained close daily contact. Whitaker (1993) expressed a preference for leadership rather than management. He identifies management as being concerned with:

- orderly structures;
- maintaining day-to-day functions;
- ensuring that work gets done;
- monitoring outcomes and results;
- efficiency;

whereas leadership is concerned with:

- personal and interpersonal behaviour;
- focus on the future;
- change and development;
- quality;
- effectiveness.

Whitaker states a need to emphasize a growing understanding of the human and interactive aspects of organizations.

This leads into our second area: ethical issues. The ethical issues involved in an interventionist project of this kind were also of especial concern to the team. Simons (1984) confirmed our feelings on this matter and served us well as we grappled with procedures and protocols. She identifies impartiality, confidentiality, negotiation, collaboration and accountability as being salient principles in school self-evaluation. Her principle of accountability did not particularly apply to this project, as the schools were not accountable to the university. However, the other principles were incorporated into the project in different ways.

Simons' perspectives accorded with Whitaker's views on the appropriateness of a leadership construct with its concern for personal and interpersonal behaviour. If the project was to assist staffs in adopting a systematic approach to review and development, within a limited period of time, and if it was to offer a level of familiarity that would bring about enhanced staff effectiveness, then the project had to be concerned with 'the centrality of learning within the learning school' (Holly and Southworth, 1989).

Our third key area was informed by the procedures and frameworks of School-Based Review. Bollen and Hopkins (1987) provided us with a working definition of SBR as a 'diagnostic activity undertaken by school staff in a school improvement process'. Hopkins (1989) identifies at least six characteristics:

1   It is a systematic process, not merely reflection.
2   Its short-term goal is to obtain valid information about a school or department's condition, functions, purposes and products (effectiveness).
3   The review leads to action on an aspect of the school's organization or curriculum.
4   It is a group activity that involves participants in a collegial process.
5   Optimally the process is 'owned' by the school or sub-system.
6   Its purpose is school improvement/development and its aspiration is to progress towards the real goal of the 'problem solving' or 'relatively autonomous' school.

The Schools Curriculum Development Council GRIDS project (McMahon *et al.*, 1984) formed the basis for the project in schools, but was adapted to encourage the use of expertise to assist in evaluation at all stages in the review cycle. Although each school had an associated university facilitator, it was also envisaged, from the outset, that other experts could be called upon as and when required.

We were also reminded by Hopkins (1991) that a project of this kind should involve a 'strategy that affects the culture of the school' and that collegiality and collaboration are in themselves not enough. Conditions must prevail in which the individual sees direct benefits for their involvement in the process if developments are to occur and be sustained.

The university project team thus based the design and implementation of the project on a number of principles, namely:

1   The management and leadership styles promoted throughout the project should strive for collaboration, collegiality and flexibility. A culture of openness, communication and mutual respect are necessary for sustained development to take place.
2   When employing the review process emphasis should be placed on clear focus and manageability. School-based research should be a substantial contributor in the process of evaluation and review. Teachers should be supported in developing a range of appropriate research methods.
3   The schools should be supported in the adoption of the processes of school development planning and implementation. The role of the 'outsider' (that is, the university facilitator) should include provision of a guiding structure to the whole project as well as personal support for individuals and for schools.
4   Appropriate expertise relating to each school's focus for evaluation and development should be called upon to assist both the identification of evaluation criteria, methods and evidence and the improvement of practice.

5   Ownership of the project report should be extended to all parties in the project. Confidentiality should also be assured.

THE PROJECT

Participants in the project were:

- a team of three university facilitators, each tutor supporting two schools – a pool of university tutors with expertise in a range of areas relating to primary schools, to be involved as required;
- six primary schools from one LEA, each of which identified a project management team, including the headteacher and a project co-ordinator;
- an LEA adviser with a brief for management, development and training.

The six schools subsequently identified the following foci for review and development:

- the links between the teaching of spelling, phonics and writing;
- National Curriculum technology;
- whole-curriculum planning (two schools);
- working towards a self-managing school;
- the methods used to review the school development plan.

The range is considerable. In some cases the focus pre-dated the project's commence-ment. Facilitators felt it important in every case to seek consensus regarding whole-staff commitment and urged management teams to include a stage of staff consultation in the very early stages of the project.

It is not possible here to look at any one case in detail. This chapter is concerned with the structuring and evaluation of the project as a whole and implications for insider–outsider partnerships.

The structure of the project

The project was in three phases all of which were to be completed in the nine-month duration of the project:

- *Phase 1: Start up – identification of focus*
  - investigating approaches to evaluation
  - exploring roles and responsibilities: contracting
  - planning strategies
  - identifying a focus;

- *Phase 2: Evaluating the focus – collecting evidence*
  - identifying objectives
  - identifying expert support
  - analysing and refocusing
  - maintaining momentum;

- *Phase 3: Evaluating the focus – planning for development*
  - drawing evidence together
  - linking outcomes to future action
  - evaluating the project as a whole.

Each school was asked to commit approximately forty hours to the project over a nine-month period. They were assisted in deciding on a time-scale for each phase of the project, and asked to identify available resources. These included photocopying, secretarial time, staff time (occasionally headteachers provided staff cover) and budget availability. It was also suggested that the project should be integrated into the normal processes of the management of the school, and that extra time should not be asked of those outside the central project management team, which consisted of the headteacher and co-ordinator. Consequently normal staff meetings were used and the staff were not involved in extra work.

Managing the project

Whole-project meetings and *individual school support* were the main contexts within which the project was managed.

Throughout the project a central intention was to assist schools in maintaining a clarity of purpose – to keep them focused. There was understandably perhaps a tendency, initially, to allow competing demands to deflect from stated intentions. Time-scales were made clear at the outset, although there was some leeway for schools to devise their own, as discussed above. Schools accepted the need to establish realistic time-scales and then adhere to them. It is perhaps worth mentioning at this point that the schools ultimately felt that one of the strengths of the project had been the expectation and demand of realistic, negotiable deadlines and targets.

Procedures were defined through the use of *documents* to be completed and submitted at mutually agreed intervals. These documents were designed to be helpful in a number of ways:

- maintaining the momentum of the project;
- keeping the focus clear and attainable in the time available;
- highlighting changes to the focus;
- acting as a resource to be used when the school staff reflected on the process through which they had passed.

Documents included:
- A Framework for Action and Review (*the initial focusing upon the area for development*);
- Sharing Initiatives (*individual schools reporting to one another*);
- Preparing for the Evaluation of the Project (*serving two functions – the evaluation of the project as a whole and assessing the impact of the project within school, in relation to both staff development and children's learning*).

Training, support and development

Whole-project meetings involved the central project team from each of the schools, the university facilitators and the LEA representative. The meetings were used to provide:

- mutual support for everyone involved;
- an occasion for sharing ideas and concerns;
- a forum for discussing review and evaluation;

- an opportunity to share understandings and therefore add to the coherence of the project;
- an opportunity to benefit from the experiences of others.

Agendas for whole-project meetings were open to negotiation but were also planned and timed to progress the project through the phases. There were three whole-project meetings:

1 introduction of the project;
2 sharing initiatives;
3 update and evaluation: drawing ideas together.

These corresponded with the circulation and discussion of the procedural documents.

Summaries of meetings were also circulated in an effort to clarify ideas and provide a model for the principle of documenting all developments. Each school endeavoured to keep records of its own school meetings, decisions made and action taken. This proved to be arduous work but was recognized as being of value, especially to those school staff who joined the project midway. As with the completion of whole-project documents, outlined above, the university facilitator also assisted this aspect of documenting the project, repeatedly modelling the appropriate action until school staff began to see the significance. With hindsight this project requirement proved to be important in, for example, the tracking of where collective decisions had been taken. We noted that staff began to say, 'Shall I minute this decision?' Such procedures assisted in a deepening understanding of evaluation processes and team building.

Individual school support was the second context in which schools were supported. A named facilitator for each school aimed to develop a positive and personal relationship with the school and to ease the way of the project by supporting both the management team and the school staff. They took on the role of critical friend, working flexibly depending on circumstances, maintaining regular contact with the school via visits and telephone calls and generally responding to the level of support that each school staff felt they required.

As mentioned above, emphasis was placed on the identification of a manageable focus and the use of systematic methods for evaluation. West and Ainscow (1991) proved particularly helpful to schools as they decided how they were to collect data that would be of use to them. This was an area in which the HE partner could be of particular service to the school. The facilitators provided reading material directly relevant to the phase of the project and to the school's work. The idea of using a research method caused some initial consternation, but each school selected methods appropriate to their purposes. As with the recording requirement, in some cases data gathering was modelled, that is, undertaken by the facilitator. However, at such times the facilitator endeavoured to involve the school's project co-ordinator in both the gathering and analysing of such data, so as to ensure that such expertise remained in school once the project had finished. The use of research methods was felt to have reinforced the imperative that clarity and focus are essential components of successful evaluation and subsequent development and also enabled the school to take ownership (Bollen and Hopkins, 1987).

The partnership with HE allowed the schools to draw on other expertise in addition to that provided by the facilitator. In general, the facilitator assisted in identifying and refining the initial focus. Further input pertaining to the focus was then provided either by the facilitator (according to that person's own area of expertise) or by a relevant colleague. In cases where the facilitator acted in a general *and* a specific capacity there were some tensions associated with the temporary transition from critical friend to 'expert'. The additional expertise was used in a number of ways. Some schools used the 'expert' to help them identify the focus or to map out the area on which they were focusing. Some used the 'expert' to help clarify their evaluation criteria. Others, having conducted an initial evaluation, recognized where they needed help and looked to the expert for up-to-date information on the area in question. Some used such expertise for both stages in the review. One school supplemented the university-led INSET provision with expertise from the LEA advisory service.

The three university facilitators met regularly to share perspectives on process in each of their two schools and to review individual procedures and practice. The discussions tended to focus on the first of the five principles that underpinned the project: collaboration, collegiality, communication and mutual respect. There was felt to be a need to emphasize the issues of ownership and collaborative decision-making. In effect, we found ourselves attaching 'invisible reins' to some of the management teams, persuading them that a speedy transition towards new ways of working ran the risk of leaving de-motivated and disempowered staff behind. Balanced against this was the need for all staff to believe that progress was being made towards their identified focus.

The project structure enabled the schools to adopt the process to meet their own needs, the *evaluation process* being seen as an essential part of the *review cycle*, with most schools moving on to implementation and further evaluation. The project helped to bridge the gap between review and development.

DID THE PROJECT FULFIL ITS AIMS?

Throughout the project the university team made formative evaluations of the progress and endeavoured to respond accordingly through planning and action. However, evidence from facilitator observations (each facilitator kept an evaluative journal), the minutes of whole-project meetings, and the reports written by the schools have also been used in an evaluation of the project against its aims as described at the beginning of the chapter. This is reported in the next section.

To develop an understanding of evaluation processes in all staff members

As the project progressed participants became more aware of the need to collect information from a broad base. There was a tendency to depend on questionnaires, semi-structured interviews and staff perceptions of needs rather than look for other types of evidence. Staff involvement was paramount, and perhaps it is understand-able, particularly given the time-scale and the emphasis on ownership and collegiality which the facilitators promoted, that such survey methods were seen as useful and manageable. There was evidence, however, that schools were also looking for additional evidence to support or challenge their general perceptions. All schools collected some information through methods such as resource audits, observation of practice and the examination of documents.

In their own project evaluations schools articulated a feeling of having been through a clearly structured process leading to an identifiable product and outcome with inherent whole-school benefits.

> We have worked through a process which can transfer to future curriculum/management initiatives.

> Using the process we hope to identify assumptions which may underpin our thinking.

> It has given us the incentive to tackle another large area of development within our curriculum with enthusiasm.

> We feel that we have developed a model for future reviews of the SDP which is much more objective and sharply focused and places ownership firmly in the hands of the staff.

To use evaluation processes in the review and development of a selected area of the School Development Plan

On the whole, the six schools became better focused as the project progressed. With this came an associated understanding of the relationship between 'manageable focus' and the 'associated time-scale for the attainment'. There was evidence to suggest that the schools gained information that was of use to them and would form the basis for improvement. Teams that had set clear and manageable goals seemed most successful at achieving them. Each school felt that it had made some progress and some schools felt that progress had been considerable.

> Staff agreement that clear targets were defined.

> A very useful learning process which has encouraged thoughtful evaluation of various recording systems.

> Our general understanding of technology has improved. An indication of this improvement has been shown in the half-term/weekly plans being submitted by the teachers.

> The consideration of curriculum research and enquiry skills being introduced into our development planning has given it authority and credibility.

Overall, the project seemed to begin slowly and then accelerate. With hindsight, the slow start has seemed beneficial. Therein were the foundations laid for personal and interpersonal perspectives, for whole-staff participation, for nurturing skills, procedures and approaches. However, in some cases it had seemed initially frustrating, particularly to headteachers, hence the 'invisible reins' mentioned earlier, and in some cases lengthy discussions between facilitators and heads.

To strengthen teamwork within the school

The strengthening of teamwork was felt to be the most clearly evident success of the project and confirms Hopkins' comments on the limitations and expectations associated with the early stages of adopting a whole-school process such as GRIDS.

> The first cycle serves to generate shared experiences, team work, ownership of process and confidence. Realistically, it is in the second and subsequent cycles that one would expect increased rigour in procedures, application of set criteria to present practices, greater openness with consultants and others and a readiness to cope with external pressures and accountability.
>
> (Hopkins, 1989)

> *Anonymous returns were made by the staff with positive comments in part due to the process promoting a sharing of ideas and ownership.*

> *A forum for open discussion with positive and relevant feedback.*

> *The process of mutual respect established a firm basis for staff development.*

> *The project continued to improve the teamwork and co-operation already existing within the school.*

It is perhaps worth mentioning briefly that there had been occasions when facilitators had found themselves mediating between school staff and management teams. Headteachers, project co-ordinators and staff each shared confidential information about procedures, desires and individual colleagues. In fact, facilitators could use such information, while respecting confidentiality, to progress the project. It required tact and diplomacy, but as a team we felt this to be part of the school's entitlement.

To improve the quality of teaching and learning in the schools

Participants recognized that evidencing improvements in teaching and learning is both long-term and difficult. Ideally, the project should have been extended to provide an opportunity to re-evaluate the focus with special attention being paid to the quality of teaching and the learning outcomes of the children. The time constraints and original brief limited the scope of the project and therefore 'improving the quality of teaching and learning' featured as an anticipated rather than measurable aim of the project. However, there was a strong feeling that teaching and learning would inevitably improve as schools were now better prepared in their planning, their provision of resources and their devising of policies.

> *A formulation of a Key Stage 1 plan geared to the needs of our school gives a clear overview – ensuring continuity and progress.*

> *We feel that this initiative will improve the children's learning because they will have a wider variety of experiences, together with the progression and continuity. Necessary resources will become available for the pupils.*

The initiative should improve children's access to learning through a whole-school approach to planning with built in coverage and progression.

It is impossible to quantify the effect the project will have on learning outcomes. But we now have in place a system which will enable us to address needs which have been identified by the whole staff.

It is also important to ask whether the structure of the project proved to be adequate and whether there are lessons to be learnt about conducting a project of this kind.

The project passed through three phases which proved to be appropriate for this type of project. The time-scale was dictated partly by the funding and partly by the management decisions that are made yearly in primary schools. The time-scale also set parameters for a manageable piece of evaluation and proved to illustrate that clarity and breadth of focus go hand in hand with time available. Schools were asked to document meetings, decisions and actions. While demanding much of participant's time and energy, this proved to be essential to the success of the project. The following comments illustrate the range of concerns and insights:

Written records enabled the new incumbent to see the background and decision-making process.

Absent staff were kept informed and working parties gave feedback to the staff.

It has been useful to keep written records of the process, particularly because [of] the discussion which has been necessary before the completion of the records. We intend to make use of them in the future.

Whole-project meetings were seen to be important, although, interestingly, participants viewed them differently at different points in the project. At first, there was an articulated need for the sharing of ideas and initiatives. As each school became more confident in its own school evaluation, they felt less of a need for reassurance and group clarity. Despite some reservations about the value of meetings, latterly voiced by the schools, it is felt that they served the purposes that were intended and that they were of value. But their purposes and format would certainly have been reviewed had the project continued.

The meetings were of interest in so much as we became aware of initiatives within other schools, but we didn't feel that the actual meetings took us forward with our own evaluation.

To listen to how other people have tackled the project has been an interesting learning experience. We might be able to use some of their strategies and ideas for future projects.

These were well organized with a clear agenda, but were quite demanding on cover for senior staff. Although these meetings were interesting and fostered empathy between schools they were rather divorced from the activity in our own school. The final meeting in March was most essential for clarifying a written report.

The original project remit did not include an evaluation of the HE–school partnership. However, in their project evaluations individual schools inevitably commented on the relatively intense relationship that had built up over the nine months. It is this aspect that became of particular interest to the team and which led to successful proposals for a research bid.

Evaluations of the insider–outsider partnership were positive:

An outsider helps to keep to time-scales.

Outsiders can give a voice to different participants.

An outsider gives perceptions and emphases from a different point of view.

To have the support of an outside agency, in this case the university, has proved very useful. It has added another dimension to our work.

It has proved useful and supportive to have an outsider's view of the school.

To return to the question posed earlier: How can schools be helped to resist the temptation to turn to short-term expediency and thereby run the risk of neither satisfying inspection nor contributing to the curriculum and organizational practices in the school?

As was discussed at the beginning of this chapter, the LEAs are undergoing a change of role. Most of them are, of necessity, adopting a predominantly inspectoral role, rather than the developmental one of the past. The devolving of in-service moneys to governors, alongside a coherent development plan, gives schools an opportunity to be selective, focused and systematic in determining and meeting their organizational and professional development needs. Yet, at the same time, it is tempting for them to become inward-looking and self-satisfied with their performance. The developmental role of the LEA by its very nature allowed experiences to be shared within the LEA; this has now been lost. This project provides evidence to suggest that HE, an outsider to whom the school is not accountable, can successfully assist schools in the process of review and development. The inherent flexibility and the sharing of outsider expertise would seem to have considerable potential for supporting change while locating ownership and agenda setting within the school.

REFERENCES

Bolam, R. (ed.) (1982) *School Focussed In-service Training*. London: Heinemann.

Bollen, R. and Hopkins, D. (1987) *School Based Research: Towards a Praxis*. Leuven: ACCO Publishing.

Clift, P. (1982) 'LEA schemes for school self-evaluation: a critique', *Educational Researcher*, **24** (4).

Constable, H., Williams, R., Brown, R., Ludlow, R. and Taggart, L. (1989) *An Evaluation of GRIDS in Leeds*. University of Leeds.

Elliott, J. (1979) 'The case for school evaluation', *Forum*, **22** (1).

Elliott, J. (1981) *Action Research: A Framework for Self Evaluation in Schools*. Cambridge Institute of Education.

Hargreaves, D.H., Hopkins, D., Leask, M., Connolly, J. and Robinson, P. (1989) *Planning for School Development: Advice to Governors, Headteachers and Teachers*. London: Department of Education and Science/HMSO.

Hargreaves, D.H. and Hopkins, D. (1991) *The Empowered School: The Management and Practice of Development Planning*. London: Cassell.

Holly, P. and Southworth, G. (1989) *The Developing School*. Lewes: Falmer Press.

Hopkins, D. (1989) *Evaluation for School Development*. Milton Keynes: Open University Press.

Hopkins, D. (1991) 'Changing school culture through development planning', in Riddell, S. and Brown, S. (eds) *School Effectiveness Research: Its Messages for School Improvement*. Edinburgh: Scottish Office Education Department/HMSO.

McMahon, A., Bolam, R., Abbot, R. and Holly, P. (1988) *Guidelines for Review of Internal Development in Schools: Primary School Handbook*. Harlow: Longman for SCDC.

Simons, H. (1984) 'Ethical principles in school self-evaluation', in Bell, J., Bush, T., Fox, A., Goodey, J. and Goulding, S. (eds) *Conducting Small Scale Investigations in Educational Management*. London: Paul Chapman for the Open University.

West, M. and Ainscow, M. (1991) *Managing School Development: A Practical Guide*. London: David Fulton.

Whitaker, P. (1993) *Managing Change in Schools*. Milton Keynes: Open University Press.

Chapter 9

School Effectiveness and School Improvement: A Meeting of Two Minds

Louise Stoll

Over the past two decades, school effectiveness researchers have examined the quality and equity of schooling in an attempt to find out why some schools are more effective than others in promoting positive outcomes, whether schools perform consistently across outcomes and areas, and what characteristics are most commonly found in schools that are effective for all their pupils (for reviews see Reynolds *et al.*, 1989a; Cotton, 1990; Sammons *et al.*, 1993). Over the same period, school improvement researchers have focused their studies on the processes that schools go through to become more successful and sustain this improvement (for example, Miles and Ekholm, 1985; van Velzen, 1987; Fullan, 1991). Caught in the middle have been practitioners engaged in attempts to improve their schools. These people have wanted high-quality, practical information to support their efforts. Thus, they have taken the pieces of research from both traditions that have made most sense to them, and, albeit unknowingly, have linked the two areas through their improvement efforts. Sometimes their adoption of ideas from research has been somewhat uncritical; for example, attempts to apply findings from one specific context to another entirely different context when research has demonstrated significant contextual differences (Hallinger and Murphy, 1986; Teddlie *et al.*, 1989). At other times, they have an understanding of what makes a school effective, but not how to translate this into action, or they have a clear sense of how people need to work together, but have no framework or roadmap that shows them key areas on which to focus their attention.

If practitioners can see and make links between school effectiveness and school improvement, surely it is time for researchers studying the two areas to do the same and to work with schools to develop a deeper and more meaningful understanding of the research and its implications for practice. Examples of the latter have begun to be seen, as evidenced in a variety of British and American projects (Reynolds *et al.*, 1989b; Holcomb, 1991; Ainscow and Hopkins, 1992).

For closer links to be made between the two paradigms, however, it is necessary to examine what each can bring to a union.

SCHOOL EFFECTIVENESS
A focus on outcomes
In this age of increased accountability, it is necessary for schools to demonstrate both to themselves and the wider community that what they do makes a difference to

student outcomes. A focus on enhancing performance in the basic skills, as advocated by some of the earlier American school effectiveness studies, will not be adequate. We are becoming increasingly aware that children may have many intelligences (Gardner, 1983). Researchers, therefore, need to develop valid instruments to measure growth in a broad range of academic and social areas of students' development that match these intelligences and are seen by educators to be important.

An emphasis on equity

Many schools in their current school improvement efforts still do not pay sufficient attention to ensure that disadvantaged students in their schools make as much progress as their more affluent peers. Edmonds (1979) brought the issue of equity to the forefront of school effectiveness research. His legacy has been continued world-wide, and now there is a considerable knowledge base from which schools can draw (for example, Teddlie and Stringfield, 1985; Scheerens, 1987; Bashi and Sass, 1989). Researchers of school improvement also need to be aware of the background of the student population in a school before they assess the value added by the school's change effort over and above what the students might be expected to learn given their background, prior knowledge and attitudes.

The use of data for decision-making

Because school effectiveness research is based on measured outcomes, it offers a database to help schools in their planning. Schools need to gather information that relates to their current situation, and to determine from it where their needs lie. Through the disaggregation of student data, schools can also establish whether they are meeting the needs of different groups of students, such as females versus males, and students of different ages, social class or ethnic backgrounds.

A knowledge of what is effective elsewhere

Although not every study of school effectiveness has come up with an identical list of the characteristics of effectiveness, there is sufficient overlap of several of these elements for us to believe that there must be some consistency of impact across situations (Joyce *et al.*, 1983). It is important that schools gain access to these findings, and that researchers help to bring these to them in a meaningful form, and explain important contextual differences and areas where it is possible to generalize, so that they can become the basis for whole-school discussion and part of a school's assessment process.

An understanding that the school is the focus of change

Goodlad (1984), in a study of school effectiveness, stressed that change must be school-based. Early applications of school effectiveness research in various American districts also demonstrates that a top-down approach did not work (Lezotte, 1989). If each school has a unique population and context, as discussed above, it is clear that individual schools need to take responsibility for their change efforts.

SCHOOL IMPROVEMENT

A focus on process

There is a wealth of theoretical and practical studies that have helped advance our understanding of the initiation, implementation and institutionalization of change (for example, Crandall *et al.*, 1982; Fullan, 1982, 1991; Huberman and Miles, 1984). Change in schools is not an event or 'one-shot deal'. Rather, it is a process that takes time and considerable patience, as proponents of 'quick fix' solutions have found to their cost. School effectiveness researchers need to learn more about this process and its interplay with the characteristics identified by their own research.

An orientation towards action and on-going development

School improvement approaches do not tend to be imposed solutions. Rather 'they embody the long-term goal of moving towards the vision of the "problem-solving" or "thinking" or "relatively autonomous" school' (Hopkins, 1992). As Hopkins points out, this approach underpinned the work of the OECD's International School Improvement Project (ISIP), in itself a changing and evolutionary project. Schools do not stand still and wait to be measured by researchers. They are dynamic institutions, subject to frequent change. Only by studying this process of change and its impact can we really understand schools.

An emphasis on school-selected priorities for development

School improvement research emphasizes the importance of teacher involvement in change efforts, and ownership for the process. Consequently, it is important that staff members be involved in the selection of priorities for future development. School self-evaluation efforts in the United Kingdom in the 1970s and 1980s (Clift *et al.*, 1987; McMahon *et al.*, 1984) emphasized the need to establish priorities or goals. This has now been incorporated into the school development planning process that is a feature of the 1988 Education Reform Act (Hargreaves *et al.*, 1989; Hargreaves and Hopkins, 1991). Similar processes are found in the United States and Australia (Loucks-Horsley and Hergert, 1985; Caldwell and Spinks, 1988).

An understanding of the importance of school culture

In recent years, researchers have become much more aware of the powerful impact of school culture on change efforts (Rosenholtz, 1989; Hargreaves, 1989; Nias *et al.*, 1989; Deal, 1990; Hargreaves, 1993). Hargreaves and Hopkins explain:

> *Successful schools realize that development planning is about creating a school culture which will support the planning and management of changes of many different kinds. School culture is difficult to define, but is best thought of as the procedures, values and expectations that guide people's behaviour within an organization.*
>
> (Hargreaves and Hopkins, 1991, pp. 16–17)

In short, a culture that promotes collaboration, trust, the taking of risks, and a focus on continuous learning for students and adults, is a key feature for school improvement efforts.

The importance of a focus on teaching and learning

Change efforts have to have a focus and, above all, must have meaning for teachers if they have the chief responsibility to implement changes and make them work (Fullan, 1991). An understanding of school organization and its underlying processes may not be sufficient to engage teachers' interest or commitment. Furthermore, collaboration or collegiality for its own sake may have little impact on the culture of the school. Teachers need a focus for their collaborative efforts, an opportunity to engage in 'joint work' around topics related to the classroom (Little, 1990).

A view of the school as the centre of change

School improvement not only views the school as the focus of change but as its centre, in that it cannot be isolated from the context around it (Sirotnik, 1987). Indeed, in North America the school district (LEA) has traditionally been seen as key to school improvement, provided that it offers appropriate support to schools and is also engaged in a process of on-going learning (Rosenholtz, 1989). Schools need to be part of a wider system, networking with other schools as well as the district, community, higher education institutions and businesses.

From the outline above, it appears that the two research traditions could complement each other and that the shortcomings of each approach could be counterbalanced by the strengths of the other. Thus, a comprehensive school effectiveness project would: focus on an examination and incorporation of school effectiveness research findings; use school improvement process and development strategies; emphasize the importance of school culture; and evaluate its impact in terms of the quality and equity of student progress, development and achievement on a diverse array of relevant outcome measures as well as that on teacher attitudes. Furthermore, a project that blended the two paradigms should evaluate its process as well as its outcomes. This has been the intent of a Canadian project in which I was involved from 1986 to 1992 at the Halton Board of Education in Ontario. The rest of this chapter will describe this project and the challenges it continues to pose for the meetings of two minds, school effectiveness and school improvement.

THE HALTON EFFECTIVE SCHOOLS PROJECT

The Halton Board of Education, on the north shore of Lake Ontario thirty miles west of Toronto in Ontario, serves 44,000 students in sixty-five elementary and sixteen secondary schools. The area has traditionally been middle-class and suburban with a couple of smaller, less affluent, rural farming communities. Recently, however, there has been an influx of students from a variety of other countries, while at the same time many families are experiencing more of the difficulties traditionally associated with inner cities.

In 1986, a task force was set up to examine the findings of a school effectiveness study in the United Kingdom in which I was also involved (Mortimore *et al.*, 1988), and find ways to incorporate these within the existing culture of the district. The impetus for this initiative came from the elementary principals who had participated in annual conferences on a variety of themes and decided to focus in more detail for several years on one topic: school effectiveness.

The task force examined many schools effectiveness studies, and came up with a composite model of twelve characteristics of effective schools that fell within three broad areas: a common mission; an emphasis on learning; and a climate conducive to learning. On reflection, it is clear that many of these characteristics were also associated with school improvement, although most of the task force members were not aware of these distinctions at the time.

It was obvious that a top-down mandate to implement the characteristics model would neither work nor fit with the district's on-going emphasis on collaborative relations with its school and federations. Through meetings with Michael Fullan and visits to other districts where successful change had occurred, Halton designed a process similar to school development planning: school growth planning. The title was deliberate, the word 'growth' being used to emphasize that many schools are already effective but that there is always room for growth.

Growth planning enables a school to select, work on and evaluate its own priorities based on an examination of its own context as well as external initiatives. The process, similar to its European, American and Australian counterparts, is on-going and cyclical in nature, but broadly has four key stages:

1 *Assessment* The school gathers relevant information to determine its current strengths and areas of need.
2 *Planning* The school selects a small number of goals to which it will direct its attention over three years.
3 *Implementation* The school works through each of the goals with the support of staff development and resources.
4 *Evaluation* The school monitors its process and progress towards the achievement of its goals and their impact.

In reality, the four stages are not linear. In order to evaluate the impact of the growth plan and its activities, indicators against which success can be measured need to be identified as soon as goals have been selected. Initial assessments may be made at this stage to provide a baseline against which the school can measure progress. Furthermore, the school needs to carry out on-going evaluations throughout implementation to ensure that the activities progress as intended and to ensure that necessary amendments take place.

This process was originally piloted by six elementary (primary) and three secondary task force principals (headteachers) and their schools. Each brought a unique style to the process. Through their efforts, insights emerged related to school growth planning. It appeared that there were three fundamental prerequisites to successful growth planning.

Vision

More effective growth planning occurred in schools where the principal had a clear vision for a better future for the school that was not imposed on staff but filtered through by a process of engagement and discussion of beliefs and values such that it became a shared vision. This vision later guided planning efforts. Barth's comment, 'Vision unlocked is energy unlocked' (1990, p. 151), seemed to be exemplified in Halton's more successful schools.

Climate setting

In some schools the stage had been carefully set such that organizational and decision-making structures and lines of communication were in place to support the growth planning process. In the more successful secondary schools, in particular, attention was paid early on to teachers' concerns regarding pupil attendance and behaviour, and procedures put in place to deal with these issues. The physical environment was also an early focus in the endeavour to create a climate conducive to learning. Once these issues had been attended to, they no longer became priorities on the growth plan and, thus, paved the way for instructional and curriculum goals that were more likely to impact classroom practice and pupil outcomes.

Collegiality

The importance of a collaborative culture to school improvement has been stressed elsewhere (Little, 1982; Fullan and Hargreaves, 1991). Rosenholtz points out that norms of collaboration do not just occur. They have to be carefully structured. For teachers in schools where such norms exist:

> *instruction seems a natural subject for reflection: they set goals to improve instruction, grapple with and share teaching problems, make suggestions to overcome instructional hurdles, and show mutual concern for their collective teaching performance.*

> (Rosenholtz, 1989, p. 50)

In some pilot schools, principals were more effective in building a culture in which teachers were not afraid to try out new ideas and take risks. This occurred once there was a level of trust that encouraged people to share ideas, open classroom doors and plan with each other. Some principals also rearranged timetables to allow common planning time.

As the pilot schools became more familiar with growth planning and other schools became involved, they increasingly looked for ways to determine their needs. The school effectiveness research provided one such opportunity.

THE LINK WITH SCHOOL EFFECTIVENESS

From the start of the project, the task force promoted the model of school effectiveness characteristics and encouraged schools to discuss them as they related to their own school. Within Halton, previous planning had been very much a response to 'gut reaction' concerning a school's needs. Early on, as part of the assessment stage, several principals took their schools through a process to examine the characteristics. In 1990, however, as part of an increased orientation to data-based planning, surveys were developed for elementary and secondary teachers. These enabled them to reflect both on where they thought their school was in relation to indicators of the characteristics, and how important they perceived each indicator to be in the creation of an effective school. Through a gap analysis, between 'what is' and 'what should be' the schools were able to identify areas of strength and need. The teacher surveys were supplemented by parent and student surveys. Similar surveys have been used in Scotland to develop ethos indicators to help schools in planning and evaluating their development (SOED, 1992).

Perceptional data are not the only sources of information from which a school should draw during the assessment phase. Schools in Halton have also been encouraged to look at attendance and retention patterns, as well as course selection, completion and results at secondary level, and available achievement data at elementary level. This has enabled schools to incorporate a further principle of school effectiveness: equity. Workshops for school growth planning teams have addressed the disaggregation of data to examine differences between various sub-groups of the student population. Disaggregation of student attitude data has produced some interesting reactions from schools that might otherwise have considered themselves to be successful with all of their students. Currently, a profile is being developed for schools, to contain much of the information specified above in compact form, but it will present disaggregated and regional data against which schools can compare themselves. Background information on the student population will also be provided at school and regional levels to enable schools to assess their data in the light of their particular population.

SUPPORT FOR SCHOOL GROWTH PLANNING

The move to school growth planning has been a significant change for Halton. With it has come an increased need within schools for a variety of types of support: instructional help related to their chosen goals; knowledge in the area of group process skills, as teachers become more collaborative and involved in school-level decision-making; and support for development, analysis and interpretation of assessment and evaluation instruments. Indeed, the impetus of this project has led to a reorganization of the support staff to meet schools' needs better. Furthermore, school-based planning has been enshrined in policy as one of three strategic directions for the district. The other two are instruction, to emphasize the importance of the teaching and learning process, and staff development, to ensure adequate support for school growth planning and instruction.

The support comes in various forms. Three key programmes are outlined below.

School growth plan team training

A five-day workshop is offered for teams of teachers and administrators, who will facilitate growth planning in their own schools. Participants work through activities related to school effectiveness, change and the different stages of growth planning. Teams examine specific issues related to their growth plan and coach other teams. With an increase in teacher involvement in whole-school development, the incorporation of conflict resolution, team-building, decision-making and problem-solving skills are highlighted as vital components of these workshops, as are an understanding of school culture and people's reaction to change.

Leadership Effectiveness Assisted by Peers

Leadership development has long been a significant feature of Halton's culture, and has had a considerable impact on the institutionalization of school growth planning. Leadership Effectiveness Assisted by Peers (LEAP), collaboratively designed by principals, central office and university staff, focused on building a supportive framework for school growth planning. Its topics included: the creation of a collaborative culture; the change process; instructional and transformational leadership (Sergiovanni, 1990; Leithwood, 1992); understanding and motivating staff members; instructional strategies and classroom management. Participants worked with a partner between sessions on problems related to their own schools.

The Learning Consortium

In 1988 Halton and three local school districts entered a partnership with the Faculty of Education of the University of Toronto and the Ontario Institute for Studies in Education. Jointly, they committed themselves to study and enhance the full range of the teaching continuum, from pre-service to in-service of experienced staff. The consortium's philosophy is that school and classroom development are inextricably linked, connected by the teacher as learner (Fullan *et al.*, 1990). Each summer, teams of teachers and administrators from the four boards participate in institutes that focus on teaching and learning strategies, classroom management, change and school improvement. In 1993, the consortium organized a conference on assessment and evaluation, attended by 800 educators. Two offshoots in Halton have been local instructional institutes and the 'Partners in the Classroom' programme for first-year teachers and their mentors. Similar programmes have been presented to different groups throughout the system, to build a common language and understanding of the techniques, and to support school growth planning and its focus on instruction. Thus, the different initiatives within the system are intended to weave together.

UNRESOLVED ISSUES

Several issues related to school effectiveness and school growth planning have proved a challenge over the period of the project. Four are now described.

Assessment and evaluation

Ontario does not have a recent history of standardized testing. Halton has internally-developed mathematics and French tests, and has participated in curriculum reviews arranged by Ontario's Ministry of Education and International Mathematics and Science Studies. Results are generally very positive. It has also collected data on school dropouts and has experienced a decrease from 9 per cent in 1987 to less than 5 per cent in 1992. It would be impossible, however, to attribute these positive results entirely to the Effective Schools Project, given that it was one of several initiatives within the district. Indeed, it should be questioned whether it is appropriate to assess the success of such a project using student achievement measures. Given its focus on process and the promotion of a collaborative culture, this should be an equally important focus of evaluation. Considerable effort has been expended to monitor the implementation of school growth planning and its impact on attitudes and behaviour through teacher and student surveys and interviews (Stoll and Fink, 1992a,b; Stoll and Fink, 1994). In addition, the school board has recently passed an assessment policy that will further Halton's efforts to evaluate students' achievement as it relates to the school board's own curriculum.

Certainly, each school should also be able to evaluate its own growth in its selected goal areas, and demonstrate both to itself and to its parents that what it does makes a difference. This, surely, is the most important measure of school growth.

An interesting outcome of the lack of external accountability in Halton, however, has been that schools, as they become more involved in growth planning, increasingly want to measure the success of their goals and to prove to themselves that they do have a positive impact on student achievement and social development. Many Halton schools now have such data that provide both summative results and formative information that highlights future development priorities.

The challenge of change in secondary schools

Results of a system-wide administration of the School Effectiveness Questionnaire to 10 per cent of Halton teachers demonstrate that at elementary level, teachers are committed to, and involved in, school growth planning. Furthermore, the majority of them believe they are involved in decision-making and collaborative planning, and have a shared vision for their schools. Secondary teachers, while less positive, believe in the concept of school growth planning and show a desire to work more closely together. This, however, is a particular challenge for secondary schools, traditionally bound by their department structure, subject orientation and size. The challenge of change at secondary level is well-documented (Fullan, 1990; Hargreaves and Earl, 1990) but previous research suggests that school-wide improvement is possible although by no means problem-free (Louis and Miles, 1990).

The involvement of students and parents

Sarason (1990) cautions that all educational reforms are doomed to failure unless there is a significant shift in power relationships. In the early years of school growth planning, we have seen a considerable move to shared decision-making and collaborative planning among Halton's teaching staff, but, as yet, far fewer examples of student and parent involvement in these processes. Perhaps, particularly in secondary schools, the interpersonal issues among staff have not received sufficient attention (Reynolds, 1992), for it appears clear that until staff feel totally involved, respected and trusted, they will not afford the same treatment to students of parents.

Multiple innovations

For a researcher studying the impact of the implementation of school effectiveness research findings on a district, it became evident that this was only one of many initiatives. Initially, there was frustration at not being able to prise out the precise impact of the project. It was soon clear, however, that the initiatives, although different, complemented each other because they were blended together by the senior administration through staff development. Fullan (1991) notes that managing multiple innovations is a reality. What are the implications for the linkage of school effectiveness and school improvement? Perhaps that they are just two pieces of a larger puzzle, and even in a single school, it might not be possible to evaluate the impact of a school effectiveness project separately from all of its other activities. The school growth plan (or school development plan), however, can provide a means to prioritize multiple innovations.

CAN SCHOOL EFFECTIVENESS AND SCHOOL IMPROVEMENT REALLY BE LINKED?

The issues above and others continue to challenge us. This does not, however, mean that the two paradigms cannot be linked. What is needed is a vehicle to connect school improvement process strategies with the theoretical base of school effectiveness.

School growth planning provides such a vehicle. It incorporates all of the criteria described earlier that each paradigm brings to the union, although it clearly demonstrates that because each district or school is unique, it has to follow its own path and make amendments to suit its context and needs. Clearly, the process is free neither of problems nor flaws, but its overriding benefit is that it addresses the culture of the institution, and encourages teachers to examine their beliefs and values, and to draw on their own experience and knowledge of what has been shown elsewhere to be effective to come to a shared understanding of a better future for their school. Furthermore, it gives a school control over its own development priorities, even when the school is faced with external demands. The implications for other countries engaged in school development planning should be clear.

REFERENCES

Ainscow, M. and Hopkins, D. (1992) 'Improving the quality of education for all: some emerging issues', Paper presented at the Fifth International Congress for School Effectiveness and Improvement, Victoria, British Columbia.

Barth, R. (1990) *Improving Schools from Within*. San Francisco: Jossey-Bass.

Bashi, J. and Sass, Z. (1989) 'Factors affecting stable continuation of outcomes of school improvement projects', in Creemers, B., Peters, T. and Reynolds, D. (eds) *School Effectiveness and School Improvement*. Amsterdam: Swets and Zeitlinger.

Caldwell, B. and Spinks, J. (1988) *The Self-Managing School*. Lewes: Falmer Press.

Clift, P.A., Nuttall, D.L. and McCormick, R. (1987) *Studies in School Self-Evaluation*. Lewes: Falmer Press.

Cotton, K. (1990) *Effective Schooling Practices: A Research Synthesis (1990 Update)*. Portland, Oregon: Northwest Regional Educational Laboratory.

Crandall, D. *et al.* (1982) *People, Policies and Practice: Examining the Chain of School Improvement*, **1–10**. Andover, MA: The Network.

Deal, T.E. (1990) 'Healing our schools: restoring the heart', in Lieberman, A. (ed.) *Schools as Collaborative Cultures: Creating the Future Now*. New York: Falmer Press.

Edmonds, R. (1979) 'Effective schools for the urban poor', *Educational Leadership*, **37** (1), 15–27.

Fullan, M. (1982) *The Meaning of Educational Change*. Toronto: OISE Press.

Fullan, M. (1990) 'Change processes in secondary schools: toward a more fundamental agenda', in McLaughlin, M.W., Talbert, J.E. and Bascia, N. (eds) *The Contexts of Teaching Secondary Schools: Teachers' Realities*. New York: Teachers College Press.

Fullan, M. (1991) *The New Meaning of Educational Change*. New York: Teachers College Press.

Fullan, M., Bennett, B. and Rolheiser-Bennett, C. (1990) 'Linking classroom and school improvement', *Educational Leadership*, **47** (8), 13–19.

Fullan, M. and Hargreaves, A. (1991) *What's Worth Fighting For? Working Together for Your School*. Toronto: Ontario Public School Teachers' Federation.

Gardner, H. (1983) *Frames of Mind: The Theory of Multiple Intelligences*. New York: Basic Books.

Goodlad, J. (1984) *A Place Called School: Prospects for the Future*. New York: McGraw-Hill.

Hallinger, P. and Murphy, J. (1985) 'Assessing the instructional leadership behaviour of principals', *Elementary School Journal*, **86** (2), 217–48.

Hargreaves, A. (1989) 'Cultures of teaching: a focus for change: Part 1 and Part 2', *OPSTF News*, February and April.

Hargreaves, A. and Earl, L. (1990) *Rights of Passage: A Review of Selected Research and Literature on Innovative School Organization for the Delivery of Programs and Services for Students Aged 11–14 years*. Toronto: Ontario Ministry of Education/Ontario Institute for Studies in Education.

Hargreaves, D.H. (1993) 'School effectiveness, school change and school improvement: the relevance of the concept of culture', Paper presented to the ESRC Seminar Series on School Effectiveness and School Improvement, Sheffield, UK.

Hargreaves, D.H. and Hopkins, D. (1991) *The Empowered School: The Management and Practice of Development Planning*. London: Cassell.

Hargreaves, D.H., Hopkins, D., Leask, M., Connolly, J. and Robinson, P. (1989) *Planning for School Development: Advice to Governors, Headteachers and Teachers*. London: Department of Education and Science/HMSO.

Holcomb, E. (ed.) (1991) *A Handbook for Implementing School Improvement*. Madison, WI: National Center for Effective Schools Research and Development.

Hopkins, D. (1992) 'School improvement in an era of change', in Ribbins, P. and Burridge, E. (eds) *Improving Education: Promoting Quality in Schools*. London: Cassell.

Huberman, M. and Miles, M. (1984) *Innovation Up Close*. New York: Plenum.

Joyce, B.N., Hersh, R. and McKibbin, M. (1983) *The Structure of School Improvement*. New York: Longman.

Leithwood, K.A. (1992) 'The move toward transformational leadership', *Educational Leadership*, **49** (5), 8–12.

Lezotte, L.W. (1989) 'Base school improvement on what we know about effective schools', *American School Board Journal*, **176** (8), 18–20.

Little, J.W. (1982) 'Norms of collegiality and experimentation: workplace conditions and school success', *American Educationl Research Journal*, **19** (3), 325–40.

Little, J.W. (1990) 'The persistence of privacy: autonomy and initiative in teachers' professional relations', *Teachers College Record*, **91** (4), 509–36.

Loucks-Horsley, S. and Hergert, L. (1985) *An Action Guide to School Improvement*. Alexandria, VA: Association for Supervision and Curriculum Development.

Louis, K.S. and Miles, M.B. (1990) *Improving the Urban High School: What Works and Why*. New York: Teachers College Press.

McMahon, A., Bolam, R., Abbott, R. and Holly, P. (1984) *Guidelines for Review and Internal Development in Schools*. Primary and Secondary School Handbooks. Harlow: Longman for the Schools Council.

Miles, M.B. and Ekholm, M. (1985) 'What is school improvement?', in van Velzen, W., Miles, M.B., Ekholm, M., Hameyer, V. and Robin, D. (eds) *Making School Improvement Work: A Conceptual Guide to Practice*. Leuven, Belgium: OECD.

Mortimore, P., Sammons, P., Stoll, L., Lewis, D. and Ecob, R. (1988) *School Matters: The Junior Years*. Wells: Open Books, and Berkeley, CA: University of California Press.

Nias, J., Southworth, G. and Yeomans, R. (1989) *Staff Relationships in the Primary School: A Study of Organizational Cultures*. London: Cassell.

Reynolds, D. (1992) 'School effectiveness and school improvement in the 1990s', in Bashi, J. and Sass, Z. (eds) *School Effectiveness and Improvement: Proceedings of the Third International Congress for School Effectiveness, The Van Leer Jerusalem Institute, Jerusalem 1990*. Jerusalem: Magnes Press.

Reynolds, D., Creemers, B.P.M. and Peters, T. (1989a) *School Effectiveness and Improvement: Proceedings of the First International Congress, London, 1988*. Cardiff: University of Wales College of Cardiff, and Groningen: RION.

Reynolds, D., Davie, R. and Phillips, D. (1989b) 'The Cardiff Programme: an effective school improvement programme based on school effectiveness research', In Creemers, B.P.M. and Scheerens, J. (eds) *Developments in School Effectiveness Research*, special issue of the *International Journal of Educational Research*, **13** (7), 800–14.

Rosenholtz, S.J. (1989) *Teachers' Workplace: The Social Organization of Schools*. New York: Longman.

Sammons, P., Mortimore, P. and Thomas, S. (1993) 'Do schools perform consistently across outcomes and areas?' Paper presented to the ESRC Seminar Series on School Effectiveness and School Improvement, Sheffield.

Sarason, S. (1990) *The Predictable Failure of Educational Reform*. San Francisco: Jossey-Bass.

Scheerens, J. (1987) *Enhancing Educational Opportunities for Disadvantaged Learners: A Review of Dutch Research on Compensatory Education and Educational Development Policy*. Amsterdam: North-Holland.

Scottish Office Education Department (1992) *Using Ethos Indicators in Primary and Secondary School Self-Evaluation: Taking Account of the Views of Pupils, Parents and Teachers*. HM Inspectors of Schools.

Sergiovanni, T.J. (1990) *Value-Added Leadership: How to Get Extraordinary Performance in Schools*. New York: Harcourt Brace Jovanovich.

Sirotnik, K.A. (1987) *'The school as the center of change'*, Occasional Paper No. 5. Seattle, WA: Center for Educational Renewal.

Stoll, L. and Fink, D. (1992a) 'Effecting school change: the Halton approach', *School Effectiveness and School Improvement*, **3** (1), 19–41.

Stoll, L. and Fink, D. (1992b) *'Assessing the change process: the Halton approach,'* Paper presented at the Fifth International Congress for School Effectiveness and School Improvement, Victoria, British Columbia.

Stoll, L. and Fink, D. (1994) 'School effectiveness and school improvement: views from the field', *School Effectiveness and School Improvement*, **5** (2), 149–77.

Teddlie, C. and Stringfield, S. (1985) 'A differential analysis of effectiveness in middle and lower socioeconomic status schools', *Journal of Classroom Interaction*, **20** (2), 38–44.

Teddlie, C., Stringfield, S., Wimpelberg, R. and Kirkby, P. (1989) 'Contextual differences in models for effective schooling in the USA', in Creemers, B.P.M., Peters, T. and Reynolds, D. (eds) *School Effectiveness and School Improvement: Proceedings of the Second International Congress, Rotterdam, 1989*. Amsterdam: Swets & Zeitlinger.

van Velzen, W. (1987) 'The International School Improvement Project', in Hopkins, D. (ed.) *Improving the Quality of Schooling: Lessons from the OECD International School Improvement Project*. Lewes: Falmer Press.

Chapter 10

Creating Their Own Futures: The Use and Effectiveness of School Development Plans in Australian Schools

John Braithwaite

An educator returning to Australia after an absence of some twenty years may feel somewhat overwhelmed with the changes that have occurred to the control and management of Australia's schools. In most of the state and territory systems the previously rigid centralized control of education is now replaced by a devolved school-based decision-making process that has shifted control from the centre to the schools in what may be termed a 'loosely coupled' management system. Or that is what would appear to be the case if the official pronouncements are to be believed. Certainly, where previously the development of plans for future school growth and evaluation was the primary responsibility of centrally selected school inspectors, the current process highlights the central role of school principals in school development and evaluation. School communities now have the responsibility of producing school development or renewal plans specifying future outcomes that illustrate how the school is going to manage its resources in the attainment of these outcomes. For a previously centralized system, the current official policies represent a definite turnaround, moving from a 'top-down' model of management to an ostensibly 'bottom-up' management structure.

To explain to the visitor why this change has come about requires an exploration of the contemporary educational context in Australia. It is the contextual factors that provide substance to the official pronouncements. Following this examination is an overview of existing school development processes, an examination of a limited number of attempts initiated by schools to create workable school development programmes and then some generalizations from the limited evidence available[1] on the effectiveness of these contemporary initiatives. To carry out this analysis, data are drawn from both state and non-state school systems.

THE EDUCATIONAL CONTEXT INFLUENCING CONTEMPORARY AUSTRALIAN DEVELOPMENTS

The management and control of Australian education are the responsibility of the Minister of Education in the various states and territories, with the Commonwealth or federal government having little direct responsibility for primary or secondary education. Until the 1980s the central bureaucracies usually controlled school administration and curricula and imposed restrictive management practices on all schools. They ensured their directives were followed through an extensive inspectorial system that monitored and evaluated the educational programmes of all schools. Most major initiatives were centrally imposed and retribution often followed if schools strayed too far outside the centrally imposed mandates. School-initiated development plans were unheard of as the overall directions that schools followed were prescribed by the central authorities. For some educational authorities the position they advocated prior to the 1980s was based on a clearly articulated position, while for others it represented pragmatic policies based on long-forgotten responses.

Three major influences caused the changes in the management and control of education in Australia in the 1980s. These influences were:

- the increased professionalism of the teaching workforce;
- the greater militancy of the teachers' unions; and
- greater intervention in educational decision-making by parental groups.

In terms of the first issue the increased years of pre-service training undertaken by teachers are shown by a 1976 survey (NSW Ministry of Education, Youth and Womens' Affairs, 1990, p. 15) which indicated that in New South Wales, the largest educational system, only 13 per cent of the primary teaching force and 63 per cent of secondary teachers had undergone four years of pre-service training. By 1990 the percentages increased to 35 and 80 per cent respectively. This figure will increase substantially as four years' pre-service training is now accepted as the standard for professional training by most Australian educational employers (Baldwin, 1991, p. 3). The acknowledged increase in complexity of the classroom teacher's role (Carrick, 1989), together with their increased training, has resulted in a redefinition of teachers' workplace roles. Schools are no longer seen as places where the teachers follow the prescribed mandates of the employer, but are places where teachers choose to and are required to take a major responsibility for their professional endeavours and school development (Scott, 1990).

Second, the teachers' unions promoted the increased professionalism of the teaching workforce by mounting campaigns to improve teachers' working conditions and length of pre-service training. They also supported a substantial increase in the provision of in-service training by employers and tertiary institutions. Third, parental groups were no longer prepared to accept at face value Departmental policies and actively fought to shape and change educational policies so that their roles in the control and management of education at the local school level increased. Central educational administrations, for their part, promoted the development of school councils to take on the responsibility of local school management.

The combination of these influences, together with a greater willingness of educational administrations to devolve control to the local school level, created new responsibilities for schools. In each state and territory the administration published reports recommending some 'downside up' thinking that focused development at the school level. Statements such as:

> The school should be a dynamic environment where desirable change is fostered, where opportunities for evaluation and appraisal occur, and where there is an emphasis on professional development and collegial support.   (Scott, 1990, p. 66)

could be found in the review statements of the educational systems. Schools were now required to be well-managed, self-determining and self-renewing centres of educational quality. The means to this end were largely to be achieved through fostering school-based development and evaluation plans.

Such school-based planning started in schools in the Australian Capital Territory (ACT) in the mid-1970s and was followed by all other systems by the end of the 1980s, with the Victorian system taking a key role in promoting such changes. In many ways devolving control to schools represented a quantum change that schools have not been able to implement wholeheartedly, since a substantial minority of teachers still 'long for the days when they were told what to do' (Braithwaite, 1991).

THE 'TYPICAL' SCHOOL DEVELOPMENT PRACTICES FOLLOWED IN AUSTRALIAN SCHOOLS

In presenting the 'typical' school development or school renewal practices of Australian schools it is important to consider that individual schools depart from this generic model as local conditions or purposes require. Most systems publish Ministerial or Departmental documents outlining the framework in which school development planning is supposed to occur. Figure 10.1 presents an example of the typical system planning model for school development planning.

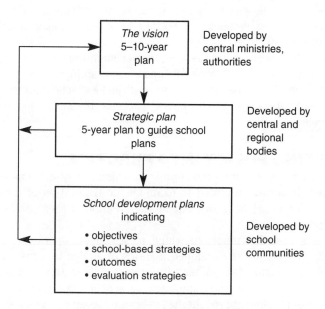

Figure 10.1 *General planning model for school development planning.*

The vision statement provides the overall framework for the establishment of policies, the strategies refine the vision statement into a more manageable time frame of three to five years, the objectives and the accompanying outcomes statements are detailed by the school community and provide an evaluative framework to determine whether the school plan achieves its objectives. The school community develops its plans within the framework of system and local regional

143

guidelines that are supposed to take into account local conditions affecting planning and decision-making. These plans are intended to describe how the school will achieve its intended goals for the year and suggest performance indicators that can demonstrate whether or not the school has achieved these goals. The school principal is charged with the responsibility of drawing up the management plans in cooperation with his or her staff and parents. Generally, the production of the formal plan is intended to help the school meet identified needs, utilize resources effectively, achieve quality outcomes and increase responsiveness. The preparation of these plans is supposed to be done in a way that publicly demonstrates the school's achievement or otherwise of its goals.

Apart from the benefits associated with schools determining their own goals and managing of their own resources, there is the intention that schools will actively involve parents and the community in the formation of their plans. Such parental involvement is a comparatively new phenomenon for Australian schools, for they have been attempting to involve parents and the community in their deliberations only since the mid-1970s. Other associated benefits claimed from the production of the plans include:

- the ability of the schools to decide their own priorities within the overall strategic plan;
- providing schools with increased autonomy in decision-making;
- the potential to establish a 'bottom-up' system that can influence overall strategic planning;
- increased innovation, creativity and experimentation;
- clear delineation of responsibility and accountability;
- integration of planning and budgeting at the local school level; and
- the publication of the school's success in achieving intended outcomes.

TRANSLATING POLICY INTO PRACTICE

The previous discussion outlined the context in which school development plans are being promoted. It is now intended to examine the translation of these intentions into reality to examine what, if any, effects the creation of these plans is having on the lives of schools.

The general planning model in which most schools operate is illustrated in Figure 10.1. Each system has developed a series of guides to assist schools in the preparation of their plans. The guides vary dramatically in the details they provide with some providing a lock step approach to school development, while others suggest a variety of possible approaches schools may choose to follow.

The response of schools to the different styles of assistance has been quite varied. At first those schools that are taking the first steps in producing their own renewal plans seek out the guides that detail the steps to follow and use them as an important crutch (see Table 10.1 for an example). The schools frequently seek the guidance of external system consultants or refer to texts such as Caldwell and Spinks (1988) when they first embark upon the task. For the beginning schools the production of such plans often represents a tremendous effort on the part of all participants and a collective sigh may be heard when the documents are finished and bound. Unfortunately, the same energy is not always followed through in the translation of the plans into action, and the documents can represent icons that are on display rather than action plans that have been translated into practical outcomes.

Table 10.1. *Example of management procedures for the development of school development plan.*

Phase	Actions
1 Initiation	• Form a management team • Explore central concerns/non-negotiables in a whole-school development process • Develop a working understanding of the model • Develop an initial time line
2 Launching the project in the School	• Develop a handbook for school development • Introduce school development to staff, students, parents • Set up an in-service day to explore values and beliefs – prepare a display, initiate student projects, liaise with consultant, plan the day
3 Conducting a needs analysis	• Develop an information matrix to establish information currently held about student, staff and parent expectations/perceptions • Liaise with consultant to plan survey strategy • Prepare resources to implement survey strategy • Process survey results
4 Compiling the school profile	• Preparation of school community profiles • Liaise with consultant to plan seminar day • Seminar day to construct school profile outlining school successes, challenges, problems and actions • Develop objectives to address major areas of concern within the value framework identified in Phase 2 • Produce draft development statement
5 Review period	• Present draft statement to school community • Accept suggested amendments • Produce second draft of development plan
6 Adoption	• Arrange printing of document • Prepare for adoption ceremony • Celebrate the conclusion of the project, implementation and on-going development

Source: D'Orsa (n.d.).

Later, with some experience in the task, the schools tend to look beyond the preparation of detailed specifications towards the preparation of documents to guide actions which can be translated into reality in the shortest possible time. It is as if the schools realize they have learnt from their initial forays into the production of school development plans and choose to use their limited time and resources more parsimoniously. The previous concentration on form is often replaced by a concern with what is achievable given their existing school resources. Plans developed under such circumstances are more likely to be implemented and adhered to by the school community.

HOW EFFECTIVELY DO THE SCHOOL DEVELOPMENT PLANS INFLUENCE PRACTICE?

To determine school development plans' effects on practice I reviewed the evidence in the available Australian databases and found numerous descriptive articles outlining the practices followed in individual schools, accounts outlining how to produce school development plans and a limited number of studies reviewing the implementation of the policies framing the developmental process. However, I found no studies attempting to evaluate the benefits to school communities arising from the production of school development plans in any comprehensive way. So I contacted twenty-one schools by telephone, based on random selection from school lists (fourteen primary and seven secondary schools in seven states and territories), and interviewed the school principals about their perceptions of the process they followed in developing their plans and the effectiveness of their endeavours. Only one of the schools contacted had not attempted to develop such a plan and the following comments are summaries of the responses received from the remaining twenty schools. While the number of schools contacted does not constitute a representative sample of all Australian schools, there is nothing I heard from individual schools to suggest they were not typical of Australian schools.

To evaluate the effectiveness of the school development processes the schools followed, the principals were asked their views on the value of carrying out the process, the strengths and weaknesses of their procedures, the extent to which they believed they had the autonomy to carry out the developmental and implementation task, the extent of staff, student and parent/community involvement in the process, the extent to which the school has sponsored creative and/or innovative approaches to the preparation of school plans and the extent to which the plans guide and/or control school decision-making and other activities.

Given that all of the educational systems encourage school-based decision-making and usually require schools to produce school development plans, there was great disparity in the principals' responses to the perceived value of carrying out the process. Just over 50 per cent stated that they believed the effort required did not make that much difference to the running of their schools, while 35 per cent claimed it gave staff and the community a sense of ownership in their immediate futures. When pressed as to whether they believed the production of such plans improved the teaching–learning processes in schools, the majority (75 per cent) claimed the influences were marginal and usually translated into helping specific groups within the school. 'More form than substance' was a frequently heard remark.

Surprisingly, the majority of principals (85 per cent) indicated that they did not find it difficult to organize the process, with the majority leaving the task to a staff–parent committee. They all claimed that the teachers' on-going experience with school-based curriculum decision-making had stood them in good stead and usually claimed that teachers were skilled in organizing themselves. The greatest problem they faced was the perennial one of time to carry out the task. Most claimed that the available pupil-free days allotted to them were insufficient to carry out the whole planning task. The other recurring problem concerned the production of a meaningful plan. Principals claimed there was a tendency to produce statements that were, in the words of one respondent, 'educanto' and didn't really mean much unless they clearly focused on their intended outcomes.

The greatest complaint the principals levied at the process was that they really did not have enough control over the key resources, for the major resource allocations were still determined by central or regional authorities. Sixty-five per cent claimed they spent a substantial proportion of their day trying to work out how they could supplement their resource allocations through additional means. A substantial minority (45 per cent) suggested that the most frustrating part of the process was that they developed their plans under certain circumstances only to find these plans changed because of changes in the prevailing political or economic conditions and sometimes because of changes in educational policies. The majority (80 per cent) were strongly supportive of the value some parents can bring to the process, especially in aspects of financial planning, which most principals claimed they did not know enough about.

Questions about the value of involving staff, students, parents and the community in the preparation of school development plans generated varied responses. Primary and secondary principals' responses differed on this issue, and this difference may be a function of the larger size of secondary schools and the closer relations primary schools tend to have with their local communities. Primary principals generally suggested that the majority of their staff members were involved in the process and contributed purposefully to their deliberations. The majority of secondary principals reported that school executives assumed the major responsibility for the development of their plans. Most principals saw their roles as setting boundaries for exploration, with the other members of the staff completing the details. They all commented that it was often difficult to get assistant teachers to become engrossed in the activity as they were more concerned about bread-and-butter issues.

When it came to seeing the production of the plans as an opportunity for creative developments in the schools, most principals (80 per cent) indicated they did not want to produce plans that were 'too far out' as their personal assessment was to be partly based on their achievement of their stated outcomes. These principals claimed they erred on the conservative side when it came to setting goals. However, many of them suggested that when they were more familiar with the requirements of the devolved system, they might be more 'adventurous' in the future. Where principals reported creative or innovative responses they were generally concerned with specific groups within their schools such as gifted or talented students or after-school activities.

Most of the principals (70 per cent) reported they used their plans as guides for action and frequently found it necessary to modify their intentions. In the majority of cases it appears this response reflected the specificity of their planning. Many commented that 'next year's planning will not be as specific as we have attempted so far.' Nevertheless, all of the principals commented that the process was a valuable one for all involved as it often brought school communities closer together and enabled others 'to see the difficulties I have to resolve in managing the school's resources.' The greatest difficulty principals faced (85 per cent) involved translating the plans into action, a task they all claimed they were getting better at as their relevant educational authorities made their intentions clearer.

Examining the responses received from these twenty principals it is obvious there are different perceptions of the value of the school development plans in influencing school practices. The majority of the principals appreciated the opportunity to manage their own affairs but were concerned they could not always control the resources that matter. They believed the process brought benefits to the whole school community but they were not always happy with the amount of effort the production of the plans required. One principal in commenting on this point claimed that 'we can't do a quick job on this task for it is the yardstick by which we are judged and are publicly accountable . . . in many ways it represents our success or otherwise as a school and shows the world how effective we are as managers.' Yet at the same time I got the feeling that many of the principals still viewed their major role as guiding the learning of students, with the development of such plans a necessary, but small, part of their overall roles as principals.

VIEWING THE FUTURE – WHERE CHANGES MAY COME

There is no doubt the next decade will see a consolidation of the existing practices by all Australian educational administrations as they endeavour to make individual schools responsible for their effective use of resources. The production of school development plans will play a key role in this process. Yet the scene in Australian schools is still underdeveloped as the process is still being woven into the local educational fabric.

It is apparent that the majority of schools are concentrating on the formal structural side of producing school development plans, and those I have read tend to focus on material resource needs often at the expense of human resource needs. The school personnel are generally judged to have become skilful at developing such plans since most schools have been engaged in the production of school-based curriculum documents for a number of years. Yet the production of school development plans requires school personnel to be concerned with resource issues, an area in which the majority often have limited experience and competence. Also, they have to focus more and more on outcomes as the economic rationalists tighten their grip on educational planning.

As the production of school-based programmes tends to go through a developmental process, I can only surmise that schools will switch their current emphasis on the formal production of such documents to concerns ensuring their successful implementation in schools. Schools will probably develop the realization that their effectiveness is also aligned with the promotion of individual goals as much as it is concerned with the attainment of school-based goals. At the moment there tends to be no clear nexus between individual teacher goals, faculty goals and whole-school goals in the majority of schools contacted for this review. Such alignment should come with increased facility with the task and the realization of the importance of promoting individual and whole-school goal attainment.

One of the great problematic areas in the process so far concerns the potential roles parents can play. In the system where parents have potentially had the greatest involvement, ACT, the evidence to date is not especially encouraging. Nearly two decades of actively encouraging parental involvement in the management of ACT schools has not, according to Collins (1989), resulted in parents being considered equal partners in the development process. No doubt some parents have skills and abilities that schools urgently require. The problem is that not all schools have developed processes that actively draw such strengths into their developmental processes.

An urgent need exists to link school development and curriculum planning into a cohesive whole that can be shown to improve the teaching–learning process, for it is this process which is professedly the primary purpose of formal education. If schools are not encouraged or required to demonstrate how the links between school development planning and students' learning are made we may be creating another passing facade that does not achieve and promote effective educational management. Also it has to be demonstrated that the emphasis on school-based planning will promote the 'upside down' model of school management that most systems claim are the focus of their reforms.

NOTE

[1] This evidence is culled from a search of the major Australian educational databases and from the author's collection of relevant school development initiatives. It ignores the South Australian data as these are the focus of Peter Cuttance's chapter.

REFERENCES

Baldwin, G.W. (1991) *Three Year Trained Access to Four Year Trained Salary Scale – Policy & Procedures*. Sydney: NSW Department of School Education.

Braithwaite, R.J. (1990) 'The organisation of the curriculum', in 'The Evaluation of the Organisation of Primary Schools in New South Wales', Sydney: NSW Department of School Education.

Caldwell, B.J. and Spinks, J.M. (1988) *The Self-Managing School*. Lewes: Falmer Press.

Carrick, Sir John (Chairman) (1989) *Report of the Committee of Review of New South Wales Schools*. Sydney: NSW Government.

Collins, C. (1989) 'Providing a curriculum: the ACT experiment', *Curriculum Perspectives*, **9** (1), 56–61.

D'Orsa, J.R. (n.d.) Management structure: School Development Project 1990 – primary model, Mimeo.

NSW Ministry of Education, Youth and Women's Affairs (1990) *Teacher Education: Direction and Strategies*. Sydney: NSW Ministry of Education.

Scott, B.W. (1990) *School-Centred Education: Building a More Responsive State School System*. Sydney: NSW Education Portfolio-Management Review.

Chapter 11

Towards a Contingency Approach to Development Planning in Schools

Mike Wallace

INTRODUCTION

The purpose of this chapter is twofold: to explore the hypothesis that the effectiveness of different approaches to development planning may be contingent upon the local and national context in which schools are placed; and tentatively to suggest that in turbulent times a flexible process of continual creation, monitoring and adjustment of plans, which also takes into account conflicting annual cycles, may be more effective than more rationalistic models based upon sequential annual cycles alone.

The context of schooling in England, in common with many other Western countries, has become increasingly chaotic in recent years primarily as a consequence of massive central government intervention. Education reforms for the State service include a National Curriculum phased in over several years; national testing, the results of which are being made public; responsibility for financial management and the appointment of staff falling to headteachers and governors; nationally imposed salaries, conditions of service and promotion structure; biennial appraisal of all teaching staff; a budget for staff development with an annual entitlement of closure days available for in-service training; open enrolment of pupils to promote competition between schools; the possibility of opting out of local education authority (LEA) control; and formal inspection at least every four years.

LEAs are charged with the duty of supporting schools with the introduction of these reforms. Since 1989 the central government grant to LEAs to enable them to fulfil this duty has been conditional upon LEAs ensuring that schools have an annual 'national curriculum development plan' (Department of Education and Science, 1988a). The majority of LEAs have responded to this demand by introducing, with central government approval, the more comprehensive innovation of completing annual school development plans, most of which are compulsory. They generally prescribe both a consultative planning process and a document in which priorities and implementation plans are recorded, but compulsion tends in practice to be restricted to the document. The central government advice sent to all LEAs and schools refrained from specifying any documentation, but stated that priorities for development would be planned in detail for one year with an outline of priorities for subsequent years (Department of Education and Science, 1989, 1991). School development planning is widely regarded as a key to managing the introduction of central government reforms, together with LEA initiatives, such as an equal opportunities policy, and any innovations generated within schools.

In addition to their own LEA's development planning approach and document-ation, schools have access to a range of models from other LEAs which have been published (for example, Sheffield Education Department, 1991; Warwickshire County Council, 1991) and from handbooks (for example, Hargreaves and Hopkins, 1991; Skelton *et al.*, 1991). These models tend to be based upon cycles of review, planning, implementation and evaluation lasting between one and three years. Some adopt the academic year (September to August) as the basis for the cycle; others use the financial year (April to March). The assumptions underlying such models are rationalistic: it is considered possible to orchestrate planning for development effectively through a logical, step-by-step approach proceeding from a systematic review at the beginning of the cycle to summative evaluation of the plan at the end. However, some models allow for adjustment within agreed priorities as formative evaluation brings unforeseen issues during implementation to light (for example, Hargreaves and Hopkins, 1991).

Possible influences upon the widespread adoption of a cyclic approach to development planning include a long tradition of planning for the academic year; familiarity within many LEAs with models for school self-review (for example, Inner London Education Authority, 1977; McMahon *et al.*, 1984) based on occasional cycles and developed at a time when the context of schooling was generally more stable than at present; central government imposition upon LEAs of a planning cycle for in-service training grants and for financial management of schools, based upon the financial year; the requirement that schools have a financial management plan based on the financial year under the central government's 'Local Management of Schools' initiative (Department of Education and Science, 1988b); and, in some LEAs, the popularity of a handbook advocating a yearly 'collaborative planning cycle' (Caldwell and Spinks, 1988), which drew largely upon experience of cyclic planning in an isolated Tasmanian school enjoying a relatively stable environment. Cyclic planning which draws upon the English experience is now being disseminated abroad (for example, Stoll, in press).

Most of these cyclic models have been trialled in schools in some way, and therefore have proven to be of value in guiding planning, at least when they were developed. Schools across England, however, face an increasingly turbulent environ-ment as central government ministers proceed with their reform agenda. Research carried out at the National Development Centre for Educational Management and Policy (NDC) into a small number of English primary and secondary schools in several LEAs suggests that the assumptions of cyclic development planning models, some of which were trialled under the more stable conditions of the past, may be open to question. It seems uncertain how far such models can promote stable conditions for school development in the present climate. Staff and governors in turbulent environments may now be *forced* to adopt a more flexible, evolutionary approach, largely for reasons beyond their control. A key finding is that much planning for development takes place continually, *outside* the 'official' development plan document and process, as staff and governors respond to spasmodically and often unpredictably changing circumstances which follow from the strategy employed by central government to introduce its reforms for schools. Under such circumstances, it is possible that the official process and documentation may be less effective than an alternative approach resting upon less rationalistic assumptions.

151

In the remaining sections of the chapter the notion is developed of a contingency approach to development planning; some limited research evidence is summarized; factors affecting the balance between environmental stability and turbulence are considered; and conclusions are drawn about further research and development work that may need to be done to help staff and governors to increase their capacity to orchestrate development while avoiding overload in an environment of multiple, externally imposed change.

A CONTINGENCY APPROACH

Some years ago Burns and Stalker (1961) suggested, on the basis of their research into twenty industrial firms, that different environments induce a need for different management structures. Firms tended to have a mixture of two contrasting structures, depending upon the degree to which there was stability and turbulence in their environment. 'Mechanistic' structures, with a tight hierarchical specification of roles, were found in stable situations but could prove rigid in the face of environmental changes. 'Organic' structures, on the other hand, tended to be developed (in some sections at least) within firms facing a greater degree of turbulence. Roles were more fluid and less hierarchical, allowing more lateral communication and a quicker response to changing tasks. Some firms responded to increasing turbulence by both retaining a mechanistic structure and parcelling off an organic structure, such as a research and development unit, to address changes.

Small-scale research at the NDC suggests that, at a metaphorical level, there may be a parallel with development planning. In so far as compulsory cyclic models based on rationalistic assumptions may be viewed as 'mechanistic', they appear to be retained in quite turbulent environments while a more 'organic', informal and flexible approach to development planning coexists with them. Where cyclic school development planning is not compulsory, the planning process is more continual, complemented by attempts at cyclic planning which tend to be modified in response to unforeseen changes in circumstances. It seems plausible that, to the extent that the context of schooling is turbulent, a more or less continual process of creation, monitoring and adjustment of plans is dictated. To the degree that the context is stable, there may be more scope for systematic, cyclic approaches as the dominant mode of planning for development.

Some limited research evidence

While the research does not provide sufficient evidence to test this hypothesis, the findings are broadly consistent with the claim that planning for development in environments where there is considerable turbulence must be flexible enough to allow for repeated readjustment whenever a new response is required. Selected findings from three research projects are summarized below.

The first project, on managing multiple innovations, was an exploratory study of how two primary schools and two secondary schools in one LEA, with reputations for being effective, coped with the implementation of multiple change. The LEA had just introduced a compulsory development plan for schools covering the academic year 1989–90 in detail and the following two years in outline. Interviews were carried out between October 1989 and April 1990 (Wallace, 1991a).

The second project, on senior management teams, explored how senior staff in secondary schools worked together where all involved expressed a commitment to teamwork. Part of the fieldwork consisted of observation and interviews over the academic year 1991–2 in two schools from two LEAs, one of which featured in the multiple innovations project. The LEA of this school had produced a modified version of the original development plan for the four terms from September 1990 to December 1991. The school was required to extend this plan for an interregnum of two terms and to complete another revised version covering the academic year 1992–3. The other LEA had introduced a compulsory development plan covering the academic year 1991–2 in detail and the next two in outline (Hall and Wallace, 1992; Wallace and Hall, 1994).

The third project, on multiracial primary schools, focused upon all planning activity for development in schools selected because their environment was likely to be highly turbulent. Those primary schools catering for a substantial proportion of pupils from ethnic minorities had to address changes in central government funding for ethnic minority support staff in addition to implementing innovations affecting all primary schools. Fieldwork included interviews in two schools in each of three LEAs carried out through the financial year 1991–2. Two LEAs had introduced a compulsory development plan for schools. One covered a financial year in detail and the next two in outline; the other covered the academic year. Staff from both LEAs were in the process of reviewing and revising their development plan. The third LEA required schools to complete a National Curriculum development plan, as required by central government, and invited schools to participate voluntarily in a development plan project. The staff of one school had elected to join the project and were developing a school-based plan covering three academic years from 1991. The headteacher of the other school had developed her own plan covering two academic years from 1989 (McMahon and Wallace, 1992; Wallace and McMahon, 1994).

The multiple-innovations project revealed how the LEA had introduced its development plan initiative at very short notice, representing a compulsory innovation for schools that cut across their existing processes and plans. In one secondary school the head had recently introduced a five-year (annually updated) development planning approach influenced by the work of Caldwell and Spinks. He continued to use his own version once the LEA plan had been completed. The senior management teams project illustrates how this same LEA subsequently revised its development planning initiative in the light of feedback from schools and, through the interregnum, implicitly acknowledged that it was not an essential planning tool for schools. The launch went more smoothly in the other three LEAs featuring in this research where compulsory development planning initiatives were introduced. It is noteworthy that two of them were revising their plans because the context in schools had changed as central government reforms proceeded. The remaining LEA had adopted a voluntary development plan project to enable school staff to work out an approach which suited the local context. Participants had access to a range of models and documentation.

Staff in all four schools in the multiple innovations project completed the development plan document and sent one copy to the LEA. As new circumstances arose, they subsequently modified some existing plans that had been contained within it and created new plans without reference to the original document. Some parts of the development plan became increasingly obsolete and it did not appear to

153

guide planning in the schools during the year. The document was designed to provide information for LEA staff to guide planning of in-service training and to provide a baseline for inspection. Yet as the year progressed the information less accurately represented the schools' in-service training needs or agreed development goals.

Detailed planning for some developments intended for the following year began to be made some months before the evaluation of the present plan which was designed to precede such planning activity. For example, it was imperative to undertake early planning work in the secondary schools because of the time required to advertise for new staff needed in post at the beginning of the next academic year to teach new courses envisaged within the National Curriculum.

The secondary school which was also in the senior management teams project completed subsequent development plan documents. Analysis was carried out of the major areas of planning for development in this school and the other in the second project over the autumn term 1991. In both cases there was variable linkage between the content of the document and major decision areas addressed by the senior management team. In one school, planning for a major marketing initiative was precipitated when the headteacher discovered that pupil enrolment was increasing in a neighbouring school at the expense of her own. This priority had arisen after the development plan was compiled and was not added to the document until the following year although work began immediately. Senior staff in the other school took the initiative of trying a 'critical path' approach to decision-making, so that a series of major decisions and plans would be made according to a sequence of deadlines. Two of the five main decision areas bore little relationship to the development plan document because of issues that had arisen in the year since it was compiled.

The rigidity of the critical path process proved valuable in ensuring that decisions were made by the relevant deadline or withheld until the following year. However, this rigidity also inhibited the desired modification of a decision about the number of teaching periods per week. It became evident during subsequent debate about curriculum and staffing plans that a new distribution of teaching periods was needed to support the favoured option. This option was ruled out because the critical path process did not allow for earlier decisions to be changed. Therefore, even where a deliberate attempt was made to stabilize a turbulent situation by agreeing deadlines for a sequence of planning decisions, evolving circumstances determined that some flexibility must ideally be retained.

The six multiracial primary schools in the third project were ranked impressionistically according to the degree of turbulence in the internal and external environment during the year of fieldwork. Turbulence was very roughly measured by the number of innovations classified as major and any serious short-term crises, longer term issues or other events unrelated to innovations that the schools had nevertheless to address. The proportion of areas of planning for development that lay within or outside the development plan documents was also analysed.

Planning for development coincided most closely with the content of the official document in those schools whose environment was least turbulent although, even in these cases, a considerable amount of planning took place outside it as the year progressed. The proportion of this additional planning was greatest in schools facing additional turbulence. An extreme case was a school where, alongside the externally imposed innovations, staff dealt with impending amalgamation (which was suddenly postponed); a term spent in temporary accommodation on a split site while repairs were carried out to a leaking roof; a residential field study initiative involving all year groups; a sudden increase in pupil numbers; and an arson attack which gutted three classrooms!

Planning for development in all schools in the three projects was variably affected by some or all of the following factors, most of which gave rise to new planning activity that was not heralded in the official plan. Several factors related primarily to information about compulsory innovations originating outside the school:

- lack of information needed to implement an innovation which inhibited planning (for example, several months elapsed between the circulation to schools of draft and final authoritative documents relating to each subject in the National Curriculum);
- new information that conflicted with earlier announcements (statutory 'Attainment Targets' for two subjects within the National Curriculum were combined after many LEAs and schools had implemented pupil records reflecting the larger number of targets);
- the unanticipated announcement of an initiative after the development plan was compiled (schools in one LEA were invited to submit a bid for funding within a new central government scheme to support inner-city schools);
- the introduction of an innovation at short notice (one LEA development plan initiative was launched very rapidly, allowing little time for implementation).

Each innovation was introduced into a context of on-going work which included the implementation of other innovations, leading to:

- interaction between innovations (four schools were due to be reorganized in order to remove surplus pupil places across two LEAs, entailing the redeployment of some staff. Planning for the National Curriculum was inhibited because certain staff would be unlikely to remain in school to implement plans);
- interaction between innovations and routine planning to maintain the status quo (problems over the 'local management of schools' budget in several schools affected planning of staffing, organization of classes and expenditure on material resources).

In addition, staff had to plan a response to unanticipated crises, longer-term issues or other events which were not directly linked to innovations:

- crises required a quick response which disrupted existing planning for a time (one school suffered storm damage to buildings)
- longer-term issues affecting planning for innovations (two schools were moved to temporary sites while major repairs were carried out on the school buildings. Planning connected with the move became the top priority for several months, overtaking planning for innovations).

155

- other events required a planned response (senior staff in three schools took maternity leave, precipitating arrangements being made for staff to take up 'acting' posts to replace them).

Frequently, one or more priorities identified in the plan document did not lead to implementation of anticipated developments (for example, work on drama in two schools was postponed because of other priorities which came to occupy staff). For any school, the balance of environmental stability and turbulence often fluctuated during the year. Figure 11.1 illustrates for one multiracial primary school the relationship between planning for all developments, the development plan itself, and routine planning for maintenance of existing work. In this multiracial primary school (mentioned above as facing a very high degree of turbulence) there was some overlap – but not coincidence – between the development plan and planning for all developments that actually took place. Maintenance planning in several areas was affected by innovations and several priorities in the development plan had not been implemented. The content of development plans overlapped more fully with planning for all developments in schools where there was more stability.

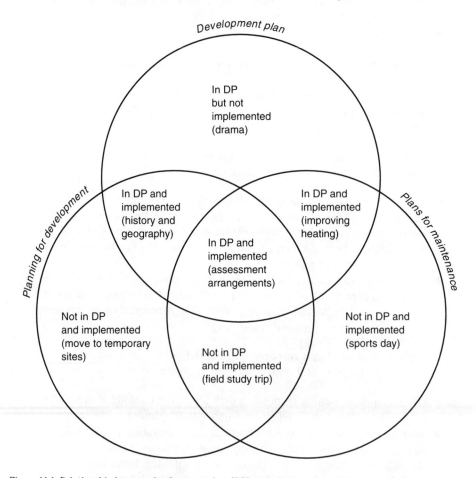

Figure 11.1 *Relationship between development plan (DP) and all planning activity in one school.*

Environmental stability and turbulence

The context of planning in schools may be conceived heuristically as a shifting balance between factors which promote stability and those which promote turbulence. Some factors relate to the external environment; others link with the internal management structure. An illustrative list of these factors, drawn from the three research projects, is offered in Table 11.1.

Table 11.1. *Factors promoting environmental stability and turbulence.*

Factors contributing to stability	Factors contributing to turbulence
Sequential goals	Simultaneous goals
Maintenance activity is routine	Maintenance activity affected by external innovations
Procedures for managing planning are routine	Procedures for managing planning are innovatory
Clarity about innovations	Ambiguity about innovations
Predictability of innovations, crises, issues	Unpredictability of innovations, crises, issues
Coterminous planning cycles	Overlapping planning cycles
Sequential planning cycles	Plan for next before complete present cycle
Paucity of innovations, crises, issues	Abundance of innovations, crises, issues
Adequate resources to achieve goals	Inadequate resources to achieve goals
High school-level control over innovations	Low school-level control over innovations
Development focuses on innovations originating in school	Development focuses on external innovations
Low staff turnover	High staff turnover

A simplistic representation of the interplay of these factors is portrayed in Figure 11.2. The left-hand extreme position represents the most stable situation, where there is bound to remain some turbulence. For example, there will be some variation between cohorts of pupils and some turnover of staff over time. The right-hand extreme position depicts a highly turbulent context, where some stability will be retained because not everything will be changing (unless, perhaps, the school is being closed). The list of factors is not exhaustive. The diagram portrays how the balance between stability and turbulence may vary. For example, as the range of innovations grows, planning for development increasingly affects planning for maintenance, so leading to uncertainty over what otherwise would remain routine; the environment becomes more turbulent as stability is reduced. The hypothesis is suggested that, as the balance shifts towards turbulence, the balance of cyclic and continual planning must shift towards the continual, although even at the most extreme position annual cycles still have to be addressed. Conversely, as the balance shifts towards stability, those at school level with responsibility for planning will have greater choice whether to employ a single planning cycle. Overall, it seems plausible that many schools in different countries may have moved from Position 1 towards Position 2 in recent years and that the assumptions behind cyclic planning may have failed to keep pace.

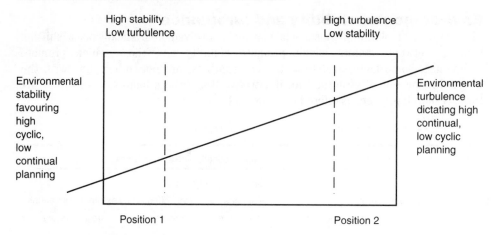

High stability
Low turbulence

High turbulence
Low stability

Environmental
stability
favouring
high
cyclic,
low
continual
planning

Environmental
turbulence
dictating high
continual,
low cyclic
planning

Position 1

Position 2

Figure 11.2 *Balance between environmental stability and turbulence and its influence on planning.*

CONCLUSIONS

The contingency hypothesis must be regarded as very tentative and in need of refinement, as it rests upon such limited evidence. However, other recent research into development activity in schools in England (for example, Bowe and Ball, 1992; Nias *et al.*, 1992) and elsewhere (for example, Patterson *et al.*, 1986; Louis and Miles, 1990), together with the study of business organizations (for example, Peters, 1987), is sufficiently consistent with this hypothesis to suggest that it should be taken seriously by researchers, trainers and policy-makers.

Research in North America suggests that requiring schools to develop an implementation plan for innovations is itself a managerial innovation (Fullan with Stiegelbauer, 1991). Unless the assumptions on which this innovation is based are in sympathy with the context where it is to be implemented, the attempt to improve schools' implementation plans can actually inhibit the implementation of other innovations (Levine and Leibert, 1987). The possibility that cyclic planning may be less than fully effective in supporting development activity in environments marked by a high degree of turbulence lends some urgency to the task of ensuring that effective planning models for such situations are found and disseminated.

One conception that may be worth further study is 'flexible planning' (Wallace, 1991b), a speculative model put forward in the light of the multiple-innovations project. This model acknowledges the limits to rationalistic planning in turbulent environments. While it has affinity with the notion of 'evolutionary planning' put forward by Louis and Miles (1990) the model also addresses an endemic tension which all schools must face. There is a need (recognized in cyclic plans) to sustain a long-term direction so that, by adhering to agreed priorities, staff overload may be avoided. Equally there is a need to respond rapidly to changing circumstances which frequently cannot be predicted at school level. The core is a continual process of creation, monitoring and adjustment of plans for the short, medium and long term. These plans roll forward over time, medium-term plans for the next few months being developed into more detailed plans and so on. Plans may be updated whenever the spasmodic and often unpredictable arrival of new information about external innovations occurs or when crises, issues or other events arise. At the same time, planning takes into account the stage reached in the overlapping academic and financial year cycles. Management procedures consist of occasional consultative and strategic decision-making exercises coupled with considerable day-to-day monitoring and adjustment. A routine procedure is established for calling a 'rapid response' review whenever information about a change in the environment suggests that present priorities and development activity may have to be adjusted. The regular consultative procedures may be cyclic: say, major reviews every year and minor, less extensive reviews every term or so. The 'rapid response' review may be inserted – and thus lead to adjustment of the cycle – whenever continual monitoring shows that it is required.

The flexible planning model is underpinned by the contingency hypothesis. It therefore seems evident that research is needed in a wider range of local and national contexts to determine under what, if any, conditions this hypothesis may hold and to provide more detail about what a largely continual development planning process with cyclic elements might entail.

The evidence presented above suggests that while compulsory LEA development planning initiatives for schools may be of positive value, their effectiveness may be limited in supporting continual development under turbulent conditions (Wallace, 1991c). Such initiatives are designed to serve the dual purpose of collecting information for LEAs and guiding development activity in schools. These purposes may be in conflict: LEAs require information annually from schools related to the support and monitoring functions for which they are held accountable by central government. Staff and governors in schools need a framework to help them continuously to retain as high a degree of control over development as is possible in an often unpredictably evolving situation. It may be more effective for LEA staff to divorce the two purposes by collecting information by other means.

Finally, the evidence suggests a further hypothesis with important implications for governments bent on education reform. The most effective way of promoting the improvement of schooling may be for governments to guard against the imposition of too many innovations in too short a time-scale, with too few resources. However, increasing the stability of school environments does not seem to be considered by politicians – the United Kingdom at least – as being a winner with voters in the 1990s.

ACKNOWLEDGEMENTS

I wish to acknowledge the support of the Economic and Social Research Council for the projects 'Managing Multiple Innovations in Schools' and 'The Role of the Senior Management Team in Secondary Schools', and the Leverhulme Trust for the project 'Planning for Change in Multiracial Primary Schools'. I would like to thank the school staff and governors and the staff in the LEAs who gave time to the research under difficult circumstances.

REFERENCES

Bowe, R. and Ball, R., with Gold, A. (1992) *Reforming Education and Changing Schools*. London: Routledge.

Burns, T. and Stalker, G.M. (1961) *The Management of Innovation*. London: Tavistock.

Caldwell, B. and Spinks, J. (1988) *The Self-Managing School*. London: Falmer Press.

Department of Education and Science (1988a) *Education Support Grant*, Draft circular. London: Department of Education and Science/HMSO.

Department of Education and Science (1988b) *Local Management of Schools*, Circular 7/88. London: Department of Education and Science/HMSO.

Department of Education and Science (1989) *Planning for School Development*. London: Department of Education and Science/HMSO.

Department of Education and Science (1991) *Development Planning: A Practical Guide*. London: Department of Education and Science/HMSO.

Fullan, M., with Stiegelbauer, S. (1991) *The New Meaning of Educational Change*. London: Cassell.

Hall, V. and Wallace, M. (1992) 'Team approaches to strategic planning in secondary schools', Paper presented at Fourth Research Conference of the British Educational Management and Administration Society, University of Nottingham, UK, April.

Hargreaves, D. and Hopkins, D. (1991) *The Empowered School: The Management and Practice of Development Planning*. London: Cassell.

Inner London Education Authority (1977) *Keeping the School under Review*. London: ILEA.

Levine, D. and Leibert, R.E. (1987) 'Improving school improvement plans', *Elementary School Journal*, **87** (4), 397–412.

Louis, K.S. and Miles, M.B. (1990) *Improving the Urban High School: What Works and Why*. New York: Teachers College Press.

McMahon, A. and Wallace, M. (1992) 'Development planning in a turbulent environment: the case of multiracial primary schools', Paper presented at Fourth Research Conference of the British Educational Management and Administration Society, University of Nottingham, UK, April.

McMahon, A., Bolam, R., Abbott, R. and Holly, P. (1984) *Guidelines for Review and Internal Development in Schools*. Primary and Secondary School Handbooks. Harlow: Longman for Schools Council.

Nias, J., Southworth, G. and Campbell, P. (1992) *Whole School Curriculum Development in the Primary School*. London: Falmer Press.

Patterson, J., Purkey, S. and Parker, J. (1986) *Productive School Systems for a Non-rational World*. Alexandria, Virginia: Association for Supervision and Curriculum Development.

Peters, T. (1987) *Thriving on Chaos*. London: Pan Books.

Sheffield Education Department (1991) *School Development Planning under LMS: A Guide for Schools*. Sheffield: Sheffield City Council.

Skelton, M., Reeves, G. and Playfoot, D. (1991) *Development Planning for Primary Schools*. Windsor: NFER-Nelson.

Stoll, L. (in press) 'Developing an effective school: linking research and practice', in Musella, D., Padro, S. and Townsend, R. (eds) *Inside School Improvement: Rethinking Our Experiences*. Toronto: OISE Press.

Wallace, M. (1991a) 'Coping with multiple innovations in schools', *School Organization*, **11** (2), 187–209.

Wallace, M. (1991b) 'Flexible planning: a key to the management of multiple innovations', *Educational Management and Administration*, **19** (3), 180–92.

Wallace, M. (1991c) 'Contradictory interests in policy implementation: the case of LEA development plans for schools', *Journal of Education Policy*, **6** (4), 385–99.

Wallace, M. and Hall, V. (1994) *Senior Management Teams in Action: The Role of the SMT in Secondary Schools*. London: Paul Chapman Publishing.

Wallace, M. and McMahon, A. (1994) *Planning for Change in Turbulent Times: The Case of Multiracial Primary Schools*. London: Cassell.

Warwickshire County Council (1991) *PRIDE (Process for the Review and Internal Development of Education) in Our Schools: An Aid to Development Planning*. Warwick: WCC.

Chapter 12

School Development Planning
in Primary Schools:
Does It Make a Difference?

Peter Mortimore, Barbara MacGilchrist,
Jane Savage and Charles Beresford

INTRODUCTION

School development plans are not new. Over the years, in many different countries, schools will have planned carefully for new developments, particularly curricular initiatives, and sought to use resources in the most appropriate way even though they might not have used the term 'school development plan' as formally as is now common.

At central and local government levels, planning for, and on behalf of, individual schools is normal practice. The new – more explicit – approach for planning began to surface in the United Kingdom during the 1980s with, for instance, a government statement which included the specific advice that:

> every school should analyse its aims, set these out in writing, and regularly assess how far the curriculum within the school as a whole, and for individual pupils, measures up to these aims.
>
> (Department of Education and Science, 1981)

This statement encouraged many of those responsible for schools to develop formal planning processes. The Schools Council also produced its 'Guidelines for Review and Internal Development in Schools' (GRIDS) after a programme of extensive development work in schools (McMahon *et al.*, 1984). The idea of school development planning was later endorsed by the Inner London Education Authority as part of its review of primary education in 1985 by the Thomas Committee.

> We recommend that every school should have a plan for development, taking account of the policies of the Authority, the needs of the children, the capacities of the staff, and the known views of the parents. The plan should have an action sheet attached to it, showing what the responsibilities of members of staff will be in setting target dates.
>
> (Inner London Education Authority, 1985, paragraph 3.94)

This new emphasis on individual school planning, following on from earlier pioneering work on school self-evaluation, fitted well with two emerging bodies of research evidence: school effectiveness and school improvement.

School effectiveness

Over the past twenty years in both the United Kingdom and the United States, a number of research studies have sought to investigate whether *individual* schools have differential effects on student achievement and development. In the United Kingdom, large-scale studies by Reynolds (1976), Rutter *et al.* (1979), Mortimore *et al.* (1988), and Smith and Tomlinson (1989) have reported positive results. At both primary and secondary levels, schools can promote or reduce achievement, good behaviour and attendance.

In the United States, studies by Weber (1971), Brookover and Lezotte (1977) and Edmonds and Frederickson (1979), although focusing almost exclusively on academic attainment in elementary schools, produced similar findings. Since the publication of Weber's ground-breaking study, there has been a flood of critiques, replications and evaluations and an increasingly theoretical debate about the value of the work and its implications for schools. A recent review and analysis of the field contains over 400 references (Levine and Lezotte, 1990) while a synthesis carried out by the Northwest Regional Educational Laboratory (NREL, 1990) traced over 700 publications on this topic. In the United Kingdom, Reynolds (1985) and Reynolds and Cuttance (1992) have charted the field. Work on school effectiveness is no longer restricted to the United Kingdom and the United States but, through the auspices of the International Congress on School Effectiveness and Improvement, has spread to many different countries. A second generation of thinking about effective schools, clarifying earlier work and substantiating its theoretical basis, is also emerging (Bliss *et al.*, 1991).

School improvement

The publication of the early school effectiveness studies in the United States led almost immediately to the implementation of programmes of school improvement. These programmes sought to intervene in the way schools were managed and, through the use of a set of correlates gleaned from the research findings, to raise the achievement of students. Such interventions, for example, took place in New York (under Edmonds), Milwaukee (McCormack-Larkin and Critek, 1982) and California (Murphy *et al.*, 1982). Since then, the field has burgeoned and a report of the General Accounting Office (1989) found numerous examples of schools drawing on the knowledge of the effective schools literature, while according to Cross (1990) more than half of the 16,000 school districts in the United States have now implemented some form of school improvement programme.

Somewhat in contrast, in the United Kingdom, according to Reynolds (1992): 'The take-up of school effectiveness knowledge by practitioners ... has been very limited indeed.'

It is not appropriate to discuss, in detail, reasons for this transatlantic distinction here, but both Reynolds (1989) and Mortimore (1991) have drawn attention to practical and cultural differences between the two nations. Such differences include a tradition of inspection and of curriculum-related public examinations in the United Kingdom and a greater dependence on general, multiple-choice tests in the United States.

In the wider context, the International School Improvement Project, sponsored by the OECD, has involved fourteen separate countries in programmes mainly concerned with curriculum change (Bollen and Hopkins, 1987).

163

School reform

The introduction of a wide-ranging series of reforms in the United Kingdom since 1988 has emphasized the need for further school-based developments. Furthermore, the increasing devolution of financial responsibilities to school heads and governing bodies, the diversification of the primary curriculum and the increasing complexity of school management have emphasized the need for individual schools to develop a much more systematic approach to planning and review (Skelton *et al.*, 1991).

As an *idea*, school development planning makes sense: rather than each teacher restricting his or her planning to the work of their own classes and reacting individually to change, the school – as a whole – seeks to act in a premeditated and concerted way, relating resources, curriculum planning and in-service training together (Hargreaves and Hopkins, 1991). Furthermore, such development plans are seen as mechanisms to support the implementation of the National Curriculum and aid the progression of learning demands made upon students and as a means of dealing with conflicting priorities. Moreover, at a time of unprecedented change in education, when national and local education authority (LEA), as well as school, priorities have altered as a consequence of legislation, a systematic, whole-school, approach to planning has much to commend it.

School development plans are now being promoted by the Department for Education, the Scottish Office and by almost every LEA in the United Kingdom.

OUR STUDY

Through an Economic and Social Research Council-funded systematic investigation – which recognizes the multiple levels of decision-making and actions of schools – we are seeking to describe and analyse the impact of plans and planning on the management of the school as a whole; the organization of classes; the learning opportunities of individual pupils; and the professional development of individual teachers. In order to illuminate the context in which schools are working, we are also investigating the attitudes towards – and the support for – school development planning by LEAs. Just as 'impact' can be seen at different levels, so too can 'timing', and we will be seeking to investigate both the immediate and the long-term effects of planning. In essence, we are seeking to test the theory that underpins the argument for the value of school development planning.

A further aim is to examine how the findings of this study can contribute to the theories of how change takes place in schools. Louis and Miles (1990) and Fullan (1991) have elaborated on the various barriers and incentives to change that occur in schools in North America. Like Wallace (1991) we will be attempting to investigate whether a practice designed specifically to bring about change can also illuminate more general patterns of institutional development in the United Kingdom.

Since change is so widespread among education systems, we think it is important to relate the findings of this study to those of similar systems in other parts of the world. We will draw on published research reports of international journals in order to collect information about similar kinds of studies but we are also hoping to play a role in two replications of our study. We are currently collaborating with colleagues in universities in Australia and in Denmark who are planning to draw on our research design and to use our research tools in their own work. These comparative studies will enable the reliability of our research instruments to be tested and the transferability of any findings to be explored.

In the remainder of this chapter, we will describe our chosen methodology, report on our progress so far, and discuss the early findings of our inquiry. Finally, we will draw on our data and analyses to outline some of the issues that are emerging from this work.

Like all research carried out in the busy world of schools, our study will be subject to interruptions and disturbances, and we will need to be flexible in how we operate. Accordingly, we have chosen to use an eclectic range of methods.

Sources of information

Local education authorities (LEAs)

In order to provide as accurate a picture as possible of the national context of school development planning, we began our study with a questionnaire survey of all LEAs in the United Kingdom. One hundred and thirty-five LEAs were sent a wide-ranging questionnaire to complete: England (110), Wales (8), Scotland (12) and Northern Ireland (5). More detailed work is being carried out in three LEAs containing schools in urban, suburban and semi-rural settings.

Schools

From these three LEAs, eighteen schools were identified by local inspectors as having a particular interest in development planning. A semi-structured telephone interview with the headteacher was then used to gather additional information about the size of school, type of building, staffing and school status, number of students and organization of teaching groups. Headteachers were asked about their experience and whether this was their first headship, how many development plans had been produced in the school, the length and type of the planning cycle, the main components of the plan and the involvement of other key people and their attitudes towards SDPs. Information was also collected on the socio-economic features of the catchment area, and on student and staff turnover.

Nine schools were then selected from this group in order to give as wide and as varied a sample as possible. The chosen schools range from a small rural school of forty students to a large inner-city primary with 450 on the roll. The sample also varies in experience of development planning, from a headteacher and staff in their first year of the process, to a school with more than six years of planning.

Research instruments

We are seeking to collect a wide variety of information from as appropriate a group of respondents as possible. We hope to be able to triangulate the accounts of past developments and to compare these with any available documentary evidence. We are also seeking to observe classroom practice and audit students' work as a way of investigating the impact of the plan at the classroom and individual student levels. Techniques of analysis will range from a detailed content analysis of the respondents' interview responses to qualitative and quantitative analyses of the LEA data and, where appropriate, of classroom observations and students' work.

Questionnaire for LEAs

We have developed, piloted and used a postal questionnaire for LEA respondents. This addresses the attitude and practice of the LEA towards school development plans and planning. It also explores the nature of any formal guidelines that have been developed and the freedom of individual schools to vary the format of the plan.

Interview schedules for schools

A set of related semi-structured schedules have been designed, piloted and used in schools. Separate versions for headteachers, class teachers and LEA link personnel, governors and parents have been created. In developing these instruments we have drawn on earlier work (Hargreaves and Hopkins, 1991; Constable *et al.*, 1991; Skelton *et al.*, 1991) as well as on the experience of our visits to schools and local education authorities.

Fieldwork

We are investing considerable resources in field visits to schools and LEAs. Each of the schools had a preliminary visit from at least two members of the research team in order to establish relationships and to clarify the purpose of the research. Since then, background information about each school – and, in particular, about the headteacher and the two class teachers involved in the initial class observations – has been collected. Members of the research team have also attended some staff meetings and LEA meetings concerned with development planning.

We are following groups of students from nursery through to year six (from 4 to 11 years old). We intend to track them through two full academic years until the completion of the project in June 1994. Observations centre on the priorities for development being implemented in each school. We are striving to overcome one problem described by recent reviewers, and to measure progress over time rather than just at one point in time (Reynolds and Cuttance, 1992).

Early findings

Two-thirds of the way through our study, we are able to report positively on the interest, and on the high level of co-operation and help, that we have received from all those working in the schools and LEAs with which we have been in contact. We can only report on our progress on the initial analysis of the LEA questionnaire and other completed instruments.

We have received returns from all the 135 LEAs giving a remarkable response of 100 per cent. Many LEAs have also responded to our request for guidelines and other relevant documentation. We now have an interesting range of documentary evidence about LEA policy, guidelines and use of development plans. We have also attempted to monitor the continued changes affecting the roles and responsibilities of LEAs.

At the school level, as noted, we have collected the views of different types of respondents in order to analyse the perceptions of the different participants in the planning process. Headteachers, chairs of governors, parent governors, LEA personnel and the two cohorts of eighteen class teachers have all been interviewed using our semi-structured interview schedules.

We completed all data collection in our sample schools by Easter 1994.

We began the project with a set of six expectations drawn from the literature of school improvement (Mortimore, 1991). Briefly, these were that schools are likely to improve if various conditions are met. The expectations, and the ways in which we hope to examine whether or not they are being met, are listed below.

- *Most staff and the headteacher can agree on a clear mission for the institution.* This is being investigated through the analysis of documentary evidence and through the perceptions of those involved.
- *A systematic audit of current strengths and weaknesses is carried out.* The accounts of the processes of planning related by the participants are an important indication of whether this took place, as are the records of any audits.
- *A change plan is thoroughly thought-through.* The evidence of who was involved, how the planning was conducted, and of whether the implementation monitoring and assessment as well as the formulation of the SDP was addressed, is being used to explore this issue.
- *An outside agent is involved.* The use and type of external help from the local inspector/adviser or a consultant, as well as the role of governors, parents and representatives from other LEA local school and community groups is being investigated.
- *The implementation of the change plan is supported by all appropriate external authorities.* The interviews with the school staff, chair of governors, and local inspector/adviser are being used to explore how far this support is available.
- *An evaluation of progress is used formatively to support the implementation.* Our observations of, and questions about, the evaluation of progress are being used to judge whether the planning is static or dynamic and whether feedback is being used to modify its operation.

It remains to be seen whether these expectations will be found to be true, or whether they will need to be modified in the light of our fieldwork.

It is clear from the initial analyses of the LEA questionnaire that Authorities support the idea of school development plans. Three-quarters of the LEAs have clarified expectations or agreed a formal policy that all primary schools should have development plans in the three school years between 1989 and 1992. Most of the remaining LEAs already had such policies in place, leaving only two LEAs in England and Wales and half the Scottish regions without such a policy at the time of the data collection (Spring 1992).

Most LEAs have produced support materials to help schools with this process. Some are derived from guidelines and in-service materials developed earlier with secondary schools, but many address the particular attitudinal and practical issues facing small organizations in a context of multiple change. In Scotland, HMI have produced supportive materials and encouraged schools to link school development planning with the use of ethos and performance indicators in self-evaluation.

The extent to which such policies are being translated into practice varies, though about three-quarters of the LEAs reported that all, or almost all, schools had SDPs in 1991–2. The proportion of schools using SDPs at that time was smaller in Scotland and Northern Ireland.

All LEAs expect schools to include curriculum and staffing matters in their school development plans. Most also expect organizational development to be included. It appears that the inclusion of financial issues may be linked with the stage that the LEA has reached in introducing LMS to primary schools. Property issues do not follow the same patterns, and some of the LEAs most advanced in LMS do not necessarily expect schools to include such issues in their development planning.

The headteacher is expected to involve others in the planning process in almost all the LEAs. Teaching staff, the deputy head and governors are said to be involved in more than 80 per cent of the LEAs, and most also involve inspectors/advisers. Only a quarter of the LEAs have sought to involve parents, the proportion being highest in inner London and lowest in Wales and Northern Ireland.

Most LEAs want to promote planning processes as part of helping schools to cope with change, whether this originates nationally or locally. However, a quarter of the LEAs in the United Kingdom still expect schools to submit their plans or their priorities to the LEA for approval. Over a half of the LEAs collect the complete plans and a third require a summary of priorities. All but 5 per cent of the LEAs analyse aspects of the plans, and a third of them claim to do so 'extensively'.

Four out of every five LEAs refer 'often' to school development plans in their inspection and monitoring of schools, but only three out of every five use them as part of their support for schools. This variation may reflect the increasing polarization of the advisers' roles into curriculum support work, carried out by advisory teachers, and monitoring, carried out by inspectors.

EMERGING ISSUES

As has been stressed, this chapter is reporting an on-going research study. Even the findings that have emerged from initial analyses of the LEA survey must be regarded as provisional. We cannot yet fully describe the way that the planning process is operated in schools, let alone report on its efficacy or on the difference between rhetoric and reality.

Nevertheless, there are four methodological and four substantive issues on which – even at this stage of the project – we feel able to comment.

Methodological issues

Sampling

We have chosen nine case studies from a potential of over 700 primary schools in the three LEAs. These LEAs were, themselves, selected from 135 possibilities. Our technique of narrowing our choice to three contrasting authorities, and then using local inspectors to screen the selection of potential schools, has obvious limitations. The sample is far from random and, as a result, our ability to generalize from the findings will be limited. Nevertheless, we have a range of schools of different sizes, a mixture of county and voluntary institutions and a selection of established and new headteachers. Within this purposive sample of case studies, we hope we will be able to contrast and compare the experience of development planning and be able to relate any patterns we may discern to the context of the LEAs that we have already surveyed.

Halo effect

Like most social researchers, we are working with active respondents. We recognize that the head and class teachers – and all the other respondents to our questions – will also be studying us. Inevitably, therefore, our presence will affect their behaviour. Thus, in the nine schools in which we are working intensively, school development planning is likely to be invested with an extra importance. We are not seeking to claim any special status for our research team, but merely to recognize that, in such a situation, we may influence behaviour merely by posing questions. We have attempted to note instances where it has appeared we are affecting the course of events in a particular school. We recognize, however, that the experience of the sample schools is likely to become rather different from that of their non-researched neighbours.

Confidentiality and other ethical issues

We have guaranteed confidentiality to all respondents and agreed to report findings only in an anonymous form. Confidentiality has been assured within schools as well as to the sample group as a whole. This has enabled the research team to gather valuable information on the differing perspectives and roles of those working within and with schools. In this way, we hope our respondents will seek to report – as truthfully as possible – the impact of planning on their classes and schools. We are not seeking permission from parents of the children in our sample, though we will respect their rights – and those of any others – to refuse to participate. Like many other school researchers, we are restricting our attention to the formal life of the school and will not seek to use other information acquired in casual conversation or observed in teachers' off-duty behaviour.

Causality

We are aware of the limits of most social science research designs in tracing causal patterns. Like many other educational researchers, we will have to content ourselves with making inferences about the impact of developing planning. Especially difficult will be the task of tracing the impact of planning through the management of the school and the work of the class teacher to the progress of the students.

Substantive issues

School culture

Like Fullan (1991) we are interested in how the process of planning is related to the shared values, expectations and ethos of a school. The methods used and the people who are involved in the process of developing a plan are two major areas for investigation. How these methods are then translated into curriculum and instructional practices via the structures and practices of schools (as recently investigated by Chrispeels, 1992) and of individual teachers in order to impact on students, is another major focus of our investigation.

External support

LEAs appear to vary widely in the nature of the support that they offer to schools and in the styles of guidance materials. In some LEAs, policy statements express explicit requirements about school development planning. However, as most of the growth in SDPs has taken place since the accelerating devolution of responsibility encouraged in the 1988 Act and subsequent publications, most LEAs have issued written guidance backed up with in-service opportunities and advisory support.

The perceptions by LEAs of their changing roles have clearly influenced their approach to school development planning. A desire for uniformity of approach and style from all schools has advantages for LEAs which can conflict with the autonomy, ownership and individuality of a school's response (Fullan, 1991).

Information gathered from some of the headteachers in our sample group reinforces the comments received in our LEA survey that headteachers recognize increasingly that the responsibility for planning strategies rests with them and their colleagues. Where schools have individually developed these approaches, subsequent LEA guidance will tend to be rejected. Such guidance is more likely to be valued where LEAs have involved headteachers and others in developing approaches to school development planning, in showing colleagues how such planning can contribute to improving the quality of their schools, and in generating a sense of shared ownership of the guidance materials that are developed.

Significant influences

It appears that significant influences on our headteachers' and on our classroom teachers' thinking have been professional colleagues and externally imposed factors such as LMS and the National Curriculum. In addition, the work of Hargreaves and Hopkins (1991) on school development planning is well known. There is also emerging evidence of the role of key individuals in disseminating training and common approaches to the planning process.

Another key area appears to be the relationship between in-service training for staff and the adoption of particular priorities within the plan. Furthermore, the tension between the maintenance and continuation of priorities from previous years (as noted by Nias *et al.*, 1992) and current needs has emerged as an interesting issue.

Style of management and leadership

Finally, our initial investigation has revealed that planning of this nature has implications for the general management of schools, and the style of leadership used by the headteacher. Like Chrispeels (1992) and Nias *et al.* (1992), we are interested in how professional relationships change as class teachers become involved in whole-school planning. It remains to be seen whether the models of management from outside schools (Handy and Aitken, 1990) will help explain these processes.

CONCLUSION

We do not yet know with what certainty we will be able to trace the impact of development plans. Our attempts to tease out, in each case study, the influence of particular strands of the development plan need to be considered in the context of many other changes in school and classroom life. Nevertheless, we will endeavour to understand the nature of any changes that do occur and, through our research design which allows for a series of replications in the United Kingdom, as well as in Australia and Denmark, we will be in a strong position to recognize common patterns as they emerge. We will also seek to assess how much impact the processes of planning have on the four target areas: school management; classroom management; the individual teacher; and, ultimately, whether it makes a difference to the opportunity for learning offered to students within the school. We intend to publish further accounts of our work at a later stage of the project.

ACKNOWLEDGEMENTS

We wish to record our thanks to the headteachers and staff of our sample schools and to the local education authority officers who responded so fully to our questionnaire.

REFERENCES

Beresford, C., Mortimore, P., MacGilchrist, B. and Savage, J. (1992) 'School development planning matters in the United Kingdom', *Unicorn*, **18** (2), 12–16.

Bliss, J., Firestone, W. and Richards, C. (1991) *Rethinking Effective Schools: Research and Practice*. Englewood Cliffs, NJ: Prentice-Hall.

Bollen, R. and Hopkins, D. (1987) *School Based Research: Towards a Praxis*. Leuven, Belgium: ACCO Publishing.

Brookover, W. and Lezotte, L. (1977) *Changes in School Characteristics Co-incident with Changes in Student Achievement*. East Lansing Institute for Research on Teaching: Michigan State University.

Constable, H., Norton, J. and Abbott, I. (1991) *Case Studies in School Development Planning*. Sunderland: School of Education, Sunderland Polytechnic.

Chrispeels, J. (1992) *Purposeful Restructuring: Creating a Culture for Learning and Achievement in Elementary Schools*. Basingstoke: Falmer Press.

Cross, C. (1990) 'National goals: four priorities for educational researchers', *Educational Research*, **19** (8), 21–4.

Department of Education and Science (1981) *The School Curriculum*. London: Department of Education and Science/HMSO.

Edmonds, R. and Frederickson, J. (1979) *Search for Effective Schools: The Identification and Analysis of City Schools That Are Instructionally Effective for Poor Children*. Eric Document Reproduction Service number ED170 397

Fullan, M., with Stiegelbauer, S. (1991) *The New Meaning of Educational Change*. London: Cassell.

General Accounting Office (1989) *Effective School Programmes: Their Extent and Characteristics*. Washington, DC: General Accounting Office.

Handy, C. and Aitken, R. (1990) *Understanding Schools as Organisations*. London: Penguin.

Hargreaves, D. and Hopkins, D. (1991) *The Empowered School: The Management and Practice of Development Planning*. London: Cassell.

Inner London Education Authority (1985) *Improving Primary Schools* (Report of the Thomas Committee). London: Inner London Education Authority.

Levine, D. and Lezotte, L. (1990) *Unusually Effective Schools: A Review of Research and Practice*. Madison, WI: National Center for Effective Schools Research and Development.

Louis, K.S. and Miles, M.B. (1990) *Improving the Urban High School: What Works and Why*. New York: Teachers College Press.

McCormack-Larkin, M. and Critek, W. (1982) 'Milwaukee's Project RISE', *Educational Leadership*, **40** (3), 16–21.

McMahon, A., Bolam, R., Abbott, R. and Holly, P. (1984) *Guidelines for Internal Review and Development in Schools*. Primary and Secondary School Handbooks. Harlow: Longman for SCDC.

Mortimore, P. (1991) 'The nature and findings of research on school effectiveness in the primary sector', in Riddell, S. and Brown, S. (eds) *School Effectiveness Research: Its Messages for School Improvement*. Edinburgh: HMSO.

Mortimore, P. (1991) 'Effective schools from a British perspective: research and practice', in Bliss, J., Firestone, W. and Richards, C. (eds) *Rethinking Effective Schools: Research and Practice*. Englewood Cliffs, NJ: Prentice-Hall.

Mortimore, P., Sammons, P., Stoll, L., Lewis, D. and Ecob, R. (1988) *School Matters: The Junior Years*. Wells: Open Books.

Murphy, J., Weil, M., Halinger, P. and Mitman, A. (1982) 'Academic press: translating high expectations into school policies and classroom practices', *Educational Leadership*, **40** (3), 22–6.

Nias, J., Southworth, G. and Campbell, P. (1992) *Whole School Curriculum Development in the Primary School*. London: Falmer Press.

Northwest Regional Educational Laboratory (NREL) (1990) *Effective Schooling Practices: A Research Synthesis*. Portland, OR: Northwest Regional Educational Laboratory.

Reynolds, D. (1976) 'The delinquent school', in Woods, P. (ed.) *The Process of Schooling*. London: Routledge & Kegan Paul.

Reynolds, D. (ed.) (1985) *Studying School Effectiveness*. Lewes: Falmer Press.

Reynolds, D. (1989) 'Research on school and organisational effectiveness: the end or the beginning?', in Saran, R. and Trafford, V. (eds) *Research in Education Management and Policy: Retrospect and Prospect*. Lewes: Falmer Press.

Reynolds, D. (1992) 'School effectiveness and school improvement: an updated review of the British literature', in Reynolds, D. and Cuttance, P. (eds) *School Effectiveness: Research, Policy and Practice*. London: Cassell.

Reynolds, D. and Cuttance, P. (eds) (1992) *School Effectiveness: Research, Policy and Practice*. London: Cassell.

Rutter, M., Maughan, B., Mortimore, P. and Ouston, J. (1979) *Fifteen Thousand Hours: Secondary Schools and Their Effects on Children*. Wells: Open Books.

Skelton, M., Reeves, G. and Playfoot, D. (1991) *Development Planning for Primary Schools*. Windsor: NFER-Nelson.

Smith, D. and Tomlinson, S. (1989) *The School Effect: A Study of Multi-racial Comprehensives*. London: Policy Studies Institute.

Wallace, M. (1991) 'Coping with multiple innovations in schools: an exploratory study', *School Organization*, **11** (2), 187–210.

Weber, G. (1971) *Inner City Children can be Taught to Read*. Washington, DC: Council for Basic Education.

Name Index

Subject Index

Page numbers in bold type refer to figures. Page numbers in italic type refer to tables